Remediation in Rwanda

THE ETHNOGRAPHY OF POLITICAL VIOLENCE

Tobias Kelly, Series Editor

A complete list of books in the series is available from the publisher.

Remediation in Rwanda

Grassroots Legal Forums

Kristin Conner Doughty

PENN

UNIVERSITY OF PENNSYLVANIA PRESS

PHILADELPHIA

Published by
University of Pennsylvania Press
Philadelphia, Pennsylvania 19104-4112
www.upenn.edu/pennpress

Printed in the United States of America
on acid-free paper

10 9 8 7 6 5 4 3 2 1

Library of Congress Cataloging-in-Publication Data

Doughty, Kristin, author.
   Remediation of Rwanda : grassroots legal forums / Kristin Conner Doughty.
      pages cm.— (The ethnography of political violence)
   ISBN 978-0-8122-4783-1 (alk. paper)
      1. Rwanda—History—1994– . 2. Restorative justice—Rwanda. 3. Transitional justice—Rwanda. 4. Peace-building—Rwanda. 5. Postwar reconstruction—Law and legislation—Rwanda. 6. Gacaca justice system—Rwanda. 7. Rwandans—Social conditions. I. Title. II. Series: Ethnography of political violence.
   DT450.44.D68 2016
   967.57104'31—dc23
                                                                    2015026168

To Josh, Natalie, and Noah, with love

Contents

Harmony Legal Models and the Architecture of Social Repair

This book tells the story of how the Rwandan government aimed to remediate the country's social ills in the aftermath of the 1994 genocide, and to rebuild the social fabric through revitalizing a traditional practice of mediation and embedding it in grassroots legal forums. Government officials hoped to use local courts as part of a broader architecture of social repair to help re-create families, repair communities, and rebuild a unified nation, consistent with the global rise in transitional justice. The three legal forums at the heart of this book—genocide courts called *inkiko gacaca,* mediation committees called *comite y'abunzi,* and a legal aid clinic—used mediation by third-party actors with the power of punishment to advocate compromise solutions across a wide range of disputes. This book describes how people's lives were shaped by law-based mediation. It illustrates how people contested collective belonging through the micro-disputes that formed the warp and woof of daily life, and how people negotiated moral community and imagined alternative futures through debates in these new legal forums. By looking across a range of legal forums, it connects the exceptionalism of disputes about genocide to the ordinary disputes people faced living in its aftermath.

Mediation-based models are by no means limited to Rwanda; they are increasingly implemented by state and international actors, especially in postconflict contexts, often in the name of customary law, local solutions, or restorative justice. This is therefore a story about rebuilding in Rwanda, but also a broader story of how the global embrace of law, particularly in postconflict contexts, shapes people's lives. Though law-based mediation is framed as benign, and is often promoted on the basis of local culture—by domestic governments such as Rwanda as well as by the transitional justice movement more broadly—I show that its implementation involves coercion and accompanying resistance. Yet, perhaps unexpectedly, in grassroots legal forums that are deeply contextualized, processes based on promoting unity can open up spaces in which people reconstruct moral orders, negotiating what Kimberly Theidon has called the "micropolitics of reconciliation" (Theidon 2012).

Legal Disputes in the Aftermath of Genocide

This book adds another strand to the complex story of how Rwandans rebuilt their social lives in the wake of genocide.[1] From April to July 1994, devastating state-led violence designed to exterminate the country's minority Tutsi population spread from the capital, Kigali, throughout the country.[2] The extraordinary violence was perpetrated by the military and ordinary civilians, and it extended deep into everyday landscapes, touching all Rwandans. It was framed by a civil war and subsequent violent political and military struggles, ultimately claiming up to a million lives. Since the moment the worst of the violence abated, victims, perpetrators, bystanders, their families, and the recently returned diaspora population have lived side by side across the country's tightly packed hillsides.

In the mid-1990s, as bodies lay unburied, and refugees streamed out of Rwanda fleeing retaliatory violence, equal numbers crossed into Rwanda after years in exile. These diaspora people replaced, and eventually exceeded, the dead. Within little more than a decade later, this cosmopolitan mixture of people mingled in markets and manually tilled their adjacent fields, they rode pressed hip to hip and shoulder to shoulder in minibus taxis, and their children sat together in schoolrooms. Reports and documents produced by the Rwandan government and international nongovernmental organizations (NGOs) commonly diagnosed postgenocide Rwanda as suffering from a "devastated" social fabric among these people, including the "destruction of family bonds" (Biruta 2006:155; Ministry of Finance 2000; Ndangiza 2007).

In an effort to create a break from the past, and consolidate power, the Rwandan government focused on reconciliation as the foundation of its governance strategies to restore peace and rebuild a prosperous

nation-state. In 1999 the government established a National Unity and Reconciliation Commission, which worked at the national level in collaboration with ongoing government programs, as well as at the grassroots level
educating the population.[3] The purported goal was to "bridge the deep rifts
in society and heal the wounds inflicted by the genocide," creating cohesion
out of division and exclusion (Ndangiza 2007:1). In that vein, Rwanda's
new 2003 constitution underscored the importance of "eradicat[ing] ethnic, regional and any other form of divisions," "emphasizing the necessity
to strengthen and promote national unity and reconciliation," and recognizing that "peace and unity of Rwandans constitute the essential basis
for national economic development and social progress" (2003: Preamble,
Articles 2, 4, 5). National unity was justified on the basis that, as the constitution enumerated, "we enjoy the privilege of having one country, a common language, a common culture, and a long shared history which ought
to lead to a common vision of our destiny" (2003: Article 7). The public
reconciliation discourse was ubiquitous, from political speeches to NGO
conferences to sporting and music events, and was taught in schools (King
2014) and solidarity camps (Thomson 2011b).[4] Rwanda's policy of unity
and reconciliation formed what Sharon Abramowitz (2014) has described
in Liberia as a "total environment of post-conflict transformation," and it
was emblematic of how peace building and reconciliation emerged as global
master narratives of the late twentieth century (Nader 1999a:304, 2002b:38;
Scheper-Hughes and Bourgois 2004).

Grassroots legal forums in Rwanda were a central site for promoting
national unity and restoring the social fabric. Specifically, Rwandan government authorities identified local mediation-based courts as an antidote for
the divisive politicized understandings of ethnicity at the heart of the genocide ideology. As the president Pasteur Bizimungu explained in 1999, law
was intended not just to punish or to make people "be afraid" of committing a crime but rather to change the "bad ideology" that caused the divisive violence and to rebuild the nation (Bizimungu 1999:6). These forums
were designed to create the rules, values, and norms among the participants
that would "become the basis of collaboration and unity"[5]—since, as
anthropologist Danielle de Lame wrote in 1996, "the old representations
that unified Rwandan culture have become meaningless" in the wake of
such catastrophic violence and displacement (2005:491). As one Rwandan
legal administrator explained to me in 2008, "It would be better for the
country if people could change their mindset to accept solutions built on

unity and compromise rather than litigation." The government justified the principles of unity and compromise at the heart of Rwanda's mediation-based forums as deriving from the shared historical-cultural Rwandan identity undergirding the policy of national unity and reconciliation.

Using law to bridge divides from the past was perhaps most notable in the creation of the now widely known gacaca courts (*inkiko gacaca*), community courts in which suspects of the 1994 genocide were tried among their neighbors before locally elected judges. I sat through one such trial with a few hundred people on a rural hillside in southern Rwanda in December 2007. The defendant, a man I call Alphonse who had been incarcerated since 1995, was a fifty-five-year-old widower with six children, educated through primary school, and recently converted to the Seventh Day Adventist Church. During his trial for acts allegedly committed thirteen years earlier, Alphonse had apologized for his role in several murders, confessing in detail by providing names of co-perpetrators and describing how and where several specific victims were killed. The eighteen witnesses and victims who testified claimed to forgive him despite the severity of his crimes, and many even spoke positively about ways he had helped some people.

In the closing moments of his trial, Alphonse knelt before the five judges, his bare knees pressing into the packed dirt. He clasped his hands behind his back and bowed his head toward his chest, choking back tears as he asked forgiveness of the judges, his neighbors, and all Rwandans. As Alphonse stood to take his seat on a low bench at the base of the tree under which his trial had taken place, he drew a tissue from his jacket pocket and wiped his eyes. The prisoners on either side of him shifted uncomfortably, and looked away.

The judges rewarded Alphonse's rather dramatic performance by, after deliberating, reducing his sentence based on his confession, which allowed him to return home within weeks to live among the people who had attended his trial. Over the next six months, I saw him regularly around town, chatting with former prisoners as well as genocide survivors, listening to the radio or having a beer with other men. In subsequent trials in the following months, the judges repeatedly invoked Alphonse's name as a model for other defendants to follow. He testified regularly from the general assembly, sometimes confirming defendants' versions of events, other times refuting them. Five months after his trial, Alphonse described what it was like returning home:

People reacted better than I expected them to. When I was first released, I thought some people would not talk to me, I thought I would have to isolate myself, that there would be places I could not go, people I could not embrace. I came and stayed at my house for two weeks. When my children would talk, I would caution them to keep their voices low. I would even draw the curtains and keep the radio volume low, so no one would know I was home. Then people came to visit, making noise and singing. They asked me why I wasn't coming out, and told me not to be afraid, to come and join the others. It's good so far.[6]

Alphonse's case stood out as a particularly dramatic example of how gacaca was intended to address the seemingly intractable problem of restoring the social fabric devastated by the violence of the early 1990s. Rwanda's gacaca courts, created by national law in 2001, were designed, according to government sensitization propaganda, to "allow the population of the same Cell, the same Sector to work together" and therefore for gacaca to "become the basis of collaboration and unity."[7] Ostensibly, the courts were intended to provide a process to facilitate the reintegration of perpetrators into quotidian life, out of prison. Suspects were tried publicly onsite at the location of their alleged crimes, by a panel of locally elected judges called *inyangamugayo* (Kinyarwanda for "people of integrity"). Mandatory participation and the deliberate avoidance of lawyers or professional jurists were intended, at least in theory, to enable all Rwandans to participate actively as witnesses, prosecutors, and defenders with limited hierarchy. The gacaca process hinged on mediating compromises prioritizing the collective over the individual good: as Alphonse's case demonstrated, defendants received reduced penalty for confessions, and victims forwent demands for harsher punishment in return for information about their loved ones. At the same time, the gacaca process established criminal accountability for genocide, including fines and prison sentences of up to thirty years. The inyangamugayo, backed by police, armed prison guards, and even soldiers, could issue subpoenas and could bring charges against case participants for refusing to testify, for perjury, or for blackmail (Organic Law N.16/2004, Articles 29, 30).

This emphasis on collaborative, unity-based justice in Rwanda was not limited to genocide crimes. In the days and weeks around Alphonse's trial, I sat on the same hillside as people brought cases before newly implemented mediation committees (comite y'abunzi) that had jurisdiction over low-level civil and criminal disputes. Comite y'abunzi were established by national law around the same time as gacaca courts based on the same general procedure, in order to "provid[e] a framework of obligatory mediation" for ordinary civil and criminal disputes, where locally elected *abunzi* (Kinyarwanda for "mediators" or "reconcilers") would "seek first to conciliate the two parties" (Organic Law N.31/2006, Articles 3, 20). Even while the abunzi aimed to find compromise solutions with which parties would voluntarily comply, state-backed punishment remained an integral component. Based on comite y'abunzi judgments, authorities and the judicial police could seize land, livestock, crops, and other personal property (Organic Law N.31/2006, Article 24).

In one example, from May 2008, a woman named Joselyne had filed a case against a neighbor named Beata for saying insulting things about her in public. Both women wore the *kitenge* wrap skirt over a T-shirt common among rural women, their slim and strong frames testament to their lives of subsistence farming, their bare feet covered in light dust from the walk. The women explained they had previously taken their dispute to a local women's committee, which reprimanded Beata and told her to pay a fine of three thousand Rwandan francs (six U.S. dollars). Unable to pay, Beata had agreed to farm for Joselyne, and she spent one afternoon fetching water and tilling Joselyne's garden. Beata did not go again, claiming it was too much hardship after her child fell ill, especially since her husband was doing twice-weekly community service work as part of his gacaca sentence. Joselyne felt the debt had not been paid and filed a case with the comite y'abunzi. The abunzi had summoned Beata repeatedly before she finally complied. During the case discussion, the abunzi concluded that because Beata had already acknowledged guilt in Joselyne's defamation accusation, the issue at stake was the unpaid fine.

The president of the mediators proposed that Beata should simply pay the fine imposed by the women's committee. Beata agreed. Joselyne repeatedly rejected this solution. She complained it was unfair that Beata had been so insulting to her, and then had shown more contempt by repeatedly refusing to pay and most recently by not responding to the abunzi summons, which had wasted Joselyne's time and prevented her from farming. She wanted Beata to have to pay more than the original fine. Joselyne asserted stridently, "I do not want to forgive Beata, I want you to punish her." The abunzi who were hearing the case responded by explaining that their job was not to punish but to mediate and reconcile. They spent more than an hour reasoning with Joselyne, emphasizing a range of compromise solutions aimed at avoiding escalation. One mediator tried to convince Joselyne of the benefits of Beata's willingness to farm for her. Another likened Joselyne to a parent and Beata to an errant child who should be forgiven. This case hearing concluded not with a performance of repentance and reintegration as in Alphonse's situation, but rather with the disputants walking purposively in opposite directions, deliberately avoiding each other over the coming weeks.

I encountered law-based mediation in a third forum located a few hours' walk away, this one a legal aid clinic run by the Faculty of Law of the National University of Rwanda. The clinic's staff members, who were university lecturers and law students, provided pro bono legal advice to all clients who came to them, with cases ranging from divorce or land disputes to employment concerns or insurance claims. I was initially drawn to the clinic by an interest in exploring another legal context that addressed quotidian disputes, though one based in universal human rights and Western-style law rather than the alleged customary law focus at the heart of gacaca and comite y'abunzi. Yet I was struck to find that in the months I spent there, the majority of clients who came to the clinic requesting help with filing a case or defending themselves against a claim ended up participating in mediation. The clinic's staff members were explicit that mediation was at the core of their approach. As the head of the clinic indicated in a presentation to his funders in 2008, "Very often clients are advised about the option of mediation," and "then it is the privilege of the legal clinic to reestablish the broken social fabric." The clinic was not a formal government institution, yet its link to the national university conveyed proximity to state power and punishment that, as the director explained to me, "reminds them [disputants] of what they are required to do by the law."[8]

In a typical example, a few weeks after Alphonse's trial, in January 2008, I entered the legal aid office, located in a small room in a single-story concrete building on the university campus. I pulled up a wooden chair around a low coffee table to join a staff member while he spoke with three clients—a man who had been fired from work as a night guard and the two nuns at the convent where he had worked. The man had come to the clinic the week before seeking help filing a case against the convent for several months of back pay, but instead the clinic staff began with mediation. The nuns explained that they had fired the man because he had allegedly stolen several blankets. Over several hours of discussion, the clinic staff member reminded the nuns of the man's reliable work, and of his ongoing obligations to his family, while reminding the client of the benevolence the nuns were showing him by not reporting him to the authorities. The nuns agreed to pay the man two months' wages, and the parties all expressed satisfaction with the result, grateful that they had not had to bring in the police.

How do we understand this focus on mediation and restoring relationships across such a range of legal forums and types of disputes in contemporary Rwanda? What happens when efforts at reconciliation are embedded in legal forums, thus combining pursuit of unity between disputants with punishment, and how do such efforts shape the conditions under which people rebuild their social lives? How do people follow and adapt the guiding rules of legal mediation, and what kinds of collective belonging result? What is at stake in participants' contestation of the terms of unity? These are the questions that this book explores.

In this introduction and the book overall, I make a series of interrelated arguments that allow us to examine how and why an increasingly authoritarian state emphasized harmony and law-based mediation as a mode of power and tool of governance. I suggest we should consider these three legal forums within one analytic frame as linked by their mediation practice. Doing so captures how people experienced the exceptionalism of postgenocide justice as inextricably linked to the more mundane disputes of daily life. I further argue we should see these forums as what Laura Nader has termed "harmony legal models" (Nader 2002a) in order to identify how the forums served as techniques of state-backed community building, a form of what Nikolas Rose, building on Foucault (1982; 1991), has called "government through community" (Rose 1999:176). Analyzing these harmony models as governmentality sheds light on their coercive dimensions, and thus illustrates the dark side of harmony that is often erased by benign cultural justifications for unity. Gacaca courts, comite y'abunzi, and even the legal aid clinic could serve as spaces in which state power coerced, silenced, or pacified people through exhortations to submerge individual desires and rights in lieu of the collective good, defined in a particular way.

Yet, attending only to coercive dimensions of mediation across these diverse forums risks flattening and mischaracterizing dynamics of power in postgenocide Rwanda. I suggest that because these forums were deeply contextualized, they were relevant to people and varied in how they operated. Attending to the contested conversations within these forums allows us to analyze how people negotiated the micropolitics of reconciliation within law-based mediation as part of their efforts to reconstruct moral orders. Further, attention to the conversations themselves draws attention to the ways power and instrumentality operate at individual, interpersonal, and localized levels, in a context shaped by the macro-level global and national reconciliation agendas. What resulted was not the creation of idealistic state versions of national belonging, nor simply coercive silencing, but rather a space in which people contested the terms of moral community, actively debating what obligations they had to one another, and what it meant to belong.

Embedding Reconciliation in Law: Harmony Legal Models

Rwanda's gacaca, comite y'abunzi, and the legal aid clinic were united by a common undergirding philosophy that, whenever possible, disputes should be solved through compromise and reconciliation with the help of a third party. They were designed to bring participants together as joint problem solvers to find mutually agreed solutions, rather than one side winning and the other side losing. This approach posited that by reasoning with one another, understanding the other side's position, and making sacrifices, people would come to more desirable and sustainable solutions than if they went to regular adversarial courts, which imposed top-down solutions.

Mediation and reconciliation are similar ideas, as I use them here, expressed in the Kinyarwanda word *kunga*, or its reflexive form, *kwiyunga*. Kwiyunga is the root of the word *abunzi*, which is translated into English as mediators; comite y'abunzi are mediation committees. Similarly, kwiyunga is at the root of the word *ubwiyunge*, which is translated into English as reconciliation. For example, the government's Komisiyo y'Igihugu y'Ubumwe n'Ubwiyunge is translated as the National Unity and Reconciliation (Ubwiyunge) Commission. These concepts were used in connection with each other and often interchangeably, reflecting the broader ethos of social harmony in the reconciliation discourse. I suggest that in routing people's disputes through grassroots mediation, the Rwandan government intended not merely for mediation to serve as a dispute resolution technique, but rather for the principles and practices to stand in for reconciliation (*ubwiyunge*) and the national unity (*ubumwe*) on which the new Rwanda was ostensibly based.

I argue that we should consider these forums as harmony legal models. Nader defines harmony legal models as legal forums based on the principles of harmony ideology: "an emphasis on conciliation, recognition that resolution of conflict is inherently good and that its reverse—continued conflict or controversy—is bad or dysfunctional, a view of harmonious behavior as more civilized than disputing behavior, the belief that consensus is of greater survival value than controversy" (Nader 1990:2).

In Rwanda, law-based mediation combined the emphasis on unity with the threat of state-backed punishment, detailed in the written laws instantiating the institutions. This punitive force included consequences that directly impacted people's daily survival, such as imprisonment, property seizure, and fines. The power to punish was explicit, as when authorities told people they could be sanctioned for not complying, threatening them with fines or incarceration, and it was also represented symbolically through the physical presence of signs that indexed state power, such as sashes worn by the mediators or the presence of armed prison guards. The ability to forcibly implement judgments and apply punishments was central to people's experience of harmony legal models, and is what distinguished legally mediated decisions from informal, nonlegal alternatives. As one case participant observed: "In the past, if a man or woman had problems, they would go see the priest. Today it is changing, people seek more the rigor of the law, because these courts have binding force. If you don't comply, then you are sanctioned for it. Going to a pastor, he will only advise you, you can either abide or decide not to. But in courts, there is administrative force."[9]

I see law-based mediation in Rwanda as a form of government through community, as Rose puts it, in which governments identify "weak communities" as a problem needing to be solved through technical, governance solutions aimed at mobilizing those same communities to solve their own problems through self-government. Mediation in grassroots legal forums was a way in which people who live proximately were intended to become linked into a community or, as Rose calls it, a "moral field binding persons into durable relations" that emphasized emotional relationships and microcultures of values and meaning (Rose 1999:176). Specifically, law-based mediation aimed at shaping and directing people to manage themselves and, equally important, to manage their relationships to one another, to take on "active practices of self-management and identity construction, of personal ethics and collective allegiances" (Rose 1999:172–176). That is, gacaca, comite y'abunzi, and the legal aid clinic were designed, like other local-level mediation processes in other contexts (Abel 1982b:11; Merry 1993:58), to emphasize relationships and interpersonal conflict resolution skills, using mediation principles to (re-)create moral bonds and emotional relationships that were shattered during the political violence.

Considering genocide courts, mediation committees, and a legal aid clinic within one analytic frame is a deviation from existing literature on Rwanda, which typically focuses on genocide-related justice as analytically distinct from nongenocide disputes.[10] Separating our analysis based on externally imposed jurisdictional distinctions obscures continuities both in the top-down social engineering goals of these forums and in how most Rwandans experienced mediation as a mode of power that cross-cut institutional frameworks. The more I observed court sessions and spoke with participants themselves, the more I saw that, contrary to one mayor's claim that "comite y'abunzi has nothing to do with gacaca,"[11] these forums were indeed connected in people's lived experience. In the middle of the first decade of the new century, Rwandans who sought legal redress were first routed through mediation practices that combined harmony and punishment—whether filing a case against a neighbor for looting property during the genocide or for defamation, whether testifying against an acquaintance for participating in killings during the genocide or against an employer for wrongful termination, whether seeking paternal recognition or inheritance. I am thus arguing that "an examination of the ordinary is just as important as the apparently extraordinary or exceptional" (Kelly 2008:353), not only in understanding how people live through political violence (as Kelly argued with respect to Palestine) but also in exploring how people cope with the aftermath of genocide.

Analyzing gacaca, comite y'abunzi, and the legal aid clinic through Nader and Rose draws attention to how mediation was a technique of governance intended to reshape postgenocide Rwanda into a particular kind of community, based on exhortations to unity that were justified as cultural. There is a paradox when community is the object of government where the idea of community is assumed to be natural and preexisting, yet is also being technologically enacted (Rose 1999:177). The sleight of hand that presents "community" as apolitical rather than constituted through contestation and suffused with power imbalances warrants investigation—especially in a context like Rwanda, where efforts to rebuild the social fabric in the wake of genocide were particularly pronounced, by a government that was increasingly authoritarian. That is, we have to understand post-genocide Rwanda not as having *a priori* cohesion but rather as attempting to use these decentralized legal forums to *create* unity. Other anthropologists have underscored the importance of denaturalizing the idea of "community" as a "repository of innate solidarity" at the heart of official postconflict interventions, as Theidon has argued with respect to Peru in the aftermath of decades of violence between the government and Shining Path (2009:296; 2012:266, 269). Similarly, Richard Wilson has critiqued the ways that in South Africa, the idea of *ubuntu,* an "expression of community, representing a romanticized vision of the rural African community based upon reciprocity, respect for human dignity, community cohesion and solidarity" became "a key political and legal notion in the immediate post-apartheid order" (Wilson 2001:9). What, we must ask, was at stake in using mediation as a tool of unity, backed by punitive law, in postgenocide Rwanda?

Mediation as Statecraft: Denaturalizing the Cultural Justification

A month after Alphonse's trial, sitting adjacent to the same courtyard, an elderly *umwunzi* (mediator) held my gaze while explaining to me and my Rwandan research assistant about the cultural history of dispute resolution in Rwanda. He described:

> When I was born in 1928, gacaca and abunzi were in place as the only judicial system. The goal of these institutions in the past was to unite and to reconcile people. They gave messages of love, coming together, socializing. In the past, there were not any of the current kind of regular courts; those only came with the colonial rule of the Belgians. There were the king's courts, but even those were just a last resort in the hierarchy beginning with gacaca and abunzi. It was the duty of abunzi to follow up and make sure the two parties reconciled. People used to bring beer to share, or exchange cows, or even intermarry, and these exchanges created strong bonds. Gacaca and abunzi now are pillars for development. You must have judicial systems like that in place to reconcile and develop.[12]

This characterization was consistent with how the Rwandan government authorities legitimized the harmony legal models as, according to printed brochures and the government's websites, "traditional community courts"[13] based on "the inspiration of the traditional context of conflict resolution."[14] These authorities claimed that Rwandans historically had dispute resolution systems that eschewed the winner-take-all basis of Western courts, instead using respected elders to solve specific disputes between individuals and families to strengthen communal ties. Indeed, scholars writing on Rwanda note a long-term presence of conciliation-based, decentralized mechanisms for resolving disputes in the region now known as Rwanda,[15] as I discuss more in Chapter 2, consistent with broader-reaching customary law practices across much of sub-Saharan Africa. This philosophy was consistent with how classic analyses of African adjudication often stressed that local courts in Africa, whether formal or moots, aimed to restore breaches in relationships among members in an ongoing community in order to restore equilibrium.[16] Much like the classic ethnographic examples, postgenocide Rwanda's harmony legal models had no lawyers, incorporated broad participation, and had minimal hierarchy among disputants, judges, witnesses, and other attendees, all consistent with a spirit of compromise rather than adversity. They used wide rules of evidence, given that the issue at hand was understood as a breach of deeply embedded relationships and practices, rather than narrowly focusing on a specific point of law. Finally, the judges or mediators at the center of these processes explicitly and clearly articulated social norms in an effort to socialize litigants as well as other participants. Obarrio (2014) has recently described similar community courts in Mozambique.

Yet, there are dangers in being seduced by cultural justification. Debating whether Rwanda's postgenocide legal institutions are "customary" can disguise the degree of state involvement in so-called informal or popular mediation in the past and the present, and it can hide historical and contemporary power imbalances and coercion. For decades we have known that we cannot take the ethnographic record of African customary law at face value, given how the focus on compromise within it reflects primarily a "Durkheimian emphasis on harmony of interests and shared goals" (Starr and Yngvesson 1975:559). Even seemingly consensus-based customary practices contained hierarchy and coercion (Colson 1974; Moore 1986). Further, customary practices and institutions in Rwanda and elsewhere in sub-Saharan Africa changed significantly during the colonial period and after independence, specifically through increasing state control (as I describe in more detail in Chapter 2). Their revival in the twenty-first century needs to be understood not as a romanticized local movement but as an "invented tradition" (Hobsbawm and Ranger 1983) that served present state needs.[17] A rich body of legal anthropology has shown how so-called popular or informal institutions that use mediation are typically tied up with, not separate from, state law and even expand state control.[18] I agree with Lars Waldorf (2006) that there seems limited utility in clinging to terms like popular and informal in Rwanda, where the state is deeply implicated in gacaca in particular and the courts may in fact be deeply unpopular.[19]

Further, attention primarily to measuring degree of cultural relevance can mask the way these forums are bound up with broader-reaching global trends. Rwanda's mediation-based legal forums were extensions of the truth commission model, popular worldwide since the 1980s, which typically foregrounds victim narratives and eschews punishment in an effort to "heal individuals and society after the trauma of mass atrocity" (Minow 1998:57).[20] Government billboards across Rwanda in 2004 and 2005 publicizing the launch of the gacaca process announced *Ukuri kurakiza*, "the truth is healing." Rwanda's emphasis on mediation through gacaca, comite y'abunzi, and the legal aid clinic reflected broader international trends in transitional justice, including a move away from exclusively using international criminal courts, a shift to national ownership of legal processes, and a shift toward valorizing cultural solutions (see Chapter 2).

Looking at Rwanda's forums in comparative perspective with other harmony models underscores that though they often derive from local practices, harmony models are simultaneously "part of systems of control that have diffused across the world along with colonialism, Christianity, and other macroscale systems of cultural control such as psychotherapy" (Nader 2002a:32). The imbrications of Christianity with mediation in Rwanda are pronounced today. Rwanda has been predominantly Christian for more than a century, due to the missionary influence during colonial rule (Longman 2010a). Postgenocide Rwanda saw a resurgence in transnational forms of Christianity, particularly evangelical churches brought in from East and Central Africa by returning diaspora members, as well as by church congregants in missions from churches in Europe and the United States. Although churches were not formally involved in the legal process,

Christianity served as a broader part of the sociopolitical context that reinforced mediation principles (e.g., Richters 2010). Both local pastors (some of whom served as abunzi or inyangamugayo) and international pastors advocated harmony principles within and outside courts in Rwanda.

In a notable example, beginning in 2005, President Paul Kagame enlisted the help of American evangelical Pastor Rick Warren, author of the best-selling *Purpose Driven Life* (2002), to collaborate in a five-year project aimed to turn Rwanda into the first "purpose-driven nation" (Morgan 2005; Van Biema 2005). In addition to meeting with government officials and visiting the hospitals his project supported, Pastor Warren—who would later go on to cement his status as a global moral leader by giving the invocation at President Barack Obama's inauguration in 2009—held large revival meetings attended by thousands of Rwandans across the country, in which he preached about the importance of unity and forgiveness to restoring Rwanda (Musoni 2008b). Rwandan pastors regularly advocated for the mediation discourse from the pulpit, encouraging parishioners to confess and forgive, and even served as lay judges and mediators. Medical anthropologist Annemiek Richters has described mediation-like efforts in sociotherapeutic processes led by churches in northern Rwanda that similarly emphasized healing within the community (Richters 2010). Other scholars have noted this trend elsewhere. Wilson has argued that Christian notions of confession and redemptive healing were crucial to many people's understandings of reconciliation in the South African Truth and Reconciliation Commission (Wilson 2001:109–120). Shaw (2007) and Kelsall (2005) have described how Christian elements were crucial to the Sierra Leonean TRC hearings, Abramowitz (2014) has described Christian discourses of harmony, reconciliation, and truth that accompanied the Liberian TRC; and Theidon (2012) has detailed the interrelationships between evangelical Christianity and the TRC in Peru.

Nader's comparative examples also draw our attention suggestively to how mediation in Rwanda is linked to a third global trend: alternative dispute resolution (ADR). Harmony models, often in the form of ADR, have been a part of the package of the Americanization of law being exported around the world for decades, alongside the more retributive, adversarial dimensions of Western-style law.[21] The shift to ADR involved a transition toward viewing law as healing, an approach that "transforms facts and legal rights into feelings, relationships, and community writ small" (Nader 2002a:131),[22] consistent with the explicit focus on individual-level forgiveness and compromise brokered by community members in Rwanda's grassroots legal forums. Laurel Rose (1996) has described being sent to fact-find about ADR approaches in Rwanda as early as 1994, and Nader has suggested that the World Bank, which supports programs in Rwanda, mandates the use of mediation to solve conflicts with many assisted countries.[23] Many states in the United States made ADR mandatory in the mid-1990s, much as gacaca and comite y'abunzi were made obligatory in Rwanda a few years later, and as mediation in legal aid became increasingly common worldwide (see, for example, Englund 2006:145–169). Paralleling the rationalization of ADR,[24] there was regular justification of Rwanda's gacaca courts, comite y'abunzi, and legal aid clinic in terms of increasing efficiency and "unclog[ging] courtrooms" (Butamire 2010) consistent with nationwide strategic planning goals of decentralization (Ministry of Local Government 2008a, b), and I heard them framed as self-evidently better than, and in opposition to, adversarial law.

None of this is to suggest that there is no basis for claiming cultural roots of harmony in Rwanda, or that these three forums are identical to ADR. Rather, in the face of such clear interconnections between Rwanda's postgenocide grassroots mediation-based legal forums and global trends, I want to examine what is at stake in the insistence that these forums are naturally Rwandan. Challenging the benign cultural framing of harmony legal models in Rwanda is vital, especially given the growing acknowledgment that the Rwandan government is increasingly authoritarian, manipulates identity politics, and uses law and "lawfare, the effort to conquer and control . . . by the coercive use of legal means" (Comaroff 2001:306) selectively as another strategy to consolidate the ruling elites' power and suppress dissent (e.g., Chakravarty 2015; Hintjens 2008; Longman 2010b; Morrill 2006; Reyntjens 2005; Straus and Waldorf 2011).

Indeed, while the postgenocide Rwandan government claimed to promote a unified national identity that superseded ethnic divisions and officially banned ethnicity, its official history erased reference to deep structures of political economic exclusion and exploitation, and actually reinscribed division by defining citizenship categories in relation to the genocide: Hutu were *génocidaires*, Tutsi were victims (see Chapter 1).[25] Other hierarchies of power and inequality existed across dimensions of gender, class, age, or region. Further, national unity was promoted alongside the implementation of increasingly repressive laws that proscribed ethnic labels and criminalized "divisionism," "revisionism," or "genocide ideology," anything seen as "marginalizing . . . degrading . . . [or] stirring up ill feelings" (Law N.18/2008 of 23/07/2008, Article 3). These laws served to reduce political dissent, especially when coupled with ongoing detentions, and state-backed violence at home and in the neighboring Democratic Republic of Congo (Thomson 2011c:442; Waldorf 2011:49).

I suggest that the cultural justification for harmony was an effort to insulate against international critique of, and interference in, Rwandan governance. For Rwandan leaders to claim they could rebuild Rwanda based on their own rather than foreign cultural principles served to protect against persistent allegations that domestic legal forums did not meet international legal and human rights standards (e.g., Amnesty International 2002; Penal Reform International 2004). This echoes how cultural justification for customary law was used in many contexts in Africa both to insulate institutions from colonial interference and to support nationalism at Independence (Chanock 1985:24; Colson 1974:77–78). It parallels Nader's argument (1990a) that harmony can be a counter-hegemonic strategy, though in Rwanda the move appears directed not at colonial leaders or state law but at the hegemony of international regimes of law and human rights.

What was particularly problematic, I suggest, was the cultural justification for unity itself. Given that mediation was presented as a practice natural to all Rwandans, to reject overtures to "be mediated" or "reconciled" was to reject the unity of all Rwandans, and even to reject shared citizenship and the legitimacy of the state. By a decade after the genocide, many scholars argued that Rwandans "rehearsed consensus" (Ingelaere 2010a:53) or "pretended peace" (Buckley-Zistel 2009), which papered over much deeper divisions (Thomson 2013). This is consistent with Nader's caution that harmony ideology "may be used to suppress people's resistance, by socializing them towards conformity by means of consensus-building mechanisms, by valorizing consensus, cooperation, passivity, and docility, and by silencing people who speak out angrily" (Mattei and Nader 2008:77).[26] Recent research underscores how most Hutu who had been in Rwanda during the genocide felt that strident resistance to gacaca risked conveying criminally divisive intentions.[27] Many Hutu men and women described to me confessing and requesting forgiveness under duress, fearing that not to do so would invite arbitrary accusations, false convictions, and heavy sentences, as well as other social sanctions. For example, as Alphonse returned home from prison after his gacaca trial and took on the role of model reformed perpetrator, he furtively told me that he remained cautious in what he said and did, under watchful eyes. Similarly, victims often described feeling pressured—by defendants, by inyangamugayo, by pastors, by neighbors— to forgive perpetrators or to accept less than they were due in property cases, for the benefit of community and country. The coercive potential of harmony in gacaca was particularly strong, perhaps inescapable, because of how tightly it linked unity principles to state punishment. People were essentially told to forgive and reconcile with a thinly veiled "or else": risk state-backed punishment as someone who did not value unity, and who therefore probably embraced divisionism as a propagator of genocide ideology and an enemy of other Rwandans and the state.

A growing anthropology of transitional justice has similarly shown how coercion and silencing are core elements of many truth and reconciliation commissions, in sub-Saharan Africa and elsewhere. Wilson has argued that the South African TRC's invocation of ubuntu could "coerce individuals into compliant positions that they would not adopt of their own volition" (2003:189), and Ross (2003) has shown how despite its purported attempts to give voice to victims, the TRC silenced and depoliticized women in particular through its narrow institutionalized definitions of violence. Shaw (2005) and Kelsall (2005) similarly showed how Sierra Leone's TRC, while ostensibly more attuned to people's needs than the United Nations–backed Special Court of Sierra Leone, overwrote cultural practices of forgetting through the Judeo-Christian valorization of talk, which rendered the TRC at worst coercive, at best irrelevant. Abramowitz has argued that the Liberian TRC "served to close doors for personal expressions of grief and memory" (Abramowitz 2014:209). Theidon has similarly illustrated how the "victim-centered" approach of the Peruvian truth commission inadvertently created "resentful silences" (Theidon 2010:110) and "systematic distortions" (Theidon 2012:28) that flatten and depoliticize people's stories. Ethnographic work in other contexts in sub-Saharan Africa has shown how local practices to cope with the past and reintegrate ex-combatants get overlooked, distorted, or erased by a focus on the standard transitional justice toolkit, as in Angola and Mozambique (Honwana 2005; Irega and Dias-Lambranca 2008), Uganda (Allen 2008; Finnstrom 2010), and Burundi (Nee and Uvin 2010).

Overall, Rwanda's harmony legal models located the solution to the genocide in interpersonal relations, not in structural and political or economic changes.[28] In the aggregate, gacaca courts, comite y'abunzi, and the legal aid clinic excluded most Rwandans from having access to Western-style courts, lawyers, and professional judges. Though the harmony legal models were framed as beneficial to reduce unnecessary conflict and promote unity, they meant that in practice governing authorities attempted to impose resocialization through harmony principles on mostly rural, typically poor, and less educated Hutu and Tutsi survivors, thus reinforcing a divide between elites and nonelites, urban and rural. With less economic, social, and cultural capital to negotiate postgenocide Rwanda's multifaceted and shifting legal terrain, these people typically had little option other than to comply with mediated solutions. Women often had even fewer options, or felt the brunt of mandatory unity principles more strongly, as I illustrate across the later chapters. These effects are consistent with how Nader has extensively argued that the focus of harmony models on relationships over root causes ignores political economy and deflects cases away from the courts that threaten to challenge the status quo, thus serving as an antilegal movement restricting certain people's access to justice (Mattei and Nader 2008:18; Nader 1988:280, 1999b:107, 2002a:53) and serving as a tool of "pacification and control" (Nader 1999a:305, 2002b:37, 42).

My analysis here is consistent with Juan Obarrio's recent book describing similar exclusionary dimensions of the "spirit of the laws" in postwar Mozambique, though with an important distinction: by illustrating how these dynamics are not isolated to legal forums framed as customary law (such as gacaca courts and comite y'abunzi) but are also found within a legal aid clinic rooted in Western-style law, I suggest we identify it as mediation-based citizenship rather than "customary citizenship" (Obarrio 2014:109). Obarrio argued that in Mozambique, "While a small minority of the population had access to the mechanisms of the urban official judiciary, the vast majority of the population in rural and periurban areas was both included and excluded from national citizenship, through the enactment of localized forms of rights, which blended official state and customary norms" (Obarrio 2014:174–175). He names this effect "customary citizenship," which "articulate[es] elements of official law, custom, and kinship" where "acquiescence to official law is filtered through 'traditional' norms and the subjection to the authority of customary chieftaincy" (2014:109). Akin to my claim that law-backed mediation in Rwanda is a central element of post-genocide governance (Doughty 2014, 2015), Obarrio asserts that customary citizenship is not a derivative effect but one of the "main defining features of the political in contemporary Mozambique" (2014:11). Ultimately, Obarrio and I agree that grassroots legal processes are a defining feature of how people are unevenly subject to the law in contemporary Africa. Where I disagree is in naming the exclusionary process as "customary" citizenship, which I fear obscures how the effects can occur in institutions explicitly not defined as customary, and risks further reifying "customary law" rather than interrogating the category itself.

Beyond Coercion: Negotiating the Micropolitics of Reconciliation

While it is crucial to recognize the potential for, and experience of, coercion within mediation in Rwanda, as the examples throughout the later chapters illustrate, equating mediation in Rwanda with what Nader calls "coercive harmony" (2005) across a diversity of forums and types of disputes oversimplifies dynamics of power in Rwanda. The examples throughout this book remind us that we must attend to how coercive state power coexists with resistance (e.g., Foucault 1978; Scott 1985; Scott 1990) to avoid mischaracterizing how law-based harmony operates as a mode of power. The governmentality critique of mediation, following Rose's government through community, risks overstating the seamlessness of how people self-regulate according to official policy (see Briggs 2013). That is, it can suggest that everyone from government authorities to case participants performed unity principles, and did so uniformly. Instead, as the examples in the following chapters show, participants and even mediators took on mediation practices to varying degrees, contesting the hegemony (Nader 1990) of mediation and imperfectly self-regulating (Rose 1999) along mediation principles.

Alphonse's seemingly total embrace of repentance for the greater good was an exception, as evidenced by the discomfited reactions of the other prisoners seated alongside him. The following chapters show that Rwandans were not simply "pretending peace" (Buckley-Zistel 2009) or "rehearsing consensus" (Ingelaere 2010a) in these forums; rather, they contentiously expressed disagreement with respect to principles of collective cohesion, individual rights, the common good, and ultimately moral community and belonging. The cases I illustrate in the coming chapters, like Beata and Joselyne's case, involved heated contestation and disagreement rather than straightforward accordance with harmony principles. People situated in a variety of positions alternately enacted mediation principles or contested them at varying moments across a given case discussion, and dynamics of power shifted across moments and in relation to different charges and allegations. Unity in Rwanda was not a dominantly expressed legal ideology among disputants of the kind Nader (1990) and Laurel Rose (1992) have described in other contexts. The two recent ethnographies of postgenocide Rwanda—Jennie Burnet's *Genocide Lives in Us* (2012) and Susan Thomson's *Whispering Truth to Power* (2013)—both provide rich detail of the sources and expression of disagreements in postgenocide Rwanda, among everyday Rwandans as well as between people and state policy. Thomson explicitly analyzes these disagreements as everyday acts of resistance to the nationwide policy of unity and reconciliation.

I am thus suggesting that we must analyze the historical and political-economic context, to be sure, but not allow it to obscure the smaller-scale interpersonal interactions that make up ordinary life. This argument is consistent with much recent work by anthropologists on warscapes who argue that focusing on violence and the macro-political struggles of war as the "only primary feature" of life in war zones overlooks, as Sharika Thiranagama writes, "myriad mundane (and perhaps more severe for being mundane) experiences of life in protracted war zones," such as Sri Lanka (Thiranagama 2011:5).[29] I suggest here we can extend that analysis to the so-called postconflict period, especially in a context like Rwanda, where, in many people's perspective and experience, protracted political violence has not ended but has merely transmuted. Stephen Lubkemann has argued, based on work in Mozambique, that exclusive attention to violence and state-level political dynamics, and to interpreting people's reactions as a response to national-level macro-political struggles, erases attention from the "other struggles" related to "gendered or generational power configurations within households, to seeking socioeconomic advantage, and to the pursuit of redress for personal grievances" (2008:162) that shaped people's lives during war. Those same dynamics in postgenocide Rwanda, I fear, are overlooked through overemphasis on silencing, coercive effects of state-backed unity programming.

Throughout this book, I therefore attend to how people maneuvered within Rwanda's legal architecture of social repair, which is a way of conceptualizing how legal forums and logics constructed particular concepts, aesthetics, and practices of time and space, some stated and some implicit, in which Rwandans maneuvered, during the period of my fieldwork, 2004–2008. I build here on Abramowitz's description of how the "architecture of post-conflict time" in Liberia created a liminal postconflict space and time in which the fundamental rules of the social order were being reworked (Abramowitz 2014). In Rwanda, the architecture of postgenocide legal time was likewise active, and intentionally transformative. It created a set of processes into which all Rwandans were drawn, to varying degrees.

I illustrate in the following chapters how people used these spaces to debate the terms of social connection and collective belonging, what Theidon has called "reconstructing moral orders" in a "micropolitics of reconciliation" (2006:436). Alphonse's case, like many others that I present here, involved situated debates over how much people should compromise and sacrifice for each other, and thus served as part of an ongoing debate about the terms of moral community among Rwandans. We have long known that in legal disputes people debate over not simply circumstances of disputes but normative paradigms and the meaning of relationships (see, e.g., Comaroff and Roberts 1981; Merry 1990). Further, we know that discussions within courts are shaped by, and shape in turn, power dynamics and relations of dependence in the broader social context—Lubkemann's "other struggles," or what Sally Falk Moore has called the "micropolitics of local social standing" (1992:33). Ben Jones, for example, has recently shown how discussions in village courts in rural Uganda were framed by political debates about the violence, and how people used them to settle private disputes, articulate public concerns, and develop ideas of seniority and propriety (Jones 2008:65).

I suggest that the focus on oral testimony across gacaca, comite y'abunzi, and the legal aid clinic—whereby sessions involved what I call "contextualized conversations," which I discuss more in Chapter 3—further heightened these relational and political dimensions of testimony. I suggest that we understand discussions in mediation sessions as episodes in ongoing negotiations over how the details of ubumwe and ubwiyunge—the unity and reconciliation often proclaimed by the Rwandan government—played out in practice in people's lives, at different interconnected levels of scale. The polysemy of the term "unity," which was invoked as a ubiquitous but vague principle on which to make legally binding judgments and allocate resources, opened up space for discussion. What resulted, I argue, was not the creation of official normative versions of national belonging, nor monolithic coerced silence, but rather a terrain in which people contested moral community.

One significant component of such negotiations in legal forums was that people confronted head-on what Theidon calls the "economics of memory": how in an industry of truth telling and postconflict justice people instrumentally "narrated with new possibilities and aspirations in mind," including "hope for some economic relief" (Theidon 2012:109). Catherine Bolten has similarly underscored the importance of "material loyalty—relationships forged and sustained in complex, often compassionate acts of resource exchange" (Bolten 2012a:4) in explaining how people survived the civil war in Sierra Leone and rebuilt in its aftermath. Rwandans' discussions in legal forums confronted the material and financial dimensions of living together, which have long been understood as central to reconciliation but are often sidelined in prevailing discourses about reconciliation that emphasize affective dimensions, moral imaginaries, and intersubjective communication.[30] Collective belonging in postgenocide Rwanda was intimately bound up with land and other assets, continuous with earlier time periods (De Lame 2005:165). Exchanges and transactions of material goods and labor have long been tools of social integration in Rwanda (De Lame 2005:15, 105, 305), and they were at the heart of debates in legal forums, as I describe further in the social-history overview in Chapter 1 and in the discussion of gacaca in Chapter 3.

I also draw attention throughout to the ways gender roles, relations, and ideologies were sites of contestation and renegotiation through law-backed mediation.[31] Rwandans, particularly in rural areas, were heavily influenced by normative ideas of gender both before and after the genocide (Burnet 2012; De Lame 2005; Jefremovas 1991; Taylor 1992). In her recent ethnography that provides the most sustained ethnographic analysis of gender dynamics in contemporary Rwanda, Burnet argues: "Women are viewed positively when they are reserved, submissive, modest, silent, and maternal, when they maintain a 'respectable' household, and when they raise 'wise' children. They are viewed negatively when they gossip, are loud and overly emotional, or have a dirty house or rude children. By contrast, men should be self-assured, dominant, logical, brave, and physically strong" (Burnet 2012:44). These assumptions about gender roles permeate the examples throughout the book, captured also in the categories of "virtuous wives, "timid virgins," and, more pejoratively, "loose women," which Villia Jefremovas (1991) described in pregenocide Rwanda. The cases I explore throughout the book show how people brokering compromises in grassroots legal forums tended to adhere to these essentialist or naturalized roles for women (as wives, mothers, or conflict avoiders), a framing that could circumscribe possibilities for individual women, even while it sometimes helped them to achieve specific legal rights.

Specifically, I draw attention to how people negotiated the socially embedded, relational nature of their rights, which is a feature of African customary law more widely (Weeks 2013). Rwandan women's lives were shaped by patrilineal kinship norms in which unmarried girls, married women, and widows derived their social identities as well as their rights to access to resources from the men to whom they were related (Burnet 2012:43). In the postgenocide context, even as efforts were made to improve women's rights and individual security—including changes in national law to assure ownership rights for women, increased legal protections, and more representation by women in government decision-making bodies—women remained vulnerable, especially in rural areas, in part because of persisting normative assumptions that women's access to resources were linked to unequal relationships to particular men, especially in a context of widespread death and dislocation. As Burnet explains, "Women's economic lives were circumscribed by contemporary interpretations of patrilineal inheritance systems whereby women remained economically harnessed to economic units controlled by male relatives" (2012:76). Yet, while the relational nature of women's rights could render women more vulnerable, it also increased space for negotiation, as women debated prevailing assumptions about care and obligation within these social categories. Burnet argues that it is precisely women's role as the "primary social mediators between households, kin groups, and community" (2012:13) that gave them some space to help transform Rwandan society.

Finally, I show one of the ways legal forums shaped conceptions of ethnicity in postgenocide Rwanda, by creating what I call "genocide citizenship." I build on work by contemporary anthropologists who explore how ethnic logics persist in Rwanda today, as ethnicity remains one among many salient factors of Rwandans' identity, intertwined with other forms of identification, such as class, gender, age, and region (Eltringham 2011; Hintjens 2008). I supplement their focus on ethnicity in everyday life, including among youth (McLean Hilker 2009, 2011, 2012), educated urban residents (Eramian 2014a, 2014b), women (Burnet 2009), and members of the diaspora (Eltringham 2004) by showing how ethnicity shapes, and is shaped by, discussions in legal forums. As I discuss more fully in Chapter 3, I argue that within the postgenocide context marked by the official erasure of ethnicity, legal forums perhaps paradoxically solidified social categories linked to one's position with respect to the genocide, which were formalized by the state and carried access to state-backed resources (hence serving as a form of genocide citizenship).

Overall, this book adds to contemporary anthropological scholarship on Rwanda by providing detail on how people maneuvered within the legal architecture of social repair that was such a pronounced part of Rwanda's postgenocide reconstruction efforts, showing how law-backed mediation shaped the meanings of institutions and practices such as exchange, gender, and ethnicity in other social fields. Analyzing mediation practices, specifically how they combine calls for unity with punishment in legal forums, allows us to attend to the processes through which rule of law is produced and naturalized in a "moral economy of justice" (Clarke 2009), and to how legal categories create and acknowledge specific categories of guilty and innocent personhood (Kelly 2011; Niezen 2010), while also attending to how people "search for normal" (Abramowitz 2014) and reestablish collective belonging across, within, and containing deep divides following violence (Bolten 2012b; Finnstrom 2010; Hromadžić 2015; Ring 2006; Schuetze 2010; Theidon 2006). Participants expressed their knowledge of not only the fictions of justice (Clarke 2009) but also the fictions of harmonious community, showing that people are always contesting what it means, and their place within it. Conversations in legal forums shed light on the contested cracks at the core of official ideas about justice and unity.

Consider the following excerpt from a later portion of Alphonse's trial. An older woman I call Grace stepped forward to testify, indicating she would speak as *umuhohotewe*, one who was victimized (a privileged designation distinct from *abatangabuhamya*, those who testify as witnesses). Grace explained that during the genocide Alphonse had taken her children to protect them but then had demanded money from her to pay the killers to spare their lives. She asked to be reimbursed for the cash, approximately $6. Alphonse responded to her charges by admitting to receiving the money and describing how he had taken it to a local authority in order to procure false Hutu identity papers for the children. As Grace renewed her demands, one of the inyangamugayo, whom I call Faustin, himself a genocide survivor, chided her that she should be grateful that her children had survived.

Rather than pressing Alphonse for money, Faustin continued, Grace should recognize he had done her a favor. People in the assembled crowd laughed aloud at Grace's claim and at Faustin's gentle remonstrance.

In this example like many others, the inyangamugayo had to actively intervene to advocate compromise. Yet, the inyangamugayo pressuring Grace had experienced the same violence as she had, had also lost family members, and currently lived in an equivalent position of poverty. These shared structural and experiential dimensions do not erase coercive potential, of course, but they suggest to me there is limited utility to an analysis that reduces every interaction to coercion or that distrusts any performance of unity and forgiveness as disingenuous. Similarly, even as some participants suggested Alphonse's confession was coerced, other participants implied that he may have been the one exerting pressure on others, such as Grace. I fear that focusing analysis on measuring coercion risks reproducing the hierarchy of suffering contained in the government's dominant narrative of the genocide, which silences and delegitimizes particular forms of experience (Burnet 2012; Doughty 2008; Lemarchand 2009).

Likewise, in the comite y'abunzi example with Beata and Joselyne, while we can and should ask how coercion shaped the women's participation, we need to move beyond coercion to explore the complex dynamics around why Joselyne would come to a legal forum to address Beata's accusations that she engaged in sexual acts with passing men, or to examine what was at stake in the kinds of logics and language that mediators used to reason with the participants. Similarly, the employment dispute between the watchman and the nuns before the legal aid clinic does not seem to be adequately captured as a "crime of exploitation," which Harri Englund writes of in connection with legal aid as mediation in Malawi (2006:123– 169). More generally, Rwandans routinely told me that they perceived the call for compromise within comite y'abunzi and the legal aid clinic as relatively benign, because individuals, not the state, served as plaintiffs and there was no armed police presence. People in structural positions that tended to render them vulnerable through gacaca sometimes felt the abunzi or the legal aid clinic staff could, in fact, challenge status quo power relations, such that the people likely to feel coerced were those with comparatively high economic, social, and political capital.

Overall, I suggest that it behooves us to move beyond the broad brush of coercive harmony, to attend equally to the fraught and iterative processes through which people varyingly took on and contested the self-regulating practices of mediation. My attention to coercion and negotiation may seem part of a theoretically dated discussion of structure and agency, yet these themes remain a central conundrum in contemporary scholarship on Rwanda (Burnet 2012; Clark 2010; Straus and Waldorf 2011; Thomson 2013), and in Rwanda itself, thanks to the strongly centralized, and increasingly authoritarian, state. Ultimately, I see acts of agency in Rwandans' use of grassroots legal forums, wanting to ensure I do not reduce Rwandans who participate in these forums to automatons, even as I recognize the deeply controlling and threatening nature of the state, and the way state power penetrates people's ordinary lives, as Thomson (2013) has richly described. Instead, I ask, how do people contest meanings of gender, guilt and innocence with respect to the genocide ("genocide citizenship"), access to resources, family, and ethnicity within postgenocide Rwanda's architecture of social repair? Examples throughout this book raise complex questions about why, when, and how people advocate for and against unity, and what, ultimately, is at stake in the debate over the legitimacy of mediation principles. The ethnographic chapters that make up the body of the book explore these contested negotiations in order to examine how people attempted to remake moral communities within frameworks of mediation.

Notes on Fieldwork and Field Sites

This book is based on eighteen months of ethnographic research I carried out in Rwanda between 2002 and 2008, including participant observation, interviews, and document analysis, conducted in Kinyarwanda, French, and English. I attended fifty-six gacaca sessions during an extended stay from July 2007 through July 2008, as well as fourteen mediation committee sessions and twelve legal aid clinic sessions. I supplemented attendance at gacaca sessions with repeated semistructured interviews with a cross-section of people in each area, including more than thirty gacaca judges, mediators, local authorities, and religious leaders. These numbers do not include the countless informal conversations I had with residents. For broader context, I conducted research in Kigali and at the International Criminal Tribunal for Rwanda (ICTR), including more than eighty interviews with NGO and ICTR staff and members of government in Kigali. I have changed all names in the text.

In order to work with the intended target of grassroots courts—most specifically the rural population, *abaturage*—and recognizing the importance of interacting with rural Rwandans rather than political and economic elites in the capital (De Lame 2005; Ingelaere 2010b:54; D. Newbury and C. Newbury 2000; Thomson 2010), I worked primarily in two field sites in southern Rwanda, one rural and one a midsize town, supplemented by periodic gacaca sessions in the neighborhood of Nyamirambo in Kigali. People in Ndora and Nyanza lived lives broadly representative of Rwanda's predominantly rural population—people in these sites participated in the same legal forums that were implemented nationwide, and they were broadly representative of national trends in economic activity (primarily agriculture), educational level (primary school), and religious activity (predominantly Christian). That is, their daily lives were recognizable to most rural Rwandans, and the problems they faced were familiar, in their reliance on agriculture, their targeting by government programs, and their recovery from genocide. Thus, my findings can be seen as suggestive beyond specific hillsides, even though, given the salience of regional variations in Rwanda (Burnet 2010; De Lame 2005; C. Newbury 1988) and how local dynamics of history and violence shaped the specific hurdles faced in rebuilding, I do not suggest my findings were uncritically identical for all areas of Rwanda.

South Province

The South Province is one of five provinces constituting Rwanda. The genocide plan faced initial resistance in the South Province in 1994. For the first two weeks after President Juvénal Habyarimana's plane was shot down, the region remained calm, as a handful of administrators—both Hutu and Tutsi—worked to suppress conflict amid national calls for attacks. The late historian and human rights activist Allison des Forges hypothesized, "Perhaps this reflected the history of the area, the heart of the old kingdom, where bonds between Tutsi and Hutu were multiple, long-standing, and strong, disposing the Hutu to defend Tutsi more vigorously. Remote from the major military posts, resisters in the region also had more time to organize their efforts before substantial military force was brought against them" (1999:496). Before the genocide, the region had high rates of interethnic marriage and a higher percentage of Tutsi than the national average of 15 percent. For example, Butare, the largest city in the South, home of the National University of Rwanda and the former colonial capital, was a quarter Tutsi before the genocide, higher than Kigali's 17 percent (Des Forges 1999:353, 432).

Killings only began when the genocidal regime sent militias from the capital, at which point the bloodshed escalated to new levels of scope and intensity (Des Forges 1999). Ultimately the violence was perpetrated by militias as well as civilians, people from inside the area and people who came from outside. Thousands of Burundian Hutu refugees, who had been living in the province since fleeing national massacres in 1993, participated once the situation deteriorated. Confusion increased further as tens of thousands of Rwandans passed through on the way to Burundi or the Democratic Republic of the Congo (DRC) for safety. This history—which combined coexistence, protection, and catastrophic violence—made the South Province a particularly compelling place in which to learn how people more than a decade later were rebuilding their lives, particularly using legal forums and understandings of the past to shape collective belonging. By 2004, people living in the South Province represented a range of experiences from the genocide, including those who lived through it and others who returned after living as refugees or citizens in Burundi, the DRC, Uganda, Kenya, Tanzania, or Europe. The province's population was diverse across class, from farmers to civil servants to university professors, as well as across religion.

The South Province's population highlighted the challenge of rebuilding the social fabric across varying lines of identification. Grassroots legal forums in the South Province had high hurdles to overcome in terms of creating community. The province was among the worst affected by the genocide, where the consequences seem to have had the most severe and enduring effects (Des Forges 1999; Ndangiza 2007:4). Despite representing 25 percent of the population, the province housed 47 percent of cases of people accused as planners of the genocide (4,357 cases out of a total of 9,362), who were tried before Western-style domestic courts.[32] The province also had the most gacaca cases. Further, according to a nationwide 2007 survey, it had the highest levels of self-reported poverty, where 68 percent of people lived below the poverty line (Frw 90,000, or U.S. $180, per year), and 90 percent self-identified as somewhat poor, rather poor, or very poor (Ndangiza 2007). The same survey showed that the South Province had the lowest levels of meat consumption and mattress ownership in the country. Southerners also expressed the strongest preference for continuing to live on agriculture rather than engaging in land reforms, which were aimed at the "transformation of agriculture into a productive, high value, market-oriented sector" as part of the national economic development plan in Vision 2020 (Ministry of Finance 2000:3).

People's faith in and respect for the legal institutions which privileged their neighbors' knowledge, and which depended on lay judges and their neighbors' testimony, could not be taken for granted. According to the National Unity and Reconciliation Commission's 2007 report, compared to the rest of Rwanda, inhabitants of the South Province were more skeptical of decentralization and had "lower levels of interpersonal trust and a perceived lower ability to work together among citizens" (Ndangiza 2007:4). Thus, government through community in this province was particularly visible in people's efforts to create or defy binding relations and a shared moral field.

Ndora

Ndora, the sector capital of Gisagara district, was a rural agricultural community approximately eighteen miles south of the university town of Butare, near the Burundian border. The population as of December 2007 was 20,340 people.[33] Ndora was one of thirteen sectors in Gisagara district (which had a total population of 262,426).[34] A typical rural sector capital, it had a weekly market, a small town center with a handful of individual storefronts, a primary school, a health clinic, and several churches.

As of July 2008, when the main ethnographic research for this book was completed, as the gacaca process was winding down, 2,842 gacaca cases had been completed in Category Two (killing) in Ndora, and 5,824 cases had been completed in Category Three (crimes against property). Thirteen cases were outstanding on appeal, with thirty-three undecided requests for appeal. In general, officials and the population in Ndora reported that the gacaca process had proceeded relatively smoothly, though all expressed concern and frustration at the lack of resolution and enforcement of judgments in property cases as an ongoing problem. The comite y'abunzi in Ndora sector heard approximately 125 cases between June 2007 and May 2008. About 25 percent of those cases were refiled in the first-instance ordinary courts at the sector level.[35]

The patterns of genocide in Ndora were similar to elsewhere in the country, in terms of how from April to July 1994 groups of civilians armed with traditional weapons (farming machetes, sticks studded with nails, sharpened sticks, or knives) and occasionally guns chased people out of their homes or fields where they hid and killed them publicly, during daylight as well as at night. Civilian militias set up roadblocks to prevent people from escaping, and required passersby to show identity cards—if marked Tutsi, that meant death. As elsewhere in the country, there were collective killings at Gisagara district's health clinic and a church. The violence in Ndora was committed both by residents and by civilians and soldiers from outside.

Nyanza

Nyanza was an administrative town located on the main road from Kigali to Butare. It was the seat of the monarchy from 1899 to 1961, and a strong Tutsi presence remained there afterward (Des Forges 1999:353). It was named the capital of the South Province after decentralization in 2006, which brought new infrastructure and administrative development. The town of Nyanza had a population of fifty-six thousand, and the district as a whole had a population of 239,707.[36] I attended gacaca in Busasamana sector, which encompassed the center of town.

Given its size and central location as compared to Ndora, Nyanza had a more dynamic economic sector, before and after the genocide. Its market was vibrant and open daily, and the town had long been home to a hospital, several primary and secondary schools, courts, and offices of national companies like Electrogaz. The main national dairy plant, Nyabisindu Dairy, was located there, as well as a national museum at the home of the former *mwami* (king). Nyanza had several churches and a mosque. It was easily reached by public minibus, which ensured regular movement of people in and out, and it had several small hotels. Its population was more diverse and well educated than that of Ndora, with people having relocated there from other regions of Rwanda, with livelihoods not exclusively based on agriculture. Gacaca sessions for Busasamana sector were heard across the road from the High Court, up the hill from the newly opened Institute for Legal Policy and Development. In Busasamana sector, by mid-2008, 2,206 gacaca cases had been submitted in Category Two, 2,079 cases had been submitted in Category Three, and 538 cases were appealed.[37]

During the genocide, the *bourgmestre* of Nyanza, Jean-Marie Vianney Gisagara, a Hutu, refused to ally himself with the Hutu power movement, and he helped the area resist the genocide in the initial weeks. He repelled attacks against Tutsi from outsiders, and kept order locally, punishing and imprisoning those who attacked Tutsi (Des Forges 1999:469). The military found and killed Mr. Gisagara in late April, at which point the massacres intensified, and victims attempted to flee (Des Forges 1999:497). The patterns of violence in Nyanza were similar to those in Ndora and elsewhere nationwide, in terms of how perpetrators included a mixture of civilians and militias, and how they chased victims out of their homes and rounded up and killed them in central locations like hospitals or schools. Administrators and civilians set up a network of roadblocks to prevent escape, manned by armed civilian militias. Dynamics of violence further intensified as the Rwandan Patriotic Front (RPF) gained ground in Rwanda, bringing increased military skirmishes between the RPF and the army around Nyanza beginning in May (Des Forges 1999:585). Gacaca sessions in Busasamana included extensive testimony about events at local hospitals, orphanages, schools, and churches, as well as the actions of individuals at roadblocks.

Gacaca in Busasamana was complicated by the movement of people in and out of Nyanza during the genocide. This meant that victims and killers often had not been, and were not now, residents of the area. Some were only passing through Nyanza in 1994. Many accused perpetrators had to be summoned from where they now lived in Kigali, for example, or others could not be located and were tried in absentia. This challenged the idea, implicit in gacaca, that cases were tried among people who knew one another then and now. The composition of gacaca sessions in Busasamana demonstrated the more fluid, contingent constellations of people who lived together during and after the genocide. Another issue complicating gacaca in Nyanza was the military's heavy involvement there, meaning many victims' deaths had no obvious perpetrators to accuse before gacaca. Many cases involved complicated discussions of complicity—for example, how responsible a defendant was for handing over a victim to the soldiers or for cutting down bushes to inhibit Tutsi from seeking shelter, whether by independent initiative or on authorities' orders.

Property cases were a significant concern in Nyanza, as looting was rampant. More expensive property was taken in towns, and so the resolution and enforcement of these cases was as difficult as in Ndora, if not more so. Overall, alongside the higher education level of participants (though still only a minority had completed secondary school) and the more cosmopolitan nature of economic and social connections, there was more skepticism in Nyanza than in Ndora about the suitability of customary-style law for handling genocide crimes. This skepticism translated to comite y'abunzi as well. People often tried to find ways to circumvent comite y'abunzi and take their complaints, such as a failure of contract in a business transaction, straight to courts. Often these disputants had only a passing acquaintance with one another.

Methods, Analysis, and Ethics

When I began my fieldwork in 2002, there seemed to be no way to avert one's gaze from or close one's ears to the discourse about gacaca, or the profound social force of law. New training facilities were established, including faculties of law at the growing number of universities in Rwanda. A Bar Association was created in 1997 for the first time, and it grew from thirty to more than three hundred members by the end of 2007 (Kimenyi 2007). Existing courts and legal structures were refurbished and new ones created, including construction of new buildings. In my specific field sites in 2007–2008, a new Institute for Legal Policy and Development was built and opened in Nyanza, and two new court buildings were constructed in Nyamirambo. The ability of "rule of law" to create order was a visible sign of the law's presence as a form of social control used to regulate the conduct of citizens (Foucault 1982; Rose 1999). This was particularly clear in Kigali, which residents and visitors described as orderly and safe in comparison with regional cities like Kampala and Nairobi. New laws took many forms, such as banning the use of plastic bags, prohibiting the raising of animals within city limits, and removing beggars and ad hoc venders from the streets. While in 2005 the ubiquitous moto-taxi drivers were bare-headed, by 2007 they and their passengers wore newly mandated helmets, and even the most regally dressed women were required to straddle the bike, prohibited from riding side-saddle. Minibus drivers respected passenger capacity limits, and their money collectors no longer leaned awkwardly over tightly packed passengers but instead took their own seats. Across the country, groups of pink-clad prisoners engaged in work projects, whether constructing buildings or digging drainage ditches, a constant reminder of the state's power to lawfully incarcerate. Police officers lined the tarmacked roads, ensuring compliance with new traffic regulations, such as speed limits and seat belt requirements. Billboards across the country advertised the impending launch of inkiko gacaca.

This effect was even more pronounced when I came to Rwanda for the extended period of my research, from July 2007 through July 2008, midway through the gacaca process. Thus, even though I did not intend to study legal processes when I first arrived in Rwanda in late 2002, nor when I began preliminary work as a graduate student in 2004, I was quickly drawn in. Of course, it has become an anthropological trope to assert that one "did not go into the field expecting to study *xyz*" but rather "stumbled upon it," as a means of performing authenticity and expertise. I revert to this explanation here in part to reflexively illustrate the palpable force of "law" in this period but more centrally to make explicit the temporal framing of this research. The unique temporal dimensions of my research came into even clearer relief when I returned briefly to Rwanda in 2013, several years after the close of the gacaca process, when the rhythm of life was no longer marked by regular interruption of the "state of exception" (Agamben 2005) of gacaca days. This book tells a story tightly linked to a particular time period, even as I make claims that may extend beyond it.

Many scholars have noted particular challenges of conducting research in postgenocide Rwanda, including government interference in research (Burnet 2012:25; Chakravarty 2012; Ingelaere 2010a:42, 50; Pottier 2002; Thomson 2010:22) and people's subsequent "selective telling" (King 2009:128). They note that "simply asking ordinary Rwandans about their experiences before the *gacaca* courts is unlikely to produce reliable results" and emphasize that "researchers must be able to recognize the government's version of events" (Thomson 2011a:375–376) in order to avoid "taking the 'mise-en-scene,' or stage-setting for granted" (Ingelaere 2010a:42). As a close Rwandan friend and colleague commented, "People will often just tell you what they think you want to hear." These challenges are arguably best met by ethnographic methods (Burnet 2012:33), with the focus on long-term engagement, repeated social interactions across diverse social fields, and participant observation as well as interviews.

Focusing on specific sites over an extended time allowed me to contextualize the social interactions in the gacaca courts as part of broader life. I spent several days a week in each field site over a full year, and so I became a familiar presence. In analyzing case sessions, I took note of who was speaking, what and how it was said, and how people spoke across sessions, and I compared and contextualized their comments with other conversations and observations in and outside sessions, and over time. Consistent with ethnographic studies of law, I studied legal forums "in context," aiming for "thick understandings of law *in* everyday life" (Nader 2002a:71). This meant, for example, not looking at the courts as autonomous institutions but seeing how people and disputes moved in and out of these forums, and how they were linked to other dimensions of daily life. Studying gacaca, comite y'abunzi, and the legal aid clinic ethnographically meant examining not just legal procedures and regulations but also meanings, and seeing not just what should happen de jure but what de facto occurred. As Moore writes, "The goal is to try to understand what is going on, and what it means to the actors, and to the collectivities in which they are embedded" (Moore 2005:3). Throughout the book, I use several specific case examples in detail as exemplary of the many other cases I attended.

Further, consistent with ethnographers of law, I situated my fieldwork, conducted in a specific place and time, in historical and global context to identify how contemporary legal practices are a complex product of past practices and global processes (Moore 2001; Nader 2002a). In my analysis I attend to how, as Mary Moran has written with respect to gender ideologies in particular, "profound transformations . . . that emerge from any post-conflict situation must be seen as grounded in *both* pre-war social institutions and forms of authority as well as in the new opportunity structures characterizing both the wartime and post-war contexts" (Moran 2012:52). Much of this framing analysis is provided within Chapters 1 and 2.

I worked closely with a research assistant, for several reasons. While I am fluent in French (and my native English), my Kinyarwanda could not always keep pace with fast-moving, dialect-inflected discussions in case sessions or interviews. Further, our discussions enriched my analysis and aided with professionalizing a Rwandan researcher. Lastly, presenting myself alongside a Rwandan accompanier together with my official paperwork was necessary for following channels of authority and operating in the open to reduce unnecessary suspicion (Burnet 2012:25; Thomson 2010:23). I did translations myself, or with his help. The vignettes included below are condensed from the detailed written notes I took of the proceedings in each case (sometimes supplemented with audio recordings and photographs, for which I had government permission, and which I used sparingly); I spent hours fleshing out my notes each evening.

Conducting ethnographic research during and on the gacaca process brought its own particular challenges. Anxieties were high, and people were cautious about talking, not surprising in a context of public criminal trials where people's loved ones could go to jail or return home based on oral testimony from neighbors. Government surveillance was pronounced, of me as well as of the Rwandans with whom I worked, given the strong government control over the production of knowledge in and about Rwanda that other ethnographers have noted (Burnet 2012; Pottier 2002; Thomson 2010). I took a conservative approach to following up on specific cases outside of trial sessions, making myself available to talk and asking open-ended questions, while also demonstrating my willingness "to leave some stones unturned, to listen to what my informants deemed important, and to demonstrate my trustworthiness by not prying where I was not wanted" (Malkki1995:51), as Liisa Malkki influentially said of her work with Burundian refugees two decades ago. Probing questions designed to ferret out the truth of motivations that influenced case sessions often risked being met with silence or hostility, or risked resulting in revocation of my research permit. I sometimes decided *not* to ask. I listened intently to silences, as Burnet also described doing during her research in postgenocide Rwanda (Burnet 2012:33). I made the choices I deemed to be most ethical in not exacerbating an already fragile situation, and, like many other ethnographers in so-called conflict or postconflict settings,[38] I see this empathic, active listening (Borneman 2002) as a strength in humanistic social science research. If I am cautious in my analysis at times, it is to avoid overstating or overimposing certainty upon a complex situation in which people themselves tended to feel unsure.

Crucially, I lived with Rwandans (both in the South Province and in Kigali) throughout my time in Rwanda, including people from different social positions, sharing a roof, meals, and housework on a daily basis. Living with Rwandans (not with other Western expatriates, and not alone) enabled me to at least begin to penetrate the "veil of secrecy" that characterizes much of Rwandan life, with its heavy distinction between private and public (Burnet 2012:36, 144; see also De Lame 2005). This intimacy exposed me to quotidian dimensions of postgenocide life that allowed me to more richly contextualize the discussions I saw in legal forums. For example, lying in bed at midday, curtains drawn, with a friend suffering from headaches and stomachaches she attributed to secondary genocide trauma helped me to understand the pervasive and even destructive force of the genocide commemoration period. Talking with a housemate on gacaca day as he worked from home and would not even venture out to the garden so as to avoid drawing attention to his not attending court that day underscored the realities of state enforcement on participation.

Attending weddings or bringing food to ill family friends illustrated the moral economies of care that formed the fabric of daily life. Sharing the news that I was pregnant in the final months of my fieldwork was one of the most unexpected forms of intimacy, as it brought into even more vivid relief expectations about gender roles in relation to life stages, and the relationship between motherhood, pregnancy, and violence, as, for example, people recommended I not attend gacaca trials for fear of harming the growing baby. It also evoked explicit discussions of future-making as I became a proxy for discussions about imagined alternative futures.

Perhaps most important for my arguments here, the sustained personal and social engagement enabled by living with Rwandans allowed me to triangulate from other directions, when I could not generate the detailed linkages between case sessions and everyday life that are exemplified in the work of standard-bearing legal anthropologists of Africa, such as Max Gluckman and Sally Falk Moore. I spoke at length informally with the Rwandans with whom I lived and worked about their disputes (legal and otherwise), even if I did not participate in those case sessions myself, and I sat with them through sidebar conversations about gacaca and other legal disputes, while cooking over a wood fire, drinking tea, sharing meals, or walking slowly, fingers interlaced, through hard-packed paths. These engagements with Rwandans outside legal spaces allowed me to recognize with confidence how the discussions I saw within legal forums were connected with daily life more widely.

One of the greatest ethnographic challenges in Rwanda is remaining open and even neutral, walking a tightrope among people carrying harrowing experiences that are often shaped by very different perspectives. For me, the most important measure of legitimacy of the findings I present in these pages lies in whether, and how, the Rwandans who blessed me with their time and trust recognize that I was listening and hearing. Perhaps from this comes the greatest claim to accuracy in the narratives and arguments within this book: if they can see themselves and one another in these stories and recognize how they are engaged in a fragile, iterative, hopefully commensurable process to rebuild.

Outline of the Book

Chapters 1 and 2 provide background and framing, setting the stage for the ethnographic argument in the subsequent chapters. I begin Chapter 1 by

examining the production of history and politics of memory in postgenocide Rwanda. I illustrate the dominant version of history the government
used from 2004 to 2008 through a speech provided by President Kagame at
the ten-year anniversary of the genocide, in order to show how the government framed belonging and justified current configurations of power, connections, and exclusion. Specifically, I argue that the dominant narrative's
lacunae served to discredit the international community, emphasize
national rather than regional dynamics, and mask divisions, which rendered thinkable the use of grassroots harmony models and mass prosecutions for genocide crimes. In Chapter 2, I situate the postgenocide legal
forums in historical context, showing how contemporary trends toward
local legal forums and inequality in law have echoes in earlier periods in
Rwanda. I argue that analyzing Rwanda's postgenocide legal forums as harmony legal models overcomes three persistent dichotomies within transitional justice discourse: it allows us to overcome a reification of transitional
justice to see how disputes about ordinary concerns and political violence
are intertwined; it corrects an elusive focus on pure customary law as distinct from universal legal principles by attending to the importance of contextualization; and it foregrounds how harmony and punishment are
inextricable in these institutions.

In Chapters 3, 4, and 5, I focus on how people maneuvered within the
architecture of social repair of gacaca courts, comite y'abunzi, and the legal
aid clinic, respectively. In each chapter, I explore how people experienced
mediation efforts combined with punishment across these different forums.
In Chapter 3, I show how gacaca sessions were deeply contextualized, and
thus served as spaces in which people could reconstruct moral orders,
debating the meaning of collective belonging and negotiating the micropolitics of reconciliation in relation to genocide citizenship and material loyalty. I suggest that the contentious conversations in gacaca sessions brought
to the fore some of the disagreements and divisions lurking behind Rwandans' superficial public agreements, and illustrated the widespread disagreement with the simplified notions of causality, guilt, and innocence in the
master narrative.

In Chapter 4 I shift to an examination of comite y'abunzi as a harmony
legal model in which law-backed mediation combined harmony and punishment. I show how, as with gacaca, comite y'abunzi sessions entailed contextualized conversations in which people negotiated the micropolitics of
reconciliation, specifically in relation to family and community. Cases

before comite y'abunzi were both within families and between families and often centered on land, and thus they were intimately intertwined with the economics of memory and negotiating the meaning of exchange in relation to social networks. These cases in particular show the overlaps between genocide-related disputes and quotidian disputes in the aftermath of genocide, complicating assumptions about among whom and about what "reconciliation" needed to occur in postgenocide Rwanda.

I turn to the legal aid clinic in Chapter 5, examining how harmony and punishment combined in similar and different ways in a legal forum based not on customary law but on universal legal principles. I show how clients at the legal aid clinic were frequently directed to mediation as in the other forums, and consider how the contextualization again allowed for people to use these mediation efforts as spaces to contest the meaning of family, community, and justice. Cases before the legal aid clinic bring to light tensions between legalization and mediation, and they show how mediation was situated within a broader system of dispute resolution. These cases further show the limitations of focusing exclusively on genocide crimes versus ordinary disputes, or on customary-style law as distinct from Western-style law.

In Chapter 6, I focus on the mediators at the heart of these legal forums, showing how they served as intermediaries between professional representatives of government and their neighbors. Lay judges' deep insider status illustrates the deep contextualization of these harmony models. Attention to lay judges reveals the textured ways the government-through-community approach unfolded. I claim that lay judges showed a side of state power that was improvisational and ambiguous, which is crucial to moving beyond coercion to understand how people experienced variations in state power in Rwanda. In the Conclusion, I briefly offer three cautions for transitional justice and peace-building practice: to relinquish the search for a pure cultural solution; to recognize that while coercion and instrumentality may be increased by legal forums they are not uniquely created by them; and to recognize that reconciliation processes may indeed be inherently violent and fraught.

Silencing the Past: Producing History and the Politics of Memory

Like many outsiders visiting or living in Rwanda—expatriate aid workers, researchers, tourists—I visited the Murambi genocide memorial early in my time there, in July 2004, as I was conducting several months of fieldwork on the politics of commemoration at the ten-year anniversary of the genocide. Murambi is located three kilometers outside the town of Gikongoro in the southwest of Rwanda. It was the site of a massacre in which tens of thousands of Tutsi men, women, and children were killed while seeking refuge in April 1994 at a technical school that was under construction. Murambi was (and still is) one of the most publicized genocide memorials in Rwanda, in large part because more than eight hundred corpses have been disinterred and remain preserved in chalky white limestone, carefully resting on low tables in room after room of the original school.

What made my visit different from the visits of most others who went to Murambi between 2004 and 2011 is that I was invited to come inside the two-story administrative building, which was added in 1998, to see the exhibit a few weeks before it was due to be formally opened. I had ridden to Murambi that morning with a Rwandan staff member of Aegis Trust, the British NGO that just three months earlier, in April 2004, had successfully opened the national genocide memorial in the Gisozi section of Kigali. Aegis also had a contract to turn Murambi into one of the Ministry of Memory's seven designated national genocide memorials, and there were plans to have an official opening later that month.[1] The day I visited the Murambi site it was buzzing with activity, as dozens of people worked outside and inside, finishing reexcavating a mass grave from which bodies had been disinterred years before, smoothing cement on the collective burial site, erecting a flagpole, laying carpet, adjusting lights, washing windows, painting walls and fences. A landscape architect walked around on his own, surveying the site. My Aegis colleague first accompanied me on a tour, in which the primary guide—an elderly man whom I saw on later visits, with a pronounced divot on his skull where, as he explained, he had narrowly missed being killed by a bullet during the massacre at Murambi—opened doors to room after room filled with ghostly bodies of those killed by the massacre.[2] My colleague then suggested I go inside on my own to look at the exhibit, which was almost complete, while he did further consultations.

Inside, after I recovered (as much as one can) from the emotional and sensory assault of the seemingly endless corpses, I saw confirmation that the work on the memorial was indeed nearly complete. I recognized the floor-to-ceiling panels that lined the walls (Figure 1) as very similar to those at the Gisozi genocide memorial in Kigali. They told the story of Rwanda's history in virtually the same way, with a combination of enlarged photographs and images interspersed with text in three languages (English, French, and Kinyarwanda). The final sections emphasized the history specifically of what had occurred on this site (see the text in the box at the end of this chapter). One wall prominently featured a six-minute video including interviews with survivors and some of the alleged perpetrators of the Murambi massacre. A survivor's narrative was prominently displayed on another wall. My host later told me that, as the text indicated, officials planned to "scientifically pre-serve" (cryogenically freeze, another Aegis staff told me) three corpses in the interior room, and to reinter the remaining corpses outside, pursuant to the wishes of many survivors to provide proper burial for victims.

At the close of the day, as we returned to Kigali, my host invited me to return to Murambi to attend the official opening a few weeks later. For the next several months, as I continued to follow up with him, he or his colleagues repeatedly told me that the official opening had been postponed, for this or that simple reason. When I returned to the States, the interior space remained unopened. In later years as I returned to Rwanda and at times visited Murambi, the interior remained closed, except to allow visitors to enter, sign a guest book, and make a donation. I was told by a variety of guides that there was "nothing inside," or it was "not open yet," or it would "open sometime soon." Behind the main building in the original rooms of the technical school, the excavated bodies remained in their places on wooden slats. Meanwhile, changes to the exterior spaces reflected

Figure 1. Murambi genocide memorial interior, July 2004; some of the text on the panels inside the memorial is given at the end of this chapter (photo by author).

the ongoing professionalization of the site, consistent with a global lexicon of memorialization, including additional signage, and an aesthetically haunting display of victims' clothes strung on lines in an open-ended school room. Evidence of the unraveling of diplomatic ties between Rwanda and France surfaced, including two new signs marking "Place of French Flag during Operation Turquoise" and "French soldiers were playing volley here" atop a knoll that guides repeatedly emphasized was the location of the original mass grave.

The exhibit eventually opened in May 2011, seven years after I saw it the first time. For the doors to stay closed for so long while the exhibit was virtually complete points to a broader set of issues that characterized the treatment of Rwandan history and memory at that time, which I explore in this chapter. According to hushed conversations I had with many people working on the site, though funding or logistical issues may have been the voiced justifications for delay, the main reason the exhibit stayed closed over the years was concern about the written history included inside. This underscores the sensitivity and contestation around Rwanda's history, as well as the consolidation and control of a particular version of Rwanda's past and how it is situated within a broader professionalized politics of memory. Murambi's closed doors provide an apt illustration of how, as the late Haitian anthropologist Michel-Rolph Trouillot put it, "any historical narrative is a particular bundle of silences" (1995:27), and the closed doors lead us to question the content, production, and stakes of those silences.

Trouillot's influential book, *Silencing the Past,* thus provides the title and orientation for this chapter, as I heed Trouillot's call to "focus on the process of historical production," specifically through "examin(ing) in detail the concrete production of specific narratives" in order to "discover the differential exercise of power that makes some narratives possible and silences others" (1995:22–25). Silence is a theme that figures heavily in contemporary scholarship on Rwanda,[3] and I return to it in more detail at the individual and interpersonal level in subsequent chapters. Here, I use Murambi's shuttered exhibit as indicative of the present-absences in story-telling about Rwanda's past, lacunae that were produced through deliberate, active choices made on behalf of the governing regime and people working under its surveillance.

This chapter unfolds in three parts. First, I present a brief overview of history for the reader unfamiliar with Rwanda, compiled from others' rich historiography, with specific attention to the points of debate.[4] I remain ever-cognizant here that, as Trouillot underscored, "facts are never meaningless: indeed, they become facts only because they matter in some sense, however minimal. . . . Facts are not created equal: the production of traces is always also the creation of silences" (1995:29). I emphasize the contestation in order to remind us that the "facts" I present are caught up in webs of debate with implications in the present.

Second, in order to reveal the interplay of traces and silences, and to lay bare how facts about Rwanda's past matter, I juxtapose this overview with the dominant version of history the government used from 2004 through 2008, which was part of the "total environment" (Abramowitz 2014) of postgenocide transformation created by the policy of unity and reconciliation. I provide ethnographic examples from the ten-year commemoration, including from the Murambi site and from the text of President Kagame's official commemoration speech on April 7, 2004. The government narrative of history dominated the public sphere from 2004 through 2008, intended equally for resocializing Rwandans and for the benefit of the international community. During my fieldwork, this narrative was propagated in regular feature articles in pro-government newspapers, in radio broadcasts reaching across the country, and in official government documents. It was taught in schools, narrated at public events locally and nationally, and served as the core of genocide memorialization and *ingando* "solidarity camps" attended by released prisoners, returning refugees, and students. It was ubiquitous, equally strong in its broadcast in rural and urban areas across regions in Rwanda. (In subsequent chapters I explore how people narrated the past in the ways that dovetailed and diverged from the master narrative.)

In the final section of the chapter, I analyze the implications of the inclusions and exclusions in the dominant narrative for understanding the politics of belonging in postgenocide Rwanda, and what is rendered thinkable versus unthinkable. I thus follow Trouillot in my approach throughout the chapter in "determining not what history is . . . but *how history works* (1995:25, emphasis mine). Specifically, I explicitly link my analysis and deconstruction of the official narrative to the harmony legal models at the core of my book in order to show what they render possible versus what they make "unthinkable" (Trouillot 1995:27). I show, for example, how historians' critique of the idea of precolonial unity should render even more suspect the use of culture to justify harmony in grassroots legal models. I show how the legal models emerged from the master narrative and contributed to the formalization of genocide citizenship, even as people used the models to negotiate belonging and contest implications within the master narrative. This chapter thus serves as part of my argument that in postgenocide Rwanda, people's understanding of the past mattered to how they framed belonging in the present, at intimate levels as well as more broadly in terms of citizenship. Further, it is central to my assertion that contemporary Rwanda is marked both by continuities with, and ruptures from, its past.

Overall, I intend this chapter to contribute to the rich literature that critiques the official postgenocide master narrative of history and politics of memory for their oversimplifications, erasures, and instrumentality.[5] This is particularly important for at least two reasons. First, Rwanda has proven a particularly troubling example of the interplay of political power and violence with collective memory—the concept that when we remember we do so as members of social groups, and that our understandings of the past legitimate social orders in the present (Connerton 1989; Halbwachs 1980). Scholars of Rwanda and the Great Lakes region of Africa more widely have specifically shown how people's "mental maps of history" (C. Newbury 1998:7) or "mythico-histories" (Malkki 1995) order and reorder particular social and political categories in the region, and have created imagined communities of fear and hatred (Lemarchand 2009:57, 70). Evidence shows how Rwandan political leaders have used competing interpretations of Rwanda's particularly contentious history as a central tool in solidifying, polarizing, and mobilizing group identities toward violent conflict in the latter half of the twentieth century, including the genocide.

Second, political elites in Rwanda have long controlled and centralized the production of history to justify their own rule, while obscuring their role in doing so (D. Newbury 2009; Vansina 2004). Historian Jan Vansina has argued that the royal court in Rwanda used "historical remembrance" as the "ultimate legitimation" of its rule as far back as 1780, and by the nineteenth and twentieth centuries the royal court was an "institution in charge of controlling the production of history and its representation . . . an institution of such a wide reach and such a degree of subtlety" that researchers and Rwandans alike became "caught in its cognitive glue" (2004:5, 90–95).[6] A decade after the genocide, many outsiders and Rwandans similarly found themselves caught in the "cognitive glue" of the regime's version of history (Des Forges 1995; Pottier 2002; Reyntjens 2005), while there was "ample evidence that the regime continue[d] to manipulate the historical record for the sake of an official memory" (Lemarchand 2009:105), providing "disinformation" about both the distant past and the period from 1990 through the present (Pottier 2002; Reyntjens 2009:57–58). Denaturalizing Rwanda's dominant narrative is crucial, thus, to keep us attuned to how contemporary versions of the past are actively produced in discursive, embodied, and material ways, and how they legitimate particular forms of belonging, exclusion, rights, and access in the present.

Historical Context and Points of Debate

For hundreds of years, ancestors of the people who came to be called Hutu and Tutsi in Rwanda lived side by side. They spoke the same language (Kinyarwanda), shared the same traditional religion, participated in the same economic networks, and intermarried to varying degrees. Precolonial Rwanda is most simply understood as a monarchy, ruled by Tutsi kings and chiefs. Lineages and patron-client ties figured heavily in social and political organization.

The nature of social harmony, stratification, and power has been heavily debated, characterized by the Hutu-power narrative as feudal exploitation and by the postgenocide government as harmonious. Much of this debate centers around the characterization of *ubuhake,* a controversial form of cattle clientship. Ubuhake was a contract between individuals in which the patron (*shebuja*) gave one or two head of cattle to the client (*umugaragu*) in usufruct but maintained ownership of the cattle and assured his client of protection. The client had to help his patron whenever needed, and the relationship was hereditary (Maquet 1961:129–142; Vansina 2004:47). The institution had a powerful political role in incorporating Rwandans in a dense network of social ties, yet it was a network that resulted in a social integration based on inequality, in which Hutu had access to cattle and protection, while Tutsi maintained ultimate control over cattle, the symbol of political, economic, and social power (Maquet 1961; Reyntjens 1987:72–73). Anti-Tutsi propaganda in newspapers, radio, and schools from 1959 through 1994 cast ubuhake as a historically deep form of domination and exploitation of all Hutu by all Tutsi in the precolonial and colonial periods. Much scholarship has, however, now shown that while there was indeed deep inequality in precolonial Rwanda, precolonial kings were not simply autocrats who ruled as they pleased (Vansina 2004:66, 85), and patron-client institutions did not merely involve exploitation of subordinate Hutu (C. Newbury 1988:90; Vansina 2004:33).[7]

Similarly, the peopling of Rwanda—when the peoples referred to as Hutu, Tutsi, and Twa arrived in the territory now called Rwanda—has been long contested. The dominant view was that Tutsi arrived in the region centuries after Hutu, but the details and implications of this view remain contentious. Did it mean Tutsi were destined to rule, or that they were foreigners who should not be allowed to do so? Did it mean Hutu were autochthonous and therefore had rights to govern? There remains debate about the precise amount and origins of biological difference and what the differences mean for interpreting human migrations (Cavalli-Sforza et al. 1994; Excoffier et al. 1987; Mamdani 2001:43–50), but Vansina's recent analysis suggests that what physical differences existed must go back millennia, not centuries, as posited in the migration histories (Vansina 2004:37–38, 198).

Current scholarship argues that the categories of Hutu and Tutsi were primarily socioeconomic, referring to elites or to control over wealth (particularly cattle) and power (C. Newbury 1988:11–12). As far back as the seventeenth century, the term Tutsi "referred mostly to a social class among herders, a political elite," while the term Hutu applied to everyone else, including poor Tutsi and foreigners (Vansina 2004:37, 134–135).[8] The boundaries of the ethnic categories had some flexibility, so people could move across statuses over generations as their families gained or lost wealth (D. Newbury 1998:84–86, 2009; Twagilimana 2003:55). Further, ethnicity was only one form of identity, and other forms, such as region, class, lineage (a corporate descent group), and clan (a social descent group), were often more significant (d'Hertefelt 1971; C. Newbury 1978:17, 1988; D. Newbury 1998:83, 2009). The term for ethnic group, *ubwoko*, also translates as clan. Each clan was made up of people from all three putative "ethnicities," and clans changed over time, operating as strategic alliances between lineages (C. Newbury 1988:96, 1980b; Vansina 2004:34–35, 198).

Colonial rule arrived in Rwanda when the first German colonial officer arrived in 1897. Two decades of German rule influenced primarily the royal court without interfering substantially in internal affairs. When Belgians took over Rwanda during World War I, in 1916, they extended their influence deeper than that of the Germans, such that Belgian rule had more extensive social and economic impacts. The colonial state contributed to formalizing and legitimizing the Hutu-Tutsi distinction, reifying formerly fluid boundaries, in its efforts to make more legible the existing complex ethnic configurations (Lemarchand 2009:9; Scott 1998). As part of the standardization of the administration in the late 1920s, the Belgians introduced identity cards that marked ethnicity (Des Forges 1995; Twagilimana 2003:55). The reification of ethnic groups was linked to European ideas of biological race, and it took an essentialized and hierarchical view of Hutu and Tutsi, which contemporary scholarship has completely debunked. It built on the Hamitic Hypothesis, put forth by explorer John Hanning Speke in 1863. Speke proposed that a race of tall, sharp-featured people who had Caucasian origins and were superior to the native Negro had introduced the cultures and civilizations of Central Africa.[9] Anthropologists converted Speke's conjectures into scientific truths with regard to African peoples in ensuing years (e.g., Seligman 1930; Westermann 1949 [1934]).[10]

Through the twentieth century, scholars writing on Rwanda continued to emphasize that there were three separate groups in Rwanda (Hutu, Tutsi, and Twa), and continued to imply that their current form had existed relatively unchanged since Tutsi arrived in the tenth century (D. Newbury and C. Newbury 2000:836; Twagilimana 2003:53). For example, anthropologist Jacques Maquet described Rwandans' prevailing stereotypes of each other in the 1950s as follows: "Tutsi were said to be intelligent (in the sense of astute in political intrigues), capable of command, refined, courageous, and cruel; Hutu, hardworking, not very clever, extrovert, irascible, unmannerly, obedient, physically strong" (Maquet 1961:164).[11] Explanatory models privileging biology were perhaps particularly seductive and enduring in the absence of other clear markers of difference between the groups.[12] Even as belief in the scientific validity of race began to weaken and scholars moved from biological toward other sociocultural means of identifying groups, Hutu and Tutsi did not fit easily into typical definitions of ethnic groups as marked by distinctive cultural features, such as language or religion, used to define boundaries in opposition to other collective identities (Eller 1999; Tambiah 1989; Weber 1968:389). While occupation varied, what cultural differences existed were minimal—for example, preferences in diet—and the groups had intermarried for centuries.

Further, the colonial period dramatically increased the political salience of ethnicity, while undermining the political autonomy of lineage groups and their role as a form of belonging, and changing the relations between the groups Hutu and Tutsi for the worse (Lemarchand 1970; Longman 2010a; C. Newbury 1988; Reyntjens 1985). Both the Germans and the Belgians, accompanied by the Catholic Church, ruled indirectly through the Tutsi kings and chiefs and discriminated against Hutu. Tutsi elites had preferential access to education and to administrative and church positions, because colonial leaders believed Tutsi were superior and excluded Hutu. Further, Rwandan political leaders used these outside ideas in their own efforts to articulate agendas and mobilize followers, with divisive consequences. The growing power of the colonial state privileged Tutsi's access to power while incorporating Rwanda into the world economy, which dramatically increased the advantages and disadvantages of being Tutsi versus being Hutu. While Tutsi chiefs had political power and were in a position to accumulate wealth through taxes, rural dwellers, who were predominantly Hutu, faced new demands, particularly under the Belgians, including increased taxes, compulsory cultivation of certain crops, and forced labor. Clientship institutions, particularly ubuhake, became less reciprocal and voluntary—in conditions of growing economic insecurity, people's "choice" to enter into clientship was a form of indirect or direct coercion—

and more rigid and exploitative, as they extended to less powerful people and became aligned with administrative demands (C. Newbury 1988:137–140). Overall, the condition of rural Hutu worsened, as they bore the brunt of the increasingly onerous forms of exploitation and discrimination (C. Newbury 1988:178–179; Reyntjens 1985:135–142). Yet not all the Tutsi were elites, even during the colonial period when virtually all elites were Tutsi (Codere 1973:70; D. Newbury and C. Newbury 2000:839).

The transition from colonial rule to independence is another period of Rwandan history that has been highly contested, described either as a democratic revolution framed around legitimate grievances where the majority took power from the minority or as precursor to genocide. By the 1950s, when Tutsi elites began calls for independence, Hutu activists became increasingly vocal, arguing that the elite Tutsi ruled in an oppressive and dominating manner, both under the precolonial feudal system and under Belgian rule, and benefited unfairly from the colonial administration. Hutu activists sought to address poverty, inequality, insecure access to land, inadequate access to education, and youth issues, and they argued for democracy and majority rule (Lemarchand 1970; C. Newbury 1988; Reyntjens 1985). They were successful in large part because they responded to and channeled widespread legitimate rural discontent generated by Hutu's shared structural position of oppression (C. Newbury 1978, 1980, 1988).

The United Nations set a date for independence, which Lemarchand (1970) argues propelled revolution and violence, because Hutu parties wanted to ensure they, not the Tutsi monarchy, held power before the deadline. The Belgian authorities and the Catholic Church switched their support to these newly established Hutu revolutionaries. The ensuing revolution was "powerfully assisted if not engineered by the Belgian authorities" (Lemarchand 2009:31). In 1959, the reigning king (*Umwami* Rudahigwa) died. In September 1959, Hutu parties won an overwhelming majority in legislative elections and decisively rejected the monarchy via referendum. On July 1, 1962, Rwanda regained formal independence from European rule.

The Hutu Revolution (1959–1962) was directed not against the Belgian colonial administration but against Tutsi, who faced intimidation and communal violence (Codere 1962; Lemarchand 1970; C. Newbury 1988:195; Reyntjens 1985:267–269). In November 1959, in response to a nonfatal Tutsi attack on a Hutu subchief, a group of Hutu attacked and killed four Tutsi notables. Widespread violent incidents against Tutsi spread across the country in a matter of days, sparing only three districts, though the attacks were initially limited mainly to burning and looting (C. Newbury 1988:194–195). Anti-Tutsi violence flared periodically and became more deliberate and marked with more bloodshed between November 1959 and the September 1961 elections (Lemarchand 1970).

The First Republic, from 1962 to 1973, was led by President Gregoire Kayibanda and his coalition of Hutu from the south. In 1963, exiled Tutsis invaded unsuccessfully from Burundi. In 1973, Juvénal Habyarimana seized the presidency in a popularly backed military coup, and he led the Second Republic from 1973 to 1994, with a northern Hutu power base. Scholars agree that after the transition in power at independence, Hutu leaders in the First and Second Republics did not reverse the oppressive leadership style of Rwabugiri and colonial authorities but continued to rule authoritatively, to centralize power in a small ethnic and regionally determined elite, to be intolerant of opposition, and to discriminate on the basis of ethnicity, now against Tutsi (Jefremovas 2002:124–125; Lemarchand 1970, 2009; Reyntjens 1985:521). Hutu revolutionaries in 1959–1962 and the Hutu-power government in the 1990s operated by similar logics, especially in terms of the marginalization of moderates, dynamics of fear, and winner-take-all politics (C. Newbury 1998).

The First and Second Republics created a political situation that excluded Tutsi from power and periodically victimized innocent Tutsi. In addition to the attacks between 1959 and 1961, after the failed Tutsi armed incursion in 1963 from Burundi, Tutsi political leaders were eliminated and between ten thousand and fourteen thousand Tutsi were killed, while thousands more were forced into exile (De Lame 2005:59; Reyntjens 1985:460–467). Beginning in 1973, there was another wave of violence when Habyarimana targeted Tutsi students and school staff in pogroms. Over time, this discrimination and violence created an extensive Tutsi diaspora community who became stateless but had legitimate claims to live in Rwanda. Between 1959 and 1963, two hundred thousand Tutsi were forced into exile: seventy thousand to Uganda, twenty-five thousand to the DRC (formerly Zaire), and fifty thousand to Burundi (Lemarchand 2009:31). By the 1980s, between four hundred thousand and six hundred thousand refugees were estimated to be living in neighboring countries, many the children of Tutsi who had fled earlier waves of violence (C. Newbury 1995:13). These refugees suffered as second-class citizens, unable to integrate into their host country, while the Habyarimana government claimed that due to demographic pressures, they could not return to Rwanda (C. Newbury 1995:13; Prunier 2009:13–16). For example, in 1982, thousands of Rwandan refugees in Uganda were forced to leave by President Milton Obote, but upon their arrival in Rwanda, they were refused the right to repatriate and were kept again in refugee camps until they were eventually returned to Uganda.

In 1990, a group of armed exiles, mostly Tutsi, successfully organized and invaded Rwanda as the Rwandan Patriotic Front (RPF), fighting to overthrow Habyarimana's government. Civil war ensued for the next three years. Anti-Tutsi violence intensified after the RPF invasion in 1990, when there were frequent retaliatory killings against Tutsi, as the Hutu government identified all Tutsi as RPF accomplices, who they feared were attempting to reestablish Tutsi hegemony. These massacres have been seen as "practice" for genocide (Lemarchand 2009:84; D. Newbury 1998:78).

Within Rwanda during the Second Republic, while elites consolidated power and there were advancements in public works, urban development, public health, and enrichment of a middle class, at the same time, poverty and inequality grew for rural Rwandans, both Hutu and Tutsi, often in relation to land access (Ansoms and Marysse 2005; De Lame 2005:63–64, 246; C. Newbury 1995; D. Newbury 1998; Reyntjens 1985:523). By the late 1980s, in the lead-up to genocide, tensions were exacerbated by the dynamics of the global political economy. Global coffee prices collapsed in 1989, and the International Monetary Fund implemented structural adjustment programs, including devaluing Rwanda's currency in 1990 and requiring Rwandans to "cost-share," which included paying higher fees for public services such as primary school, health care, and water. These factors both resulted in sharply deteriorating economic conditions and increased poverty for the vast majority of Rwandans (C. Newbury 1995; D. Newbury 1998:89). These economic constraints, combined with the disconnect between rural people and elites, which meant rural people were not meaningfully connected to the changing political situation, contributed to social tension and fear, especially among male youth, who were particularly vulnerable to recruitment by militias (C. Newbury and D. Newbury 1999: 91–92; D. Newbury 1998).

During this period, in the late 1980s and early 1990s, outside powers that controlled the flow of economic resources to Rwanda pushed the democratization process and legitimization of multipartyism (De Lame 2005:65). This reorganized structures of power and forced Habyarimana to open political space to others, which angered powerful members of his own regime and contributed to elites trying to eliminate challengers and reassert their hold on social, economic, and political dominance (Longman 1995; C. Newbury and D. Newbury 1999; D. Newbury 1998:80, 89). In 1991, Rwanda legitimized a multiparty system, which intensified the contest for political power. In 1993, with the support of the major Western powers, Tanzania brokered peace talks between the Rwandan government and the RPF that resulted in a power-sharing agreement known as the Arusha Accords.

Scholars have shown that during the early 1990s the organizational planning and conditions for genocide were put in place, countering interpretations dominant in the Western media that the violence was the unfortunate escalation of a civil war or a spontaneous eruption of hatred among people who were inherently violent (Des Forges 1999; Lemarchand 1995; Longman 1995; Mamdani 2001; C. Newbury 1995; D. Newbury 1995; Prunier 1995). They have shown that the genocide resulted not from a failed state but rather, from an unduly strong one, where state apparatuses—political organizations, military, and the administration—were used to commit genocide (Des Forges 1995; Lemarchand 2009:85). Organization involved distinct sets of actors, including Habyarimana's core group, the Presidential Guard, rural organizers at the commune level, and civilian militias called *Interahamwe*, "those who stand together." The genocide ideology of hatred targeting Tutsi was key to these efforts and was well established by 1992 (Des Forges 1995). Planning intensified after the signing of the Arusha Accords in 1993, when hardline elements within the Rwandan government and other Hutu extremists exploited ethnically based ideologies to mobilize the population as a strategy for maintaining power and simultaneously stepped up efforts to organize, indoctrinate, and arm segments of their supporters. Consistent with the dominant narrative, scholars have pointed to the role of the media and schools in fomenting ethnic division in the lead up to the genocide, particularly by propagating racist anti-Tutsi writings, cartoons, and songs, often based on the Hamitic ideology (Chrétien 1995; Des Forges 1995; King 2014; Lemarchand 2009). The international development aid system supported the processes that underlay the genocide by, for example, financing the processes of social exclusion, perpetuating humiliating practices, and ignoring growing racialization (Uvin 1998:224–238). The international arms trade in the wake of the end of the Cold War made it possible for the government to provide weapons for the newly developed militias (D. Newbury 1998:90). International actors knew about, but did not try to stop, growing anti-Tutsi massacres in the 1990s, and France even assisted the Habyarimana regime's military efforts against the RPF (Kroslak 2007; Lemarchand 2009:84).

On April 6, 1994, as President Habyarimana was flying home from finalizing details of the Arusha Accords, his plane was shot down above the Kigali airport. This plane crash, blamed by the Hutu government on Tutsi rebels, triggered a coordinated attempt by Hutu extremists to eliminate the Tutsi population. Within hours, a campaign of violence ignited in the capital and began to spread through the country. The Tutsi-led RPF broke the Arusha cease-fire and relaunched a military campaign, resuming its civil war against the Hutu regime. The country was thrown into confusion. The violence was carried out by highly organized state armies, as well as the coordinated and trained Interahamwe militias, which were groups of armed youth indoctrinated in the Hutu-power ideology who killed and openly terrorized the population. Though a U.N. peacekeeping force had twenty-five thousand troops on the ground, they were quickly withdrawn, along with foreign nationals. Adding to the confusion of the period, the vast majority of Hutu took to the roads, fleeing the violence and the approach of the RPF.

The details of the violence were horrifying, intimate, and unimaginable.[13] People targeted by the genocidal regime, whether Tutsi or Hutu opposition, had little chance of survival. Soldiers and police officers encouraged or coerced civilian involvement and forced civilians to "kill or be killed." Tutsi and those trying to protect them were massacred en masse in churches, schools, and public buildings where they gathered seeking safety, and were sought out in their homes and hunted while fleeing. Many of the people who killed their fellow Rwandans—often intimately, with machetes—had grown up together, went to the same churches and schools, and even intermarried and were related. Women of childbearing age were targeted, especially as objects of rape, sexual humiliation, and sexual mutilation (D. Newbury 1998). Identity cards—introduced by the Belgians but maintained by the First and Second Republics—were used by killers to determine victims' ethnicity. While the genocide spread nationwide, violence did not play out uniformly across the country; some politicians fought to avoid escalation of violence, and many individuals sought to save neighbors (Des Forges 1999; Janzen 2000; Jefremovas 1995; Longman 1995; Nduwayo 2002; D. Newbury 1998:80–82). In areas where peasants were relatively cohesive and empowered, they were less susceptible to ethnic appeals, and therefore violence had to be imported from outside (Des Forges 1999; Longman 1995). Many people protected others with whom they felt bonds of kin, neighborhood, religion, or humanity.

Researchers have shown clearly the egregiousness of the international community's failure to act, detailing the ways the U.N. Security Council and key actors such as the United States hesitated and did not intervene in ways that could have saved lives (Dallaire 2003; Power 2002; Prunier 1995). Members of the French government are widely understood, within Rwanda and outside, to have supported the genocidal regime and to have led a controversial intervention (Operation Turquoise) that resulted in aiding the escape of thousands of perpetrators (Kroslak 2007).

Debate remains on many points over the genocide: why people joined the killers, and how to understand the link between elite propaganda and individual actions; what the scale and meaning of Hutu casualties were; what the scale of participation was—how many Hutu participated versus how many tried to save neighbors, and how wide the web of collective guilt should be cast; and whether the RPF fighters were heroes or aggressors (Davenport and Stam 2009; Fujii 2009; Straus 2006; Vidal 1998). Those who call this period a civil war and negate the existence of genocide, equating all the killing during this period, are in disagreement with prevailing opinion and scholarship—and, since 2008, in contravention of Rwanda's genocide ideology law.

Further, the quantification of genocide victims remains highly contested. In the immediate wake of the genocide, scholars quoted a figure of approximately five hundred thousand victims, but consensus emerged at around eight hundred thousand victims within several years (e.g., Lemarchand 1995, 2009). In April 2004, on the eve of the ten-year anniversary commemorations, the government announced the tally was 937,000 victims, whom they claimed were predominantly Tutsi, and it said that with gacaca ongoing, more victims would likely be identified (Kazoora 2004). This official number rose to more than one million (Kagire 2009). Most scholars believe that both official figures are inflated, and that these numbers must include Hutu, including those killed by the RPF or the newly named Rwandan Patriotic Army (RPA) during and after the genocide. Davenport and Stam controversially claim that a majority of the victims were most likely Hutu, and that the events should be considered a politicide rather than a genocide (Davenport and Stam 2009).

The genocide is understood to have ended on July 4, 1994, when the RPF captured Kigali. The RPF put in place a government generally based on one that was mandated by the Arusha Accords, and it tried to govern in a situation marked by massive death and destruction, devastated infrastructure, and displaced population. The late 1990s continued to be marked by instability and violence. Hundreds of thousands of Tutsi returnees quickly began to cross the borders from Burundi and Uganda, while hundreds of thousands of Hutu refugees left the country for refugee camps in the DRC. Hutu insurgents living in these refugee camps launched periodic attacks into Rwanda, and RPA responded with attacks against them, under General Kagame. In 1996, the RPA was involved militarily in the DRC, both to clear the refugee camps in efforts to eliminate the rebel threat and to help overthrow President Mobutu, widely considered a dictator, and install Lauren-Désiré Kabila. In 1997, internal civil war resumed as rebel insurgents—former Interahamwe and members of Habyarimana's army—continued their guerrilla warfare across Rwanda, and the RPA retaliated. Again in 1998, the RPA entered the DRC to quell ongoing threats from Hutu Interahamwe. Rwanda made repeated forays into the DRC between 1998 and 2002 before officially withdrawing in 2002 because of the Pretoria Accords (Lemarchand 2009:26–27), but Reyntjens claims the RPA continued to maintain a clandestine presence (Reyntjens 2005:36). The official period of political governance transition ended in 2003 with Paul Kagame's election as president.

The Postgenocide Government's Master Narrative of History and Its Implications

The official Hutu-power narrative, propagated by the architects of the genocide to mobilize people and justify the violence, contended that the history of Rwanda was one of conquest by "foreign" Tutsi cattle herders who, through economic and military means, gradually imposed centuries of oppression and exploitation on the Hutu (Eltringham 2004; Malkki 1995; Rutembesa 2002; Semujanga 2003; Twagilimana 2003). This narrative goes on to assert that in the 1959 social revolution, the Hutu reversed this feudal situation and acquired their rightful place. They continued to defend their right to majority rule against domineering, power-hungry Tutsi who wished to reestablish hegemony and oppression, evidenced by continued Tutsi-led violent incursions into Rwanda.

The official postgenocide narrative was a renegotiation of the Hutu-power narrative, with altered evaluations and different implications for future action. It stated that the *Abanyarwanda* (inhabitants of Rwanda) were a single ethnic group, and that divisions were created by the colonial leaders. As the national genocide memorial, which opened in April 2004, explained in its text, "We had lived in peace for many centuries, but now [with colonial rule] the divide between us had begun." The dominant narrative contended that the violence of 1959, when Hutu came to power, marked the beginning of the genocide. Having lived side by side with Hutu for centuries in a relationship of mutual respect and even friendship, Tutsi then were oppressed and persecuted under the First and Second Republics for decades building up to 1994. In 1994, according to this narrative, the Rwandan Patriotic Front reversed the trend of Tutsi persecution by defeating the genocidal regime and establishing a government that restored order, including implementing such policies as abolishing ethnicity and promoting national unity.

The official postgenocide master narrative was buttressed by the genocide memorials across the countryside, which served as *lieux de mémoire* (Nora 1989), ritualized spaces in which people actively produced memory. The careful planning of genocide and the international community's failure to prevent it were manifest in the enormity of the death toll at any given memorial, often marked in hand-lettered signs—twenty-five thousand victims (Kibeho), 11,400 victims (Kibuye Parish), ten thousand victims (Kibuye stadium), 250,000 victims (Kigali genocide memorial). The scattered limbs and disconnected pelvises, the bullet wounds or machete cuts on skulls, the rosaries clutched in shriveled corpses' fingers, and the devastated physical structures of the churches or schools in which these were found materially represented victims' desperation and dehumanization. Victims' innocence was manifest in the corpses of toddlers, the skulls of children, the baby shoes, and leg braces found within the remains of the buildings. The ubiquity of sites across the landscape and the lost lives they immortalized underscore the narrative's emphasis on the heroism of the RPF in bringing an end to the terror.

At the same time that the postgenocide authorities were beginning to consolidate a new narrative of history in the wake of the genocide, Trouillot

(1995) published his call to examine power in the production of history. This exhortation remains crucial today, particularly in light of the growing critiques against President Kagame and his government, and his reputation as a shrewd information manager. Scholars who have worked in the region for decades conclude that Kagame and the RPF reproduced, rather than corrected, the pattern of politics characterizing colonial and postcolonial rule in the region, including regional and ethnic discrimination, exclusion, corruption, and disregard for the population's needs (Brauman et al. 2000; Jefremovas 2002; Lemarchand 2009; Prunier 2009; Reyntjens 2005). While the government initially appeared inclusive, within a year there was widespread Hutu flight from government, and Hutu became victims of harassment, imprisonment, and physical elimination by the RPA (Brauman et al. 2000; Reyntjens 1995; Reyntjens 2009:23–34). These patterns were particularly evident in the lead-up to the 2003 elections, when opposition leaders were arrested or mysteriously killed, newspapers were closed, and civil society was constricted (Reyntjens and Vandeginste 2005). Filip Reyntjens and René Lemarchand, longstanding scholars of Rwanda, both call Kagame's regime a "dictatorship" (Lemarchand 2009; Reyntjens 2005).

As an empirical example illustrating the themes within the government master narrative, I use portions of the text of President Kagame's speech at the official event marking the ten-year anniversary of the genocide, on April 7, 2004 at Amahoro Stadium in Kigali. President Kagame's presentation, which I transcribed from an audio recording I made when I attended the commemoration event, was part of a three-hour ceremony that launched the national week of mourning, which included similar speeches, testimonials, and burials of victims throughout the country. Kagame delivered this speech to a stadium crowded with Rwandans, most of whom had been bused there and who had waited for hours in the sun for the event to begin (Figure 2). His speech was preceded by the formal arrival of an impressive array of international dignitaries who attested to the global significance of the occasion, including sitting presidents of Kenya, South Africa, Uganda, Congo, and Mozambique, the vice president of Burundi, the prime ministers of Ethiopia and Tanzania, and high-level dignitaries from Belgium, England, Switzerland, Germany, the Netherlands, Sweden, Togo, and Mali, as well as official representatives of the International Criminal Tribunal for Rwanda, the European Union, and the United Nations. (French representatives were notably absent.) Several of the guests provided short speeches as

Figure 2. Amahoro Stadium, waiting for President Kagame's speech, April 7, 2004 (photo by author).

well, bracketed by the arrival of a Rwandan military delegation, the playing of the new Rwandan national anthem, mourning songs, and survivor testimonials. Kagame began his speech in Kinyarwanda, then indicated that since his key auditors were his international guests, he would shift to English. The speech was televised and broadcast worldwide.

Analyzing what Rwanda's postgenocide dominant narrative selectively emphasized alongside what it left out denaturalizes the government's assumptions about belonging and legitimacy of authority, and illuminates how this narrative justified ongoing configurations of power, alliances, and exclusion in the present. As I explore further in subsequent chapters, when this dominant narrative became institutionalized through grassroots legal forums, it rendered certain actions criminal and others invisible, and it contributed to the formation of "genocide citizenship," in which people's access to the benefits of citizenship were shaped by their perceived position with respect to the violence of the 1990s, defined in a particular way. Furthermore, it justified law-based (punitive) harmony as crucial to Rwanda's future.

Discrediting the International Community

Kagame's speech clearly was directed at an international audience, and it heavily emphasized the negative role played by outsiders in Rwanda for more than a century. For example, he explained, "In many ways the genocide in Rwanda stems from the colonial period when the Colonialists and those who called themselves evangelists sowed the seeds of hate and division. This is evident from the 1959 massacres and subsequent ones which had become the order of the day in Rwanda and in which the international community had become habitual bystanders. These massacres culminated in the 1994 genocide."

Placing blame on foreigners, akin to the increasingly derisive references to the French at Murambi, was a continuous theme in the master narrative. Doing so morally discredited the West over generations based on its role in sowing division and tolerating violence in Rwanda, beginning with the arrival of the Germans in 1897, continuing with the political upheavals and violence at independence, through the lead-up to genocide, and culminating in the world's inaction and even support of the genocidal regime. This served to frame Rwandans as twice victims: first of the genocidal regime and second of Western countries, based on insidious racism. In a notable example, Kagame said in his 2004 speech, "All these powerful nations regarded one million lives as valueless, as another statistic, and could be dispensed with. And of course some claimed that the dying people were not in their national strategic interests. But if the death of a million people was not a concern to them, then what is? I hate to think that this may be due to the color of the skin of these Rwandans who died or other Africans who might die in the future. Ten years after the powerful nations eventually called the mass killings by their proper name, genocide, they have not demonstrated proportional responsibility where it belongs." Comments like these positioned Rwanda in solidarity with the African continent and the non-European developing world more globally.

Further, placing blame on foreigners exonerated Rwandans (particularly Tutsi) for certain forms of oppression and division in the past *and* the present. It was a counter-hegemonic move to neutralize international critiques of the RPF in the past or present and justify the government's ongoing efforts to chart its own fate, consistent with the widespread use of culture to justify mediation in harmony legal models. Also, it allowed the postgenocide government to assert that the international community had a moral obligation to provide ongoing support, but on the RPF's own terms.

Indeed, as I discussed earlier in the chapter, the international community carries a share of the blame. For good reason, between 2004 and 2008, the Hamitic Hypothesis was mentioned in newspaper articles, narrated by taxi drivers and tour guides, included as part of Rwanda's official colonial history in the Kigali Genocide Memorial Center (Smith 2004:9), and referenced in virtually every academic and popular history of Rwanda.[14] For more than a century, Europeans had argued that Hutu, Tutsi, and Twa constituted distinctly separate racial or ethnic groups.[15] In the 1950s, the ideas at the core of the Hamitic myth were at the center of the Hutu Revolution, when leaders claimed Hutu autochthony and therefore rights to govern, while Tutsi were cast as foreign and innately domineering (Lemarchand 2009:58). In the 1990s, the same ideas played a central role in anti-Tutsi propaganda in the lead-up to genocide (Chrétien 1995:139–208). As I outlined earlier, scholars have further shown that the international community played a role in the escalating tensions and violence in Rwanda between the 1950s and 1990s and did not do enough to stop the genocide.

But placing blame on colonial leaders—and by extension on the West in the present—overlooks the problems in place under Rwandan leadership. Specifically, it erases how the reign of King Rwabugiri (1867–1897),[16] who ruled immediately prior to the arrival of colonial leadership, marked a crisis of social health and spurred the formation of resistance or liberation movements directed against the monarchy, as well as examples of anti-Tutsi violence (Botte 1985a,1985b; Feierman 1995; Vansina 2004:137–138). Under Rwabugiri, internal factional rivalry among elite families fueled competition and further territorial expansion that increased insecurity and impoverishment for the bulk of the population, herders as well as farmers (D. Newbury 2009; Vansina 2004:126–139,163). The "nearly permanent recourse to violence" created social instability and led to social disaggregation (Vansina 2004:164–195). Catharine Newbury and Jan Vansina point specifically to the role of uburetwa, a form of mandatory unpaid labor performed for a chief as payment for occupation of the land, as "poisoning" interethnic relations because it was imposed only on farmers, not herders

(C. Newbury 1980, 1988; Vansina 2004:134–139). To do uburetwa symbol-ized low status and powerlessness, and it was "difficult to exaggerate" its "exploitative character" (C. Newbury 1988:141). Uburetwa began under Rwabugiri, and although it would become even more inflexible and humili-ating under colonialism, its damaging effects were well entrenched in the late nineteenth century (C. Newbury 1980; Vansina 2004:135–139, 192).[17] Uburetwa remained relevant to understanding the meaning of exchange of labor in postgenocide Rwanda, as I discuss in more detail in Chapter 3.

In addition to silencing the existence of precolonial problems, placing blame primarily on the West overlooks how the system of "dual colonial rule" meant colonialism's negative effects were attributable not only to Europeans but also to Rwandan elites (C. Newbury 1988:53; Reyntjens 1985:161–170). While Belgian policies increased chiefs' power and provided incentives and rationalizations, through entry into the world economy, for them to take advantage of the rural population, it was the Rwandan chiefs themselves who determined how to meet, resist, or further exacerbate these demands, how much to privilege their own advancement at the expense of others, and how colonialism influenced the transformation of clientship ties (C. Newbury 1988:117–150). Many Tutsi chiefs ruled exploitatively, wielding power arbitrarily (Lemarchand 1970:35–40; Reyntjens 1985). Rwandan leaders, including Tutsi chiefs, were complicit in accepting and propagating the racial model of human diversity that Europeans brought to Central Africa. Framing the Hutu Revolution at independence as the result of colonially introduced ethnicity and as the early expression of geno-cidal ideology overlooks the long-term evolution of rural grievances under-lying the transformations of 1959–1962, and the fact that the revolution addressed the political exclusion of the Hutu peasants who composed 80 percent of the population (Lemarchand 2009:31; C. Newbury 1978, 1980, 1988:178–179, 207–208).

Placing blame on the West during the genocide also allows the RPF to claim the moral high ground and solidify its "genocide credit" (Lemarc-hand 2009; Reyntjens 2005; Vidal 2001). For example, Kagame emphasized the moral purity of the RPF in his 2004 speech, saying, "I also have to thank the soldiers of the Rwandan Patriotic Front. In the fight many gave their lives in the cause of freedom and liberation. I know that every soldier in the RPF knew that the cost was likely to be high but the cause of freedom and liberation was one worth fighting for. We were fighting a difficult and determined enemy who was supported by powerful forces. We were fighting two wars at once. Our soldiers fought by day and rescued victims by night until they halted the genocide. Thank you to all of you." He continued later, "And I say it, from the lessons we have drawn from our pasts, we will be very eager, and we are committed, to fight for our rights and fight for the rights for others who are targeted like the people of Rwanda were targeted during the genocide." This attention to the moral virtue of the RPF erases accusations against Kagame and his RPF soldiers of committing atrocities during the genocide, specifically human rights abuses and reprisal killings against innocent Hutu civilians as the RPF pushed through Rwanda to Kigali.[18] High-ranking Rwandan and international military personnel have argued that Kagame's goals as head of the RPF were first and foremost to gain political control of Rwanda, and only secondarily to halt the genocide, with full awareness of the cost this would bring to Tutsi (Dallaire 2003:515; Prunier 2009:15; Ruzibiza 2005:10). Scholars argue that the RPF (now the RPA) continued to perpetuate violence and human rights abuses in the years after the genocide. By 1995, RPA soldiers conducted reprisal killings and created domestic insecurity, while Hutu were imprisoned summarily on genocide accusations (Reyntjens 1995). While Kagame claimed that only three hundred people were killed during the closing of a refugee camp in Kibeho in southern Rwanda in 1995, other reports claim as many as five thousand innocent people were killed (Lemarchand 2009:73; Prunier 2009:37–42). Some reports claim that in 1997 at least sixteen thousand innocent Hutu civilians in the north were killed when the RPA responded to incursions by Hutu rebels into Rwanda (Reyntjens 2009:175–176). Drawing attention to these RPF/RPA abuses should *not* be confused with supporting the double genocide theory or its implication that the RPF/RPA counterattacks exonerate genocide perpetrators; rather, it is recognition of the multiple forms and sources of violence during the 1990s (Prunier 2009:12–13).

Emphasizing National over Regional Dynamics

Kagame's ten-year commemoration speech, consistent with the dominant narrative, emphasized the national dynamics of the genocide rather than situating it within a broader set of regional ethnopolitical struggles. Even as he gestured towards regional African cooperation, it was in the context of reiterating the right of a national leader to resolve internal issues. Kagame orated, "It is very important that the African countries get together, we sort out our national problems, our internal situations to do with good governance, to do with democracy, to do with socio-economic development and work together and protect each other and defend each other for nobody owes us anything as was shown in the case of Rwanda." Kagame's national focus sidelined how regional dynamics helped explain and legitimize (though not justify) some of the anti-Tutsi sentiment and the ease with which people could be mobilized by fear to violence. By extension, the national focus ignored how postgenocide governmental actions within and outside Rwanda could have similar ongoing effects on regional instability today. Erasure of regional dynamics in the dominant narrative allowed the RPF to prioritize national resocialization policies rather than macro-political and economic factors. It also continued to locate the solution at the national level, rather than opening the door to international or regional solutions that might promote corrective action in Rwanda's foreign and domestic policies.

Focusing on ethnicity within natural national borders—which were not coterminous with the Rwandan kingdom over the previous three centuries[19]—disregarded the broader entanglement of regional and international sociopolitical dynamics, particularly the waves of violence and genocide against Hutu in Burundi and ongoing war in the Great Lakes region of Central Africa (Autesserre 2010; Lemarchand 2009; Prunier 2009; Reyntjens 2009). These regional dynamics contributed to the pregenocide situation—and arguably to postgenocide dynamics as well—by enflaming fears of ethnic violence, adding fodder for political manipulation, and creating massive movements of refugee populations who were particularly receptive to ethnic-based ideologies (Lemarchand 2009:20; Malkki 1995; C. Newbury and D. Newbury 1999).

Specifically, the dominant narrative ignored the 1972 killings of Hutu by Tutsi in Burundi, massacres that sank into "near oblivion" in broader global memory (Lemarchand 2009:71). In the wake of an aborted Hutu-instigated uprising that caused the death of hundreds or perhaps thousands of Tutsi civilians in Burundi, the ensuing (Tutsi) government-backed repression from April to November 1972 resulted in the deaths of one hundred thousand to two hundred thousand Hutu, specifically primary and secondary school children, university students, teachers, and civil servants (Lemarchand 2009:71). This helps contextualize the anti-Tutsi backlash in Rwanda that paved the way for Habyarimana's coup in 1973 (Lemarchand 2009).

Ignoring the 1972 events, as well as the October 1993 assassination of the Hutu president of Burundi, Melchior Ndadaye, at the hands of the all-Tutsi army, erased the idea that there was any legitimacy to Hutu fears of power sharing or of Tutsi-generated violence. Ndadaye was the first Hutu president in the history of Burundi, and his election brought to a close twenty-eight years of Tutsi hegemony. His assassination three months after he took office unleashed violence in Burundi on both sides, with Hutu civilians killing up to twenty thousand Tutsi in October and November 1993, and the Tutsi army killing as many Hutu in retaliation. Further, the violence caused some two hundred thousand to four hundred thousand Hutu to seek refuge in Rwanda in 1993 and 1994 (Lemarchand 2009; C. Newbury and D. Newbury 1999:85). In the context of the uneasy truce between the RPF and the Habyarimana government, these events contributed to the Rwandan Hutu-power regime's anti-Tutsi propaganda and were part of the undoing of any compromise contained in the Arusha Accords.

The national focus of the RPF's master narrative obscured Rwanda's problematic role in neighboring countries, only publicizing international interventions when they were consistent with the dominant narrative—for example, claiming that incursions into the DRC were solely driven by efforts to oust génocidaires who remained intent on killing Tutsi, not by desire to control mineral resources or expand territorial sovereignty (Lemarchand 2009:17–19). Yet, Kagame faced accusations of atrocities—crimes against humanity and even possibly genocide—for events in the mid-to-late 1990s in Rwanda and in the DRC where Rwanda "exported" its war (Prunier 2009; Reyntjens 2009). Scholars, human rights activists, and a 2010 U.N. report accused Kagame and his army (the RPA) of the deaths of as many as two hundred thousand civilian refugees during the destruction of refugee camps in the DRC in October 1996, as part of a broader Rwandan desire to overthrow Mobutu and support Kabila (Brauman et al. 2000; Lemarchand 2009:26; Pillay 2010; Prunier 2009; Reyntjens 2009:80–102). Overlooking the fact that four times as many people died in the eastern DRC between 1998 and 2006 as in the genocide, in a war in which Rwanda was heavily involved (Lemarchand 2009:5), maintained the uniqueness of the Rwandan situation to strengthen the RPF's genocide credit.

Masking Past and Present Divisions

The dominant master narrative emphasized externally produced ethnicity, and how a rogue political regime misused it, to the exclusion of recognizing other kinds of social identities, divisions, and misuses of political power in the past and present. In his speech, President Kagame explained:

Genocide in Rwanda was not an uncontrollable outburst of rage by people consumed by ancient tribal hatreds as has been suggested by some western anthropologists and sociologists and even espoused by some in African scholarship. It was deliberate, calculated, pre-meditated, and cold blooded as a result of a distorted ideology that preached death and extermination of a section of Rwandan society. ... We know that they [killers] were responding to the vicious campaign of hate by the architects of the genocide, men and women who held the highest offices in the land. This elite, which had for a long time misappropriated and controlled the government army, radio and television stations, was most instrumental in fomenting ethnic division and hatred, a strategy they subsequently transformed into genocide.

This emphasis on genocide ideology propagated by government elites to brainwash ordinary people into killing their kin allowed the postgenocide RPF government to claim that erasing ethnicity would be sufficient to avoid recreating conditions for violence, even while it consolidated power in the hands of a regional and ethnic elite, with troubling parallels to the past. Emphasis on unity as an antidote to "ethnic division and hatred" erased reference to how issues of region and class were significant sources of fracture in the past and remained so in the present, and to how social identities changed in relation to changes in political organization and expansion of state power (C. Newbury 1978, 1988:10–16, D. Newbury 1980; Vansina 2004:134–139).

In the face of the deeply entrenched, fundamentally flawed, and dangerous understandings of difference in Rwanda stemming from the Hamitic myth and its legacy in scholars' writings over the following century, it is understandable why the dominant narrative so vehemently focused on unity among Rwandans. Yet, debunking the myth of precolonial harmony and unity that homogenizes Rwanda across time and territory is a first step to acknowledging more complex forms of sociality and thus bringing to light forms of difference and inequality in the past and present. Contemporary Rwandan historiography argues it is factually inaccurate to suggest there was comprehensive unity prior to the colonial period, or that ethnicity only became salient due to the actions of non-Rwandans. While a generalized unity perhaps characterized precolonial Rwanda in the seventeenth century, the territorial area at the time did not correlate with the geographic area in which postgenocide unity was justified (Vansina 2004:198). The period of Rwabugiri's reign, characterized as internally brutal and violent down to the level of ordinary people and daily life, perhaps most powerfully negates visions of enduring precolonial unity (D. Newbury 2009:131, 333–334; Vansina 2004:164–195). By the end of the nineteenth century, Rwandan society was highly stratified, and ethnicity became salient through institutionalized hierarchies along lines of Hutu and Tutsi (Lemarchand 2009; Vansina 2004).[20] Under Rwabugiri, a poor Tutsi was no longer considered a Hutu (Vansina 2004:136), and "Tutsi and Hutu became political labels; 'ethnicity,' such as it was, came to assume a political importance, determining a person's life chances and relations with the authorities" (C. Newbury 1988:52).

The narrative's preoccupation with ethnicity obscured how throughout Rwandan history ethnicity was just one form of social belonging, alongside kinship, neighborhood, age group, voluntary associations, and religious ties (De Lame 2005:238, 317; Longman 2010a). It overlooked how expanding state power that varied across the territory shaped belonging and resulting access to resources in the precolonial period through the 1990s, and surely did so in the present (C. Newbury and D. Newbury 1999:294; Reyntjens 2005:22).[21] Saying that Hutu and Tutsi originally mapped onto farming versus herding minimized the importance of changes over time and across space, particularly in relation to state expansion, ubuhake contracts, armies, and installation of local authorities whose influence derived from different kinds of land tenure and use (farming versus herding) (Vansina 2004:135), all processes that had correlates in the postgenocide government's reconstruction policies, including decentralization. The narrative thus deemphasized how disenfranchisement was a function of class, not merely ethnicity, across periods of Rwandan history.

Minimizing region and class as sources of difference, and disallowing talk of ethnicity in the present, rendered publicly unspeakable the postgenocide government's concentration of power in the hands of a regional and ethnic elite in the present: the RPF prioritized Ugandan refugees, beginning in 1995, while Tutsi diaspora elites gained predominant control over urban areas (Jefremovas 2002:125; Reyntjens 1995, 2005). Yet, this concentration of power was consistent with other periods in Rwandan history when regional and class divisions were crucial to fomenting instability and violence. Most conflicts after independence were among regionalized Hutu factions, and infighting among Hutu elites in a context of economic decline spurred instrumentalization of ethnicity for political purposes (De Lame 2005; C. Newbury and D. Newbury 1999:299).[22] Disregarding class divisions and the economic woes faced by Hutu and Tutsi rural farmers in the past shifted attention away from obvious parallels between the 1970s to 1980s and 2004 through 2008, which were both periods when the world saw Rwanda as a paragon of development and poured in international support, while the gap between the rich and the poor increased. This was problematic given that, although the postgenocide RPF policies improved some economic conditions in Rwanda, economic inequality increased (Ansoms and Marysse 2005). Elites remained disconnected from ordinary people (Ansoms 2009; Clark 2010:125). Tutsi survivors, along with other rural inhabitants, were resettled to "villagization" projects, intended to give them better access to security and livelihoods but often increasing their vulnerability to malnutrition, disease, or reprisal attacks (Ansoms 2009; Jefremovas 2002:125; Reyntjens 2005:28–30; van Leeuwen 2001).

Despite its claims of unity, the dominant narrative simultaneously promoted identity categories based on collective guilt and innocence that reinscribed ethnicity and created differentiated forms of "genocide citizenship" (see Chapter 3). As Kagame asserted in his speech, "The victims were all innocent civilians, unarmed and defenseless, burnt alive in their houses or hunted out in churches, schools, maize fields, banana plantations, forests and swamps by machete wielding neighbors, soldiers, and militia men." Thus, in the dominant narrative, all Tutsi were innocent victims, and no Tutsi were perpetrators. This included the RPF soldiers, whose actions were framed as a righteous liberation struggle, alongside claims that any civilian deaths were unfortunate collateral damage of their war against the génocidaires. It also included diaspora Tutsi, who constituted most of the political and economic elites, and who were not in the country in 1994. This interpretation created a shared status among victims of attacks between 1959 and 1994 that asserted belonging along ethnic lines even while ostensibly erasing ethnicity, while allowing government elites to speak for rural genocide survivors.

While Tutsi had a monopoly on suffering, surviving Hutu were assumed to be guilty, with no rightful claims on victimhood (Burnet 2009; Clark 2010:127; Lemarchand 2009:104; Pottier 2005:211). President Kagame's speech, characterized the perpetrators as follows: "Their tormenters and killers were fellow countrymen and women who chose to do evil because they were swayed by hate or hope of profit. They were kin to kin, raped, robbed, and ravaged. They killed their victims without remorse, and inflicted pain and agony and enjoyed doing so." Thus, perpetrators were cast as inhuman and relentless in their cruelty, and all surviving Hutu were associated with that category (since those who disagreed with the genocide were arguably all killed), while the experiences and pain of Hutu were obscured. This perspective was captured by a guide at the Kigali genocide memorial who told me, in April 2004, that the reason guides at memorials were survivors was because "survivors can tell visitors the truth about what happened, while génocidaires would try to cover up the truth." This common, and officially sanctioned, view implied that those were the only two options in Rwanda (an honest survivor or a lying génocidaire), which effaced the variety of positions in the middle ground. A wealth of research underscores how Hutu suffered, forced to flee the country as refugees, experiencing extreme hardship for many months or even years, as they faced disease outbreaks, lost family members, or themselves died in refugee camps or prisons (Clark 2010:127; Des Forges 1999; Lemarchand 2009: 36–37; Nduwayo 2002; Umutesi 2004). The dominant narrative made only perfunctory reference to the actions of Hutu who actively sought to help others. The master narrative created a contradiction in which the range of Hutu experiences during the genocide were homogenized, even while government authorities claimed that gacaca would alleviate collective guilt by identifying specific guilty individuals and exonerating the innocent. I explore these dynamics in more detail in Chapter 3.

There were some exceptions to the binary opposition of Tutsi equals innocent, Hutu equals guilty. A few Tutsi were singled out as being perpetrators, framed as "rogue" or outliers (Reyntjens 2009:182), and a few Hutu were celebrated as heroes, but controversially. For example, I attended an event at the Kigali genocide memorial on July 18, 2004 (eleven days after Kagame's tenth-year speech) designed to celebrate half a dozen Hutu heroes (Figure 3). Organizers told me that they had received hundreds of nominees but had had to disqualify most of them because during the vetting process they found that other survivors had alleged that those same nominees had victimized them. Relatively few people attended this event— only a hundred to two hundred, as compared to thousands or tens of thousands at other events honoring victims held in the previous months— suggesting that people either rejected the validation of Hutu heroes or did not accept the restriction on the meaning of the term. Further, it is

Figure 3. Empty seats at ceremony for protectors/heroes, July 2004 (photo by author).

significant that this event was held after the closure of the official genocide mourning period (April 7 through July 4, the dates marking the official genocide), rendering the attempted recognition less symbolically powerful. If anything, in the broader political context, this official recognition of only a half dozen Hutu heroes served to underscore that some people had succeeded in risking their lives to protect others, and therefore to imply that anything less counted as complicity. In the lead-up to the national launch of gacaca courts, this suggested that any accusations of guilt tarnished or even negated assertions of helping or saving, setting a standard of moral purity virtually unachievable in the tumult of the genocide, which many have described as akin to Primo Levi's "gray zone" (Levi 1988) in which the complexity of dynamics of violence, coercion, and complicity muddies the binary of guilt and innocence.

Conclusion: Legitimizing RPF Rule

Approximately one third of the way through his ten-year anniversary speech, President Kagame proclaimed: "I wish to make it abundantly clear that we Rwandans take primary responsibility for what happened ten years ago. And I stand here in the name of my government and the people of this country and apologize in their name." This claim seemed designed to differentiate President Kagame from the international community and previous Rwandan leadership, both of whom were the subject of the damning critiques that made up the entirety of the rest of the speech. I close here by showing the ways that these sentences capture the key implications of the dominant narrative that matter for the purposes of this book.

By starting with "we Rwandans," Kagame asserted national unity and spoke for his fellow citizens. He proclaimed that "we Rwandans," not the international community (which he was in the midst of thoroughly discrediting), were in the driver's seat in solving the problems facing "our country," defined nationally, in relation to a specific territory. The "we" who needed to have remorse and be rehabilitated referred to Hutu for crimes against Tutsi. This "we" did not, for example, refer to those Tutsi chiefs who ruled arbitrarily and unjustly under the system of dual colonialism and who therefore contributed to the oppression of rural Hutu, nor to those members of the RPF who killed Hutu during and after the genocide, whether episodically or systemically. For Kagame to "apologize in their name" was consistent with the broader silencing many Hutu perceived they experienced at the hands of the postgenocide regime.

The government's dominant narrative of history was a key element of the "total environment" of reconciliation. While vigorous debates on Rwandan historiography continued among scholars, the government narrative did not invite contestation but instead constrained opposition with allegations of divisionism or genocide ideology. The example from Murambi with which I began this chapter, where a highly polished, professionalized historical narrative and exhibit about the genocide remained behind locked doors for seven years, served as a concrete physical reminder of the existence of lacunae within the master narrative, and of the deliberate effort expended in maintaining certain holes in the historical presentation. Comparing the dominant narrative with the rich scholarship on Rwanda's distant and recent past brings to light how the government strategically highlighted and deemphasized specific elements, with implications for how power, belonging, and exclusion were configured.

The dominant narrative and its lacunae were crucial to legitimizing the government's authority to rule. Linking the genocide to 1959 allowed the RPF, predominantly composed of people whose families fled the anti-Tutsi violence from 1959 to 1963, to claim the right to govern a country, their motherland, in which they had never lived. It was a crucial move to reinterpreting Kagame and the RPF not as outside invaders but as rightful members and leaders of the national community in spite of, or even because of, their physical displacement. The RPF gained further legitimacy in this narrative from its liberation of Rwanda and rescue of innocent victims during the genocide. Further, by emphasizing how the genocide was planned over the decades from 1959 through 1994, the dominant narrative cast aspersions on everyone in leadership positions from independence until the RPF seized Kigali, and correspondingly on the only period of majority Hutu rule in Rwandan history. Emphasizing how multipartyism in the 1990s led directly to mass violence, as the text of the national genocide memorial did, implicitly legitimized the RPF's consolidation of power and heavy-handed rule, and served as justification for further disenfranchisement of the majority population, including a variety of restrictions on civil society and on Hutu's access to political or economic power, not least the genocide ideology law. In a related move, the dominant narrative obscured the role of Tutsi chiefs in contributing to ethnic division and Hutu oppression over time, which deflected attention from the role of Rwandan governance practices in creating and perpetuating inequalities in the present.

Overall, the government used this narrative to justify its legitimacy to oversee the rebuilding of Rwanda based on "genocide credit," casting victims' suffering in terms made meaningful by the contemporary goals of the regime (Reyntjens 2005:32; Vidal 2001). The government claimed that allegations of human rights abuses came from people who intended to sow division, as in other periods in Rwanda's past. The genocide credit proved highly successful, as Western leaders maintained a "strange fascination" with Kagame and mostly turned a blind eye to accusations of atrocities against him (Lemarchand 2009:95; Reyntjens 2005:32).

The dominant narrative provided the backdrop against which postgenocide legal institutions were put in place, as I discuss in more detail in the following chapters. It rendered thinkable the creation of gacaca courts to

mass-prosecute génocidaires, with reduced sentences for those who confessed and renounced the genocide ideology that elites had manipulated
them into accepting. Similarly, it rendered unthinkable the idea of prosecuting RPF for atrocities. And, perhaps most centrally to my story here, it
justified the creation of institutions based around mediation as the revital-
ization of a shared cultural tradition that unified Rwandans.

Text from panels inside the Murambi genocide memorial, 2004; see Figure 1.

The panels inside the Murambi exhibit in July 2004 were organized under the following headings: Colonial Period; Race, Politics and the Church; Independence; Discrimination; Habyarimana in Power; The RPF invasion, October 1990; Propaganda; Peace Process; Eve of the Genocide; 100 Nights; International Responses; Operation Turquoise 1994; A Personal Account of Genocide; Perpetrators; Murambi, April 1994; SOS Village of Children; Murambi after the Genocide. The following text was under Murambi, April 1994:

Murambi is the story of how 40,000–50,000 Tutsi men, women, and children came to perish, on 21 April 1994, in a secondary school under construction. Sensing danger, Tutsis from the town of Gikongoro, and neighbouring communes, congregated in schools and churches. The authorities directed them to the school in Murambi, saying that it was where their security could be guaranteed. The men who planned and carried out the massacre were the préfet (governor), Lauren Bucyibaruta; a deputy préfet, Frodouald Havugimana; the deputy commander of the gendarmerie in Gikongoro, Captain Faustin Sebuhura; Col. Aloys Simba, a retired army officer; Col. Rwamanywa and Felicien Semakwavu, the bourgmestre (mayor) of Myamagabe commune where Murambi is located.

The same local officials and soldiers then established a formidable network of roadblocks to control the movement of Tutsis. Many were murdered or raped before they reached the school. And then the officials and soldiers organized the militiamen, arms, ammunition and transport to decimate them. They held meetings for local residents to ask for "a hand in the war against the Tutsis."

Meanwhile, the refugees at the school were denied water and food. The water pipes were disconnected and those who brought provisions were turned back. Weak from hunger, thirst, and fear, they endured constant sniping from militiamen and wanted to die. Preparations for the final onslaught intensified after an aborted attack on 18 April. The President of the interim regime in charge of the genocide, Theodore Sindikubwabo, visited Gikongoro on 19 April and met with local officials and military officers. Guns and new machetes were distributed. Hutus living in the vicinity were taken to safety in nearby schools on the 19th.

A large-scale massacre started at 3:00am on 21 April. Taken by surprise, the refugees tried to fight back with stones. Most of them died under a hail of bullets and grenades. There was a brief respite at 6:00am when the ammunition ran out. This was replenished within twenty minutes and the shooting and explosions lasted for another few hours. Those who survived this onslaught, including the wounded, were finished off with machetes. And then the possessions of the dead were looted. At 11:00am, the préfet thanked everyone "for the work that had been accomplished."

Some of the survivors were caught as they fled to the nearby parish of Cyanika. Most of the men and women who reached the parish were killed there a few hours later by the same militiamen. The few who remained alive, mostly women and children, were taken back to Murambi to show the international community that no one had died at Murambi. To hide the evidence, bulldozers removed the corpses at Murambi and Cyanika and dumped them in various mass graves, including at Murambi itself.

In 1995 victims were exhumed from mass graves in Murambi. 18,684 men, women, and children were exhumed from one grave alone. Most people were reburied again in the communal grave at the front of the memorial centre. Nearly one thousand corpses were preserved in lime and placed in the buildings that should have been classrooms. They became a testimony to the terrible events that happened on this hill in April 1994. Remains of victims from three of the classrooms have been moved to this burial chamber as their final resting place.

Chapter 2

Escaping Dichotomies: Grassroots Law
in Historical and Global Context

> Bringing government decision-making closer to the people through
> decentralization and adjudicating crimes of genocide and building the
> basis for reconciliation through truth telling are central elements in
> the Rwandan strategy to rebuild the social fabric of the country.
> —National Unity and Reconciliation Commission of Rwanda (2007:1)

As the epigraph underscores, in postgenocide Rwanda decentralization,
legal processes, and reconciliation—key themes at the core of this book—
were intertwined in government policy. In this chapter, I consider grassroots legal forums and decentralized law first in historical context in
Rwanda, then in global context in relation to international trends of transitional justice. I thus emphasize here how the transformations in legal institutions and forms of authority in postgenocide Rwanda derived from
pregenocide, wartime, and post-genocide institutions and opportunity
structures.[1] I close by suggesting three correctives to existing transitional
justice debates.

The combined emphasis on law, reconciliation, and decentralization
was not unique to Rwanda but rather was consistent with neoliberal policies
more broadly, policies that emphasize the creation of active individual citizens who demonstrate personal responsibility in self-governance. Rwanda
formally adopted a nationwide process of decentralization in May 2000.[2]
The main thrust of Rwanda's governmental decentralization policy was to
help local populations to "participat[e] in the planning and management

of their development process" (Ministry of Local Government 2008b:4). It was part of the community empowerment framework in Rwanda's broader overarching national economic development strategy called Vision 2020 (Ministry of Finance 2000). Vision 2020 was based on an approach called Community Driven Development, advocated by both the World Bank and USAID, which aimed to "empower communities and local governments to 'take control' through a bottom-up approach that treated communities as partners in development" (Johnson 2009:10).

Specifically, decentralization aimed to disperse the functions of the national government and strengthen the administrative districts as the core local governance authority. In an administrative restructuring in 2005, Rwanda's thirty administrative districts were subdivided into sectors (416 in total), and sectors into cells (2,148 in total). Sectors served as the focus of local service delivery and were administered by several RPF appointees, including an executive secretary and a civil affairs coordinator (Ministry of Local Government 2008b:9). The cell level was intended to serve as the center for information and community mobilization, while villages (*imidugudu,* approximately fifteen thousand in total) were intended to involve community members in participatory sustainable community development activities. In each cell, there was an executive secretary at the cell level and a cell coordinator, as well as a team of ten people to help manage it. Leadership at the village level was invested in one coordinator and a four-person committee.[3]

The harmony legal models at the heart of this book were implemented consistent with the goals of decentralization. Gacaca courts and comite y'abunzi were designed to "move deep to the places where the crimes were committed" (Karemera 2004). Comite y'abunzi were implemented at the cell level. Gacaca courts were implemented both at the cell level (for cases regarding crimes against property during the genocide) and the sector level (for murder cases). The National University of Rwanda's legal aid clinic was consistent with the goals of decentralization, insofar as it explicitly aimed to provide members of the surrounding population with easier access to legal services, at reduced cost, and to help them navigate the shifting legal terrain. I describe this contextualization in more detail in chapters 3 through 6. Further, consistent with the philosophy of community empowerment linked to decentralization, both gacaca and comite y'abunzi were designed to use lay judges elected by their peers rather than professional judges or lawyers, and prioritized public participation. Similarly, the legal aid clinic staff members were predominantly students, and even the faculty on staff did not typically represent clients in court as trained attorneys. The idea of these forums was to empower citizens to solve disputes among their neighbors. For example, authorities described gacaca repeatedly as being "the responsibility of all the Rwandans with no exception and in the first place to rebuild their society."[4]

In this chapter, I first show that the historical contextualization of the three grassroots forums underscores both continuities and discontinuities in the ways central authority and state power have combined with dispute resolution over time. Specifically, scholars of law in Rwanda have shown how customary law has been intertwined with central authority and state formation since the late precolonial period, and they have demonstrated that state-backed legal decentralization and even "lawfare" (Comaroff 2001) are not merely inventions of postcolonial rulers in Rwanda but have deeper roots.

I then show that analyzing postgenocide Rwanda's grassroots mediation-based legal forums alongside each other as harmony models provides a foundation with which to critique three core assumptions in the field of "transitional justice"—which dominates debates on law in postgenocide Rwanda—as a growing body of critical transitional justice studies is doing (Hinton 2010; Nader and Grande 2002; Shaw et al. 2010). I argue that such analysis allows us to see how the "justice" of transitional justice relates to seemingly more prosaic processes; it corrects an elusive focus on pure customary law by attending to the importance of contextualization of legal forums; and it foregrounds how harmony and punishment are not separate but intertwined in these institutions.

Grassroots Harmony-Based Legal Forums in Historical Context

Four key themes characterizing contemporary decentralization in Rwanda can be traced as continuing from the precolonial period through the colonial periods and after independence during the First and Second Republics. First, there were deep roots to conciliation-based systems in Rwanda. Second, the penetration of central authority into dispute resolution began early, most notably when Belgian administrators had a hand in formalizing the customary legal system. Customary law was not a purely autonomous realm in the colonial period, just as gacaca and comite y'abunzi were not separate from state law in the postgenocide period.[5] Third, increasing state penetration occurred alongside decentralization efforts. Last, looking historically reveals how the biases and inequalities perpetuated through mediation in harmony legal models had roots in earlier periods, as there were continuing disparities in access to law and justice in Rwanda over time, particularly along lines of rural versus elite or in preferential access accorded those closer to power.

To expand on the first of these themes, there is clear evidence that principles of reconciliation- and compromise-based legal processes existed in precolonial and colonial Rwanda, even as the institutional form altered over time. Sources seem to agree on a general view of gacaca in the precolonial period without specifying precisely when it came into being or differences across centuries precolonially.[6] During the precolonial period in Rwanda, as late as the eighteenth century there existed no codified law, no formal tribunals, and no structure for appealing judicial decisions (Vansina 2004:89–90). Gacaca hearings were convened when conflicts arose within or between families over such issues as land rights, property damage, marital disputes, and inheritance.[7] They were presided over by elders or male heads of household and were based on shared social norms. The primary goal was to restore social order and create reconciliation by reintegrating the offender into the community after sanctioning the offender's violation of shared values and rules. Offenders appeared voluntarily, insofar as they were not compelled by the mwami (king). The elders could determine the sanction, without having to follow formal written rules set out by the mwami. Decisions were intended to represent a compromise between the individual interests of the participants and collective norms. Sanctions were enforced through social pressure.

Second, penetration of the central authority or state into local affairs of dispute resolution, in the name of customary law, is a continuous theme, rather than an invention of the postgenocide regime. It began as early as King Rwabugiri's reign, before the arrival of colonial leaders (D. Newbury 2001). For much of the precolonial period the mwami and the queen mother settled disputes according to their own decisions, without a distinction between a judicial session and a general audience. At lower levels at that time, local lineages enjoyed relative autonomy and resolved many conflicts, such as those over land (C. Newbury 1978:20). Rwabugiri introduced new chiefs who took over many of the functions, such as resolution of land disputes, which had previously been performed by lineage heads (C. Newbury 1978:20).

During the colonial period, authorities continued to increase regulation of dispute resolution processes.[8] A hierarchy of customary law rigidified gradually over several decades, in interplay between Rwandan chiefs and Belgians. Both German and Belgian colonial leaders created two categories of rules: they formalized the colonial legal system where written law applied to Europeans, while indigenous jurisdictions maintained the right to judge Rwandans for civil and penal affairs based on custom. In principle, then, justice for Rwandans remained in the hands of the mwami and his chiefs. In reality, custom was only allowed where it did not contradict public order as defined by the colonizers, and Rwandan people were subject to both indigenous law and Belgian written law.

Under the First and Second Republics after independence, systems based on the principles of customary law continued to exist and were intertwined with state law, though not formalized. Specifically, after independence, the new government extended Belgian written law to apply to all Rwandans, so citizens were formally subject to "modern" law (Gahamanyi 2003:266). Customary law was no longer part of the state system, though local systems of dispute resolution continued to exist and in some areas to flourish. Gacaca was in place as late as the 1980s, distinct from the formal system of law and not regulated by any codified legal texts as it would be in the postgenocide period, but not purely popular or traditional, as it was recognized and used by the state, via local authorities, to resolve community level disputes amicably (De Lame 2005:38; Reyntjens 1990; Runyange 2003:53). Gacaca sessions occurring in Ndora in the 1980s, according to a study conducted by Reyntjens (1990), had many procedural and stylistic similarities to how gacaca and comite y'abunzi operated in Ndora in 2007 and 2008. Sessions occurred once a week and were well attended. There was little differentiation made between parties to the case, witnesses, and other participants, and everyone who had something to say could speak and influence the solutions. As before comite y'abunzi, the disputing parties had the option of either voluntarily accepting the verdict and enforcing it or not accepting it, at which point the participants would bring the case before the first-instance tribunal. The people who presided—cell committee and the sector *conseilleur*— were elected officials without formal legal training, not professional judges or legal scholars.

This brings me to the third point. State penetration into customary law and local dispute resolution occurred alongside state-backed decentralization of conciliation-based tribunals, in earlier periods as well as in the postgenocide period. First, according to Reyntjens (1985), in the 1920s, to supplement the mwami's court in Nyanza, the mwami and Belgian administrators put in place fifteen indigenous tribunals, one in each territory, for which the mwami's court served as a court of appeal. These indigenous courts were seen as a success, processing 3,219 cases in 1929. Though initially the mwami's court heard all civil and criminal complaints and could provide up to one month of penal sanctions, in 1929 the Belgian administration took away indigenous courts' rights to imprisonment, meaning these courts basically lost power over criminal issues, retaining only civil jurisdiction, which is echoed quite closely in contemporary comite y'abunzi, which had only very limited criminal jurisdiction.

Then, in the 1930s, as in the 2000s, the mwami decentralized dispute resolution to the most local level, with an emphasis on mandatory conciliation before litigation. Between 1934 and 1937, the mwami (likely in interaction with the Belgian resident administrator) added a third hierarchical level to the indigenous court system, establishing tribunals of conciliation at the lowest administrative levels. These conciliation tribunals were intended, like comite y'abunzi seventy years later, to address minor disputes among Rwandans, and aimed to put parties in agreement before they went to litigate before indigenous tribunals. Cases could come before the first conciliation tribunal only if they had first been presented to the hill chief, who, along with two other notables, attempted to reconcile the parties. If the parties failed to reconcile before the hill chief and then before the conciliation tribunals, the parties could take their litigation to the territorial tribunal and then, if necessary, to the mwami's court. The mwami maintained oversight over all levels of customary courts, could serve as a judge at any of these courts, and could revise any judgments pronounced. The efficiency logic of the 1920s and 1930s persisted in the postgenocide period. The mwami in 1937 was concerned that too many cases were coming before his court (Reyntjens 1985:152), which mirrors the language of "unclog[ging] courtrooms" (Butamire 2010) behind contemporary comite y'abunzi and gacaca and within the rationale of alternative dispute resolution.[9]

The colonial era saw an unresolved relationship between mediation/ customary law and "real" law, informal and formal systems, that persisted into the postgenocide period. In the 1930s, the Belgians noted that it was improper to call the conciliation courts "tribunals," since they did not in fact settle litigation. This attempted differentiation between mediation versus "real" law was echoed in 2010 in how the Rwandan Ministry of Justice acknowledged comite y'abunzi as a compulsory legal system and referred to mediation committees as "judicial structures" (Munyaneza 2004) while simultaneously differentiating the system from formal law, claiming: "*Abunzi* [was] not designed to be a first stop into formal justice but rather a community mediation / dispute determination service."[10] The Belgians' distrust of leaving criminal matters to the system of "palaver before the chiefs" (Reyntjens 1985:150) foreshadowed critiques in the 2000s about assigning issues as serious as "genocide, crimes against humanity and war crimes" to "local justice" through gacaca (e.g., Waldorf 2006:79).

Coming to my fourth and last point, the law-based structural violence and inequalities that I have noted with regard to grassroots decentralized courts in the 2000s extend back more deeply. It is equally clear that hierarchies and inequalities, and precursors to what some scholars now identify as lawfare (Chakravarty 2015; Morrill 2006), were endemic within the court systems in the colonial period. Precolonial justice under early mwamis was typically swift, though not necessarily impartial. Under Rwabugiri's reign, at the elite level of the king, the judiciary was part of the politics of violence of Rwabugiri's regime, where courtiers used accusations before the mwami's court to eliminate their adversaries (Vansina 2004:185). Both the customary and the Belgian tribunals, as part of the system of dual colonialism, served primarily as instruments through which the ruling elites, appointed as judges and key personnel, retained privileges (Lemarchand 1970:75; Reyntjens 1985:155). Though patrons typically supported clients in lawsuits (Maquet 1961:30, 1970:118), as chiefs' powers increased, most people's opportunities for legal redress were heavily curtailed (C. Newbury 1980:103–104). Many ordinary people felt that they had no real recourse to the courts but rather were at the mercy of the chiefs, who could choose to take people's goods, force them off their land, or even threaten their lives (C. Newbury 1988:133, 143). Practically, ordinary people had little recourse to the mwami's court of appeal, due to discouragingly long delays and arbitrary fees (Lemarchand 1970:76; Reyntjens 1985:150). For example, the *mwami*'s tribunal tried about sixty cases per year and had a backlog of nine hundred untried cases by 1949 (Lemarchand 1970:76). Thus, even while

customary and Western-style law coexisted from the beginning of the colonial period, these cannot be seen as fully autonomous but often operated
in tandem, typically to the benefit of elites at the expense of ordinary rural
inhabitants.

Under independent rule, inequality in access to and application of the
law persisted. While there was a written code of law that allegedly applied
equally and was accessible to all, there was in practice unequal access to
the legal system inherited from colonial rule and postcolonial developments (De Lame 2005:386). Local authorities often interpreted the law
according to their own whims and arbitrarily imposed justice (De Lame
2005:65). In Rwanda, as in many other postcolonial contexts, the introduction of modern judicial institutions with professionalization and
Westernization reduced access to justice for the majority of people (Reyntjens 1990:40–41). Under independent rule, there remained a perception,
carried over from the colonial period, that the customary system was
inferior to the Western-style one. For example, most educated people and
wealthy merchants preferred to take their cases directly to the ordinary
tribunals rather than spend time with gacaca (Reyntjens 1990). It is clear,
then, that the inequalities perpetrated by mediation in harmony legal
models were not necessarily ameliorated by gacaca and other decentralized courts in postgenocide Rwanda, but they also were not introduced
or created by them.

International Trends in Transitional Justice

Rwanda's postgenocide legal forums must be understood in the context of
the global emergence of transitional justice. Since the emergence of the
term "transitional justice" in the early 1990s to identify a "distinctive con-
ception of justice associated with periods of radical political change following past oppressive rule" (Teitel 2008:1), the field of transitional justice
research and practice has come to span the globe (Buckley-Zistel and Zolkos 2011; Hinton 2010:1; Nagy 2008; Shaw et al. 2010). National governments and international actors increasingly create legal forums to help
people address the past and restore peace after civil war and genocide, ranging from prosecutorial courts, to truth commissions, to standardized
community-based healing rituals, even without a full understanding of how
law shapes people's everyday lives. Transitional justice mechanisms are

under debate, or have been recently implemented, in countries adjacent to Rwanda, including Burundi, Uganda, Kenya, and the DRC, as well as in other places stretching around the world, such as Nepal, Afghanistan, the Solomon Islands, Indonesia, Iraq, Lebanon, Cyprus, Colombia, and Mexico. Transitional justice has become an industry in itself, with a growing number of international NGOs, postgraduate degree programs, scholarly journals, and books. At its core, this growing global interest in transitional justice indicates the "fetishization" (Comaroff and Comaroff 2006:vii) of law as a privileged mode for marking the shift between past violence and present peace, and in its recent instantiations often moves beyond goals of promoting accountability and countering impunity to include attempts to rebuild national identity.

In this section, I first provide brief background on Rwanda's postgenocide legal framework and then give a brief overview of international transitional justice to provide the context against which the legal responses in postgenocide Rwanda were implemented.[11] I sidestep chronology to discuss two parallel strands—first criminal tribunals, then truth commissions—to capture what were long seen as binary oppositions between truth versus punishment and restorative versus retributive justice. I then consider contemporary trends in transitional justice.

Postgenocide Challenges: Detentions and Early Trials

After the genocide, the transitional government inside Rwanda immediately began dealing with detaining suspects and attempting to start trials.[12] The United Nations set up the International Criminal Tribunal for Rwanda (ICTR) to try the masterminds of the genocide, while inside Rwanda, as early as 1994, authorities began arresting people, up to a hundred to 150 every day.[13] The people detained, typically based on neighbors' denunciations which authorities did not have the resources to substantiate, were a mixture of genuine killers and people against whom accusers sought revenge, often for property quarrels or other personal disputes. By the beginning of 1998, estimates suggested there were more than a hundred thousand people in detention, and 125,000 by the beginning of 1999.

This growing prison population created significant problems. Detainees were housed across the country under deplorable conditions, marked by severe overcrowding and lack of adequate sanitation, leading to thousands of deaths in prison. Most prisoners had no files and heard no charges against them. Meanwhile, the main perpetrators remained free, as many had fled Rwanda and the ICTR had difficulty enforcing arrest warrants.

Government authorities faced significant hurdles in beginning trials. The pregenocide judicial system had been weak, with limited resources, insufficiently trained personnel, and lack of judicial independence. Genocide destruction further reduced these material resources by two-thirds. Much of the infrastructure, including court buildings, was ruined in the fighting, and those buildings still standing were empty of supplies or personnel. In the whole country only a handful of judges and lawyers remained. There was no Bar Association for attorneys until 1997, and even then only thirty or forty lawyers were accepted in the first year. The Rwandan government was willing to accept international financial support in its efforts to reconstruct the judicial infrastructure and retrain personnel. However, it rejected offers to have foreigners directly involved in the judiciary, even temporarily, claiming it would be a breach of governmental sovereignty.

By late 1996, the Rwandan government had most of its courts functioning again, passed a law that paved the way for prosecuting genocide suspects (Organic Law 08/96), and began trials for nongenocide criminal and civil cases, as well as for lower-level suspects in criminal cases. Rwanda's national courts, developed during the colonial period, were based on the Belgian system. They followed civil law, with an inquisitorial system, in which judges gathered evidence and could question witnesses, and lawyers typically served as advisers (Joireman 2001:573–574). Cases were heard before a bench of three judges (Organic Law of 30/08/1996, Article 21). The government brought charges, represented by the prosecutor's office. While defendants could be represented by lawyers, though not at government expense (Organic Law of 30/08/1996, Article 36), in reality in the first year 56 percent had no legal representation (McCourt 2009:274).

In an effort to address the lack of defense lawyers, partly in response to international critique and with international donor funding, Rwanda established the Corps of Judicial Defenders in 1997, training people who had not been educated as professional lawyers and therefore did not meet the criteria to qualify for the Bar, but who were still granted rights of audience before a court. They completed a six-month training course and two-month internship, then worked as interns for a year under a supervisor.

The judicial defenders addressed a crucial need with so many cases pending, and from 2000 to 2005 they provided representation in more than three hundred cases (McCourt 2009:277).

In the early years, conditions were not auspicious for most defendants. Initially, most trials resulted in convictions and the death penalty, and trials were criticized for not meeting international standards. In an oft-cited incident, in April 1998, twenty-two convicts, some of whom had not had a defense lawyer, were publicly executed in stadiums before large crowds in Kigali and elsewhere around the country. But the courts continued to make progress. By the end of 2003, the national courts had tried 9,721 cases, and up to 40 percent of defendants had representation (Reyntjens and Vandeginste 2005:109). There was also a clear shift in sentencing over time: by 2003, the death penalty was given in only 3 percent of the cases as compared to 30 to 43 percent in 1997, and acquittals were up from 9 percent in 1997 to 27 percent (McCourt 2009:278; Reyntjens and Vandeginste 2005:108).

And yet, by the end of 2003, seventy thousand genocide suspects awaited trial in state prisons (Reyntjens and Vandeginste 2005:110). Prison conditions had slowly improved but remained poor. Critics argued that existing trials did not meet international fair trial standards, and that the government was interfering in the judiciary. The judicial apparatus was dominated by Tutsi, which created a perception of partiality in national prosecutions, where most defendants were Hutu. The RPF's army, the RPA, continued to arrest people, while the RPA's alleged war crimes went unaddressed. Meanwhile, the burden of genocide crimes on the courts left little room for nongenocide-related concerns. It was against this backdrop that the government turned to decentralized legal forums.

Criminal Tribunals

Rwanda's domestic recourse to Western-style criminal trials was consistent with global models of pursuing punitive, adversarial court procedures in the wake of political violence. The quintessential example of transitional justice was in 1945 when, against a backdrop of calls for execution or indefinite detainment of Nazi leaders, the victorious allies agreed to hold the Nuremberg trials to prosecute Nazi leaders. This established a historic precedent for reliance on rule of law following crimes against humanity. It also created precedent for prosecution and criminal accountability led primarily by the international community, rather than national governments (Teitel 2003). In subsequent years, trends in transitional justice shifted away from the Nuremberg model in two main ways: from international to national oversight (largely due to the Cold War's constraints on internationalism), and from prosecutions toward truth commissions, as I discuss in the next section (Hayner 1995). Where trials continued, as in Eastern Europe in the post-Communist transition, they were nationally driven.

In the 1990s, in the wake of the Bosnian war and the Rwandan genocide, the establishment of the International Criminal Tribunal for Rwanda (ICTR) and the International Criminal Tribunal for the Former Yugoslavia (ICTY) marked a return to the Nuremberg model, with internationally led prosecutions. This time the courts were under the clear direction of the international community, via the United Nations, rather than simply the victors.

Specifically, in November 1994, the U.N. Security Council passed Resolution 955 that mandated the creation of the ICTR, "for the sole purpose of prosecuting persons responsible for genocide and other serious violations of international humanitarian law committed in the territory of Rwanda . . . [to] contribute to the process of national reconciliation and to the restoration and maintenance of peace" (United Nations Security Council 1994). From the beginning, Rwanda's transitional government expressed reservations at having an international tribunal on grounds of national sovereignty and asked instead for support in creating a national tribunal (which would exclude war crimes), but ultimately agreed to the ICTR (Prunier 2009:8–12). Out of concern that the situation in Rwanda at the time was still unstable, the court was located in Arusha, Tanzania. It was given a finite mandate, with the idea that it had a limited task to accomplish—to try the top leaders of the genocide—and then would cease to exist. The ICTR could indict and try people for crimes occurring only in the calendar year 1994, including genocide, crimes against humanity, and other serious violations of international humanitarian law (such as murder, torture, and rape). The ICTR had no enforcement arm, so once the indictments were approved and arrest warrants issued by the court, staff had to track down the individuals—most of whom had fled the country and were outside the reach of Rwandan transitional authorities, elsewhere in Africa or Europe—and had to rely on foreign governments to help arrest and extradite them.

Cases were held in the Arusha International Conference Center, a complex of three-story whitewashed concrete buildings in the center of Arusha in neighboring Tanzania. Courtroom personnel were a cosmopolitan mix of nationalities and languages, and practices were an improvisational blend of civil and common law that established a body of international criminal case law (Eltringham 2010). Panels of three international judges presided over cases. The two chief prosecutors of the ICTR were first from Switzerland, then from the Gambia. The office of the prosecution ultimately included a few Rwandan lawyers, but it was primarily international. Defense attorneys were overwhelmingly from France or francophone Africa. Defendants were assigned counsel paid by the ICTR budget because they met the criteria for indigence established by the tribunal. The defense attorneys were kept separate from the ICTR infrastructure, a partition that was intended to ensure independence from prosecution but in practice meant that they had fewer financial and infrastructural resources.

Cases typically lasted several years between arrest, trial, and judgment. The maximum punishment was thirty years or life in prison. The ICTR was funded by the United Nations, and by the close of 2010 had cost at least $1.5 billion (*Economist*, November 25, 2010). By December 2010, the ICTR had completed fifty-three cases, with eight acquittals, and had twenty-three cases in progress or awaiting trial.[14] All the people indicted and tried were members of the former Habyarimana government, though it was within the ICTR's mandate to issue indictments against members of the RPF for allegations of reprisal attacks. Many saw the failure to issue indictments against the RPF as a significant weakness that risked discrediting the tribunal as providing victor's justice rather than objective justice (Amnesty International 2002:11; Peskin 2008:207–231; Reyntjens 2009:183). When the chief prosecutor in 2002 and 2003 began investigating RPF crimes, the Rwandan government restricted in-country operations, successfully pressuring her to stop (Jones 2010:121; Maganarella 2000:83–84; Reyntjens 2009:183).

More broadly, the second half of the 1990s coincided with a broader international emphasis on the policing of crimes against humanity. For example, in 1998, after being granted amnesty by Chile, former Chilean dictator Augusto Pinochet was arrested and detained in Britain for crimes against humanity committed in his own country, based on an indictment issued by a Spanish judge using the principle of universal jurisdiction. Though Pinochet ultimately died with no convictions, his detention marked a watershed in international law because of the cooperation of international states in pursuing and attempting to prosecute him, a former head of government, for crimes committed in his own country. This principle of universal jurisdiction enabled trials of Rwandan genocide suspects in France, Canada, Belgium, and Switzerland (Jones 2010:12).

It is also under the principle of universal jurisdiction that judges issued recent indictments against members of the RPF for atrocities committed during and after the genocide, though not against Kagame because he maintains head-of-state immunity under international legal principles (Tunks 2002). French judge Jean Louis Bruguière carried out an investigation into the shooting down of Habyarimana's plane and concluded in November 2006 that Kagame gave the orders to shoot. Bruguière signed indictments against nine of Kagame's senior aides. In February 2008, Spanish judge Fernando Andreu indicted forty current or former Rwandan military officers on several counts of genocide and human rights abuses for their reprisal killings during and immediately after the genocide.

The ICTR and the ICTY were the only ad hoc tribunals of their kind created by the U.N. Security Council. Recognizing the expense and difficulties in creating separate ad hoc tribunals for each conflict situation, the International Criminal Court (ICC) was established by the Rome Statute in 1998 by a U.N. conference as a permanent international criminal tribunal. The Rome Statute is an international treaty, binding only on those states that have formally expressed their consent to be bound by its provisions. It entered into force on July 1, 2002, once sixty states had become parties to it. As of this writing, 123 states have become parties to it.[15] The court, based in The Hague in the Netherlands, is not a part of the United Nations but maintains a cooperative relationship with it. It has jurisdiction over genocide, crimes against humanity, and war crimes. It can only exercise jurisdiction if the accused is a national of a state that is party to the Rome Statute or otherwise accepting of its jurisdiction, or if the crime took place in a state that is party to the Rome Statute. The principle of "complementarity" provides that a case will not be referred to the ICC if it is being investigated or prosecuted in good faith by a state with jurisdiction (Burke-White 2005). The ICC requires voluntary compliance by member states to enforce indictments.

The international tribunals have had mixed results (Teitel 2008). Supporters of the ICC, ICTR, and ICTY argue that there is significant value in institutionalizing respect for rule of law and human rights principles and in creating a body of international criminal law that counters impunity and deters future atrocities (Birdsall 2007; Burke-White 2005; Maganarella 2000; Møse 2005). The ICTR established many significant contributions to international law, specifically by creating jurisprudence about genocide (Møse 2005; Nsanzuwera 2005). The ICTR succeeded in apprehending, convicting, and therefore neutralizing many high-level genocide leaders who otherwise would probably have remained outside the reach of the Rwandan courts and thus able to continue to foment trouble from outside in the uneasy sociopolitical environment in the years after the genocide (Møse 2005). It had the first conviction for genocide, affirmed rape as an international crime, and demonstrated that the principle of "command responsibility" could not exonerate perpetrators.

Yet, these institutions remain controversial. The ICTR and ICTY have been routinely criticized for being slow to deliver justice and too distanced from the populations who suffered, and therefore failing to aid the rebuilding of national legal infrastructure and being only marginally effective, if at all, in contributing to national reconciliation (Fletcher and Weinstein 2002; McMahon and Forsythe 2008). ICC indictments raise thorny questions about international versus national sovereignty and have prompted concerns of neocolonialism. Early indictments have all been against Africans (Uganda, the DRC, the Central African Republic, Sudan, and most recently Kenya and Libya), while, for example, the United States is not a signatory, and no American citizens have been indicted for their role in civilian attacks in Afghanistan or Iraq (Gettleman and Simons 2010). Kamari Clarke (2009) has shown how the ICC reflects a broader "tribunalization" of African violence and exists within a broader moral economy of justice characterized by deep-seeded inequalities. Richard Wilson (2011) has illustrated the deeply flawed processes through which historical knowledge is produced in international criminal trials.

Others claim that international tribunals are ineffectual, absent international political will for enforcement (Rodman 2008). Still others claim the ICC even inhibits peace processes and justice. This was illustrated particularly clearly with the case of the violence in northern Uganda, which was the first case referred to the ICC prosecutors. While ICC indictments arguably weakened support for the rebel group, the Lord's Resistance Army (LRA), and brought the rebels to the table, they also made negotiations more difficult, because LRA leaders used the indictments as a bargaining chip, claiming they would not stop fighting until the indictments were lifted (Blumenson 2006; Worden 2008).

Overall, during the past two decades the role of the international community in prosecuting crimes against humanity and genocide has raised concerns about national sovereignty. As in Rwanda, national governments expressed desire to be involved in, or retain control over, their own prosecutions. In response, by 2000, there was a shift toward the creation of "hybrid" courts that mixed national and international involvement, oversight, and law (Dickinson 2003; Shraga 2005). For example, the Special Court of Sierra Leone was set up in 2002 jointly by the government of Sierra Leone and the United Nations. It was mandated to try those who had committed serious violations of international humanitarian law and Sierra Leonean law since 1996, though, as Tim Kelsall argues, it failed in critical ways to adapt to local dynamics (Kelsall 2013). In 2003, in Cambodia, a negotiated treaty between the United Nations and the government of Cambodia created the Extraordinary Chambers in the Courts of Cambodia (ECCC). The ECCC was part of the domestic Cambodian court system, with jurisdiction to try members of the former Khmer Rouge of serious violations of Cambodian law and international humanitarian law. Both of these courts had a mixture of national and international judges, prosecutors, and investigators.

These hybrid courts reflected a shift away from unmitigated international policing, with a compromise on the need to address impunity with punishment but also to recognize national sovereignty and to balance national law with international law. The turn to hybrid courts also reflected questions about whether there were universal solutions in terms of transitional justice, versus how much the culture and particular circumstances of each context should be taken into account, as I discuss further in a moment. Yet the idea of punishment in the wake of political violence remained central to many transitional justice advocates, widely understood as crucial to countering impunity to break cycles of violence. Rwanda's emphasis on mass prosecutions for genocide through gacaca was consistent with this mindset (Waldorf 2010:184).

Truth Commissions

Beginning in the 1970s, truth commissions became an alternative solution to coping with transition after political violence. The first truth commission was established in Uganda in 1974. Six more were created in the 1980s, thirteen more in the 1990s, and another twenty between the years

2000 and 2009, with the highest concentration in Africa and the Americas (Sikkink and Walling 2006:308–309).

Truth commissions were established as temporary bodies, operational for a discrete period of time, with power to investigate specific time periods and types of violence. They aimed to paint a picture of a particular past violence and to fight against silences in the historical record, using documents, investigations, and testimonials (Hayner 1995). Rather than foreground perpetrators and punishment, they put victims and their voices at the center, based on a Western, Judeo-Christian, largely psychoanalytic model of the centrality of speaking and talk therapy for healing (Borneman 2002; Minow 1998; Shaw 2007). Victims gave wrenching testimony about their suffering, while perpetrators (ideally) gave detailed information about killings and disappearances. At the end of the process, results were typically published in multivolume reports, such as the *Nunca Mas* (Never Again) report that detailed tortures, disappearances, and deaths in Argentina under military rule between 1976 and 1983. These reports, though typically highly politicized, were understood to contribute to solidifying the authoritative history of the violence.

Typically spearheaded by national governments, truth commissions generally emerged in contexts where the alleged perpetrators shared political power, and therefore compromise had to be reached, rather than clear victors designing prosecutions on their own terms. Several were implemented in Latin America where, following democratization processes in Chile, Argentina, and Uruguay, military leaders who had perpetrated the violence still held significant political power, in which cases prosecutions were seen as impractical, or even as risking the provocation of further coups and violence, as in Argentina (Hayner 2011; Roht-Arriaza and Mariezcurrena 2006; Sikkink and Walling 2006). In another notable example, South Africa's Truth and Reconciliation Commission following the end of apartheid, from 1995 through 2003, came out of a negotiated settlement where ongoing involvement of National Party members in high positions of power basically precluded prosecutions (Ross 2003; Wilson 2001). From the beginning, truth commissions had an uneasy relationship with formal prosecutions, and were differentiated from formal legal accountability mechanisms. Sometimes information presented could lead to prosecutions, while at other times truth commissions granted amnesties to perpetrators in return for their testimony about what had occurred (Hayner 1995:226).

Truth commissions have attracted widespread support and critique. Proponents claim that they are crucial to giving victims a voice and to correcting the historical record, and that they can contribute to individual as well as collective healing (Hayner 2011; Minow 1998). Critics note the ways truth commissions can silence and distort victims' voices through their institutionalized processes and lack of concrete reparations, and how they can overlook citizens' desire for retributive justice (Bolten 2012a; Kelsall 2005; Phelps 2004; Ross 2003; Theidon 2012; Wilson 2001). While initially most were directed by national governments, there has been increasing international involvement in recent years.

Given the RPF's clear victory and claim to power after the genocide, it is not surprising that they did not pursue a truth commission model. There was historical precedent for a truth commission in Rwanda, however, as one was established as part of the Arusha talks in 1992, to investigate human rights abuses in the period after the RPF invasion into Rwanda on October 1, 1990. This commission was unique at the time in being sponsored by NGOs domestically and internationally (Hayner 1995:242–244). The commission traveled to Rwanda for two weeks in 1993, in a visit that provoked additional government violence before and after. Their resulting report concentrated on documenting violence by government forces, while also including rebel-led (RPF) human rights abuses. The commission was planning a second investigative trip when the genocide broke out.

Gacaca contained many elements consistent with truth commissions, including the centrality of truth telling as linked to promoting reconciliation. Gacaca put victims' narratives front and center, even among the judges (see Chapter 6), and allowed for a wider (though still limited) view of victimhood than circulated in other public spaces in Rwanda (see Chapter 3). While it did not offer amnesties, it had incentives of penalty reduction to encourage perpetrators to provide information.

Contemporary Complementary Approaches

The past twenty years have been marked by three trends in transitional justice, all of which were reflected in the embrace of local mediation models in postgenocide Rwanda: first, the joint, often contentious, role played by the international community versus national governments; second, the move to establishing multiple models simultaneously, often in efforts to balance obtaining truth versus prosecuting perpetrators (Roht-Arriaza and

Mariezcurrena 2006); and third, the move to valuing local culture over exclusively universal legal and human rights norms (Shaw et al. 2010). These trends coincide with what some have argued is a paradigm shift in the kinds of wars and political transitions occurring at the turn of the millennium. Toward the end of the twentieth century, global politics was characterized, on one hand, by persistent conflict and, on the other hand, by global discourse of justice through law and society (Teitel 2003).

First, transitional judicial institutions implemented in the past decade all reflect interplay between national and international actors. Gone are the ad hoc United Nations tribunals of the 1990s, replaced by hybrid tribunals, and even while the ICC continues to issue indictments on behalf of the international community, they are often at the request of domestic actors (such as the request by the Ugandan government for indictments of the Lord's Resistance Army). At the same time, domestic courts and truth commissions have international involvement, whether from governments, funders, or international NGOs such as the International Center for Transitional Justice. Postgenocide Rwanda demonstrated the move away from exclusively international prosecutions toward acknowledgment of national sovereignty over how to prosecute in the wake of mass violence. Gacaca was a dramatic challenge to the internationally driven prosecutions, a clear assertion of domestic authority to prosecute, based on Rwanda's own rules and guidelines that did not necessarily accord with universal legal and human rights standards. Even as gacaca courts were designed, implemented, and managed by the Rwandan government, this was done with the financial and capacity-building support of international donors, and under the close scrutiny of international academics and human rights organizations. The balance of power between national and international law and control remains contentious, in contexts around the world.

Second, along with blending national and international oversight, recently countries have put in place multiple complementary institutions in an effort to achieve manifold simultaneous ends of countering impunity, rebuilding rule of law, and promoting reconciliation (Roht-Arriaza and Mariezcurrena 2006). This can be seen in the coexistence in Rwanda of the ICTR, domestic trials, and gacaca courts, which mix types and levels of involvement. In other examples, alongside the hybrid Special Court of Sierra Leone, for the first time, a Truth and Reconciliation Commission (TRC) was implemented in parallel (Shaw 2007). The Sierra Leonean TRC, established in 2002 and operational for eight months, was a national institution with international involvement through U.N. oversight and funding but with a budget much smaller than the Special Court's. Similarly, in East Timor, to respond to the violence surrounding the 1999 referendum in which East Timorese voted for independence, a U.N.-backed hybrid court was set up (Special Panels for Serious Crimes), an ad hoc tribunal was established in Indonesia by the Indonesian government, and a Commission for Reception, Truth, and Reconciliation was set up in East Timor by the national government.

Finally, the resurgence of national control in the face of international norms, along with the focus on multiple simultaneous solutions, led to a distinct valuation of local, culturally derived solutions (Shaw et al. 2010). Rwanda was basically unprecedented in choosing to pursue a strategy of maximal prosecutions, but through a culturally situated, locally derived mechanism. Similarly, in East Timor, local spiritual reconciliation practices were incorporated into the Commission for Reception, Truth, and Reconciliation, with varying degrees of success (Babo-Soares 2005; Burgess 2006). In Uganda, discussions were waged on how to formalize a traditional reconciliation ritual called *mato oput*, which was based on principles of accountability, forgiveness, and reparations, either in addition to or in lieu of the ICC indictments (Allen 2008; Finnstrom 2010; Latigo 2008). Contemporary transitional justice debates continue to search for the right balance of universal principles versus specific cultural values and to identify how legal norms can be "vernacularized" without diluting their fundamental value (Merry 2006a; Shaw et al. 2010).

Overall, the Rwandan government's decision to implement gacaca alongside other efforts to rebuild rule of law, such as through comite y'abunzi and nongovernment legal aid clinics, did not occur in a vacuum but rather were informed by vigorous ongoing debates about the role of law in postconflict situations and the relationships between law, justice, punishment, and reconciliation. For decades, there appeared to be a trade-off where societies could either establish the truth about what happened or punish people through criminal prosecutions, but not both. That is, Western-style prosecutorial trials were seen as inhibitors to truth, because defendants had incentives and rights to withhold information. Meanwhile, truth commissions were seen to promote narratives about violent events while accountability remained elusive. Tensions between these separate historical strands remain at the heart of gacaca and other transitional justice processes. The Rwandan government's decision to use gacaca, a system prioritizing customary mediation and narrative truth telling while also emphasizing punishment, was a deliberate rebuke of international courts, on the one hand, and amnesty-based truth commissions, on the other hand. It precipitated a broader global shift toward valuing "the local" in transitional justice.

Conclusion: Overcoming Persistent Dichotomies

Analyzing the three forums (gacaca courts, comite y'abunzi, and the legal aid clinic) together dislodges an exclusive focus on gacaca and transitional justice and puts these forums in the context of decentralization and the broader history of conciliation-based tribunals for ordinary disputes in Rwanda. Considering the mediation focus in gacaca, comite y'abunzi, and the legal aid clinic together in historical and global context provides three interventions into transitional justice debates. These correctives allow us to escape reliance on persistent, pernicious terminological dichotomies between restorative versus retributive, customary versus modern, formal versus informal, and popular versus state, which break down upon close examination.

First, transitional justice must be understood as inextricably linked to the seemingly commonplace processes of ordinary justice. As the subsequent chapters show, people experienced gacaca, comite y'abunzi, and the legal aid clinic in a set of overlapping social fields, and their disputes spilled over the boundaries of a given forum, troubling a distinction between "genocide" versus "nongenocide" dispute. Examining disputes about genocide property, housing, inheritance, and employment problems together allows us to better understand the three-dimensionality of people's social struggles in the wake of genocide. My argument here is consistent with the feminist critique of transitional justice, which challenges the dichotomy between before and after, war and peace (Buckley-Zistel and Zolkos 2011:12; Ni Aolain 2009; Valji 2007), arguing that "there is no aftermath," particularly for women (Turshen et al. 2002), as forms of structural violence and inequality persist into the so-called postconflict moment. I suggest we must identify continuities in forms of grievance, disputes, and violence over time, and see how people cope with a wide variety of struggles in the aftermath of genocide. The historical and comparative framing I have provided here and the case examples I present in the subsequent chapters show that maintaining the exceptionalism of genocide-related violence as distinct from more prosaic grievances through legal processes contributes to the kinds of reification of social status and institutionalization of hierarchies that I problematized in the master narrative.

Second, I suggest that what relevance harmony models had to people's ongoing efforts to rebuild their social networks was related to decentralization, or, more specifically, contextualization, overcoming a stark distinction between cultural versus universal justice principles. The history presented here and in the prior chapter shows that understanding harmony models as customary law or cultural practices is problematic, given that "culture" is used to imply unity and an absence of power relations that are belied by the scholarship. Rather, regulation of dispute resolution has long been a preoccupation of ruling elites in Rwanda, and practices and institutions of dispute resolution have been tied up with political and economic power for centuries. Of course, I am sympathetic to renewed calls to recognize the cultural dimensions of law, in the face of the growing hegemony of international human rights and criminal law (Clarke 2009; Kelsall 2013; Merry 2006a; Renteln 2005; Rosen 2006). But given the history provided in this chapter and the dangers of cultural justification for unity detailed earlier, I agree with other scholars that we should shift transitional justice discussions away from identifying some elusive "cultural" relevance (Allen 2008; Shaw and Waldorf 2010), and suggest that we can identify ways that being embedded can foster relevance—though ideally with much more genuine local ownership than we saw in Rwanda. I show in the subsequent chapters how these legal forums were deeply contextualized, an inescapable part of the backdrop of everyday life, notwithstanding the heavy state involvement.

Third, I argue that harmony and punishment are inextricable, overcoming a chronic persistence of language of restorative versus retributive approaches. Historical context from Rwanda showed how sanctions, force, coercion, and inequality have been a part of so-called restorative-based systems across time, as in other regions. I illustrate in more detail in the coming chapters how harmony and punishment were deeply intertwined in each of these forums, even as they played out in varied combinations with multiple effects.

This chapter marks the conclusion of the first part of this book, which sought to outline the architecture of social repair and provide a framework for understanding postgenocide Rwanda in historic and comparative perspective. I turn now to the ethnographic chapters that focus on each legal forum in turn, beginning with gacaca.

Chapter 3

Gacaca Days and Genocide Citizenship

One morning in January 2008, I sat with several hundred people who had gathered beneath a jacaranda tree in Ndora to listen and provide testimony in a gacaca trial. A man I call Claude, a farmer and accused midlevel perpetrator in Ndora, was charged with killing the children of a woman named Mukatagazwa, who was his godfather's wife and lived next door. The two witnesses who provided evidence implicating Claude in killing Mukatagazwa's children were both Claude's sisters. They each said they saw him killing two of her children with a club and then leaving with the third, who was never seen again. Claude admitted that Mukatagazwa's children had been at his house before they died, but he claimed his sisters were accusing him simply to take the blame off their own sons (his nephews), who he said were the guilty ones along with Mukatagazwa's brother, Yohanni.

Mukatagazwa testified that during the genocide, she and her children fled to Claude's house one night for safety. Claude later came with a group of killers. He killed two of her children and then disappeared with a third, and she still did not know where his remains were. She said she had recently heard Claude say he would never admit to the deaths of her children because he heard that victims were given cows, and he did not want her to get any. Claude responded that Mukatagazwa was accusing him simply to take the blame off her own brother, Yohanni. Mukatagazwa retorted that Claude was simply blaming Yohanni and his nephews because they were dead and therefore could not defend themselves.[1]

Conversations like this one occurred weekly in Ndora for several years, beginning in 2005 with the nationwide launch of the gacaca process. In Ndora, every Thursday was gacaca day, when all business, farming, and transport activities were halted so that people could participate in public trials of suspects of the 1994 genocide before panels of locally elected judges. In Nyanza, gacaca day was on Tuesday, in Nyamirambo (in Kigali) it was on Sunday. By midmorning, people would gather for sessions. In Ndora, it was in an outdoor courtyard just down the hard-packed dirt road from the market, a space that other days of the week frequently hosted meetings as part of the government's broader policy of decentralized development. In Nyanza, people met in the L-shaped courtyard of a local administrative building. In Nyamirambo, they gathered under a tent in the courtyard of the sector administrative office. Cases sessions began midmorning, continuing without a break through the afternoon, often not closing until sunset.

Gacaca sessions quickly became a regular part of people's weekly routine and their habitual interactions with neighbors, whether they participated actively or sought strategies to avoid it, staying out of sight to minimize risk of sanctions for nonattendance. The launch of gacaca brought the past unavoidably into everyday life as a palpable presence. The process was intended to formally categorize people in relation to the genocide as perpetrators or victims, with duties, rights, and obligations associated with these positions. At the same time, consistent with the mediation principles, gacaca sessions emphasized process as well as outcome, geared toward reshaping relationships as well as determining guilt according to specific legal principles.

In this chapter, I explore what was at stake in the contested social negotiations like Claude's, which occurred across Rwanda every day for several years as part of a legal process purportedly designed to help restore the social fabric. I examine the social negotiations that occurred during the days of gacaca to explore what happened when people contentiously debated over what it meant to live together, shaping the present in direct relation to the past. I attend both to how gacaca was part of a global regime of law that reproduced particular configurations of unequal power and to how people themselves maneuvered within these public legal spaces.

I begin by providing brief background on gacaca to illustrate the inextricable combination of harmony principles and punishment within the framing and procedures, and to show how Nikolas Rose's (1999) notion of government through community, laid out in the Introduction, operated within it. That is, I show how gacaca was a form of governance intended to manage the relationships among people, forging them into a binding moral field, a deliberate attempt to construct "community," in and through the workings of individuals themselves a part of that community. I argue that even though the Rwandans with whom I worked recognized gacaca as a state-driven practice that used law as a tool for social engineering, gacaca courts were deeply contextualized, and sessions therefore served as spaces that people like Claude and his family and neighbors used to reconstruct moral orders, debating the meaning of collective belonging, social obligations, exchange, and even citizenship categories in the present and the future. Specifically, I suggest people used these sessions to negotiate the micropolitics of reconciliation in relation to genocide citizenship and material loyalty.

During gacaca sessions, people had to evaluate one another with respect to official categories of "genocide victim" and "genocide perpetrator," which were defined by the versions of causality, guilt, and innocence in the dominant narrative. Given the format of gacaca, rather than simply assign criminal responsibility, people actually used the process to shape the meaning of the categories themselves. Gacaca sessions unfolded as churning pools of competing recollections and assertions about what occurred in the past. The contentious conversations brought into public some of the disagreements and divisions lurking behind Rwandans' superficial public agreements, bringing into the fore to at least a limited degree discussions that otherwise remained in "hidden transcripts" (Ingelaere 2009:524, 2010b:282; Scott 1990; Thomson 2011b:445; Waldorf 2006:77; Zorbas 2009). I suggest that discussions in gacaca did not result in or reflect straightforward indoctrination in government reconciliation propaganda but rather served as a constant reminder that definitions of victim and perpetrator, guilt, innocence, and unity more broadly were still being debated in postgenocide Rwanda.

Harmony and Punishment in Gacaca

The law formally instantiating gacaca courts nationwide was promulgated in 2001 (Constitution of the Republic of Rwanda 2003, Article 143; Organic Law N.33/2001). In the previous few years, Rwandan authorities had begun talking about resurrecting and adapting a precolonial model for dispute resolution called gacaca as the answer to the weaknesses within the national courts.[2] Advocates had noted that since 1995, administrators in some areas had been encouraging the settlement of local claims by survivors against perpetrators through an informal gacaca process, which typically took place before a community gathering (Des Forges 1999:761). The gacaca process began gradually, rolling out across the country over a period of several years in the early 2000s. The government conducted extensive sensitization campaigns to educate the population about gacaca's goals and methods, regularly visiting cell-level community meetings and prisons. In October 2001, nationwide elections were held in which people selected inyangamugayo. A gacaca pilot phase began in 2002, with approximately 740 cells nationwide participating.[3] Based on the pilot phase, modifications were made in the gacaca law in 2004, and the official launch of gacaca activities nationwide quickly followed, including training judges for the initial information-gathering phase.[4] National office staff explained that the official national launch of the documentation phase was in January 2005, while the first actual genocide trials in the pilot sectors began in March 2005. July 2006 marked the beginning of trials at the national level in the remaining approximately two thousand cells.

The gacaca process was under the control not of the Ministry of Justice but of a separate office called the National Service of Gacaca Jurisdictions. Gacaca courts were thus established in parallel with, and with equal authority to, the national court system. The gacaca system included three levels of courts: cell courts, sector courts, and appeals courts. Cases could not be referred to the ordinary courts, and defendants could not be tried for the same charges in ordinary courts as well as gacaca.

The gacaca process followed three stages: documentation, trials, and appeals. In the first stage, documentation, people came together to develop inventories of who had lived in the area during the genocide, who had died, and who was accused. Observers noted that in most areas of the country participation was high during the documentation phase. Many of the people for whom dossiers were compiled were already prisoners, while others were newly accused. Dossiers were compiled on each individual, and the charges were organized based on categories of genocide crimes that had been established by the 1996 law.[5] Category One included "planners, organizers, instigators, supervisors and leaders" and people with political authority, as well as people who had committed acts of sexual torture. Category One defendants (leaders accused of planning the genocide and anyone accused of rape) were referred to the national courts, though by 2008 the law was amended to include certain Category One offenses before gacaca (Organic Law N.13/2008, Article 2). Category Two included "notorious murderers," perpetrators, conspirators, or accomplices of intentional homicide or assault, and Category Three included perpetrators of crimes against property. One of the key challenges gacaca faced was to establish individual accountability for collective violence, which required careful codification of degrees of participation and complicity. Gacaca was mandated to deal with crimes committed from October 1, 1990, through December 31, 1994, starting with the period when the RPF invaded Rwanda, which launched the civil war, and therefore included the retaliatory attacks against civilian Tutsi and three and a half years of planning for genocide.

In the second phase, the trial stage, trials were held based on the compiled dossiers. This is the phase that was under way during the main period of my research. Category Two murder cases were tried at the sector level, while Category Three cases regarding crimes against property were tried at the cell level. Trials took anywhere from a few hours to several days. Some cases were conducted against specific individuals, one dossier at a time, while sometimes judges chose to hear related cases simultaneously. Fugitive defendants were tried in absentia, on the premise that if and when they returned to the country, they would have the right to appeal. During trials, each defendant (*uregwa*) spoke on his or her own behalf, and judges directed the questioning, with active input from victims, witnesses, and the general assembly. People who registered to testify as witnesses (*abatangabuhamya*) were required to wait out of hearing range and were separated from one another until their turn to speak, in an effort to ensure integrity of their testimony. People registered as victims (*abahohotewe*) were allowed to sit through the ongoing testimony, based on the premise that they could more accurately assess the accuracy of participants' claims. As punishment, in Category Two cases, inyangamugayo had the authority to imprison defendants for up to thirty years, to require them to do community service work (*travaux d'intérêt général*, or TIG), or simply to allow them to return home. In Category Three property cases, inyangamugayo had authority either to require defendants to repay victims with cash or in-kind goods or to exonerate them of financial penalty.

In the third and final stage, dissatisfied defendants could request that their case be heard before the appeals court (Organic Law N.16/2004, Articles 85–93). Cases were not automatically forwarded to appeal; rather, defendants had to demonstrate how the case had been wrongfully handled based on a substantive issue of law or prove bias among judges.[6] The assembly of gacaca judges for each sector decided on which cases warranted review, and the cases were heard by a separate panel of gacaca judges.

Mediation, harmony, and compromise were explicitly part of the framing rationale of gacaca, intended to "allow the population of the same Cell, the same Sector to work together" and therefore for gacaca to "become the basis of collaboration and unity."[7] The gacaca process was designed around the idea of reduced penalties in return for confessions, consistent with the 1996 law that codified genocide within the national penal code, and it established punishment for genocide that was lower than in the standard penal code. The goal was for defendants to confess to what they had done and to provide information about victims and other perpetrators, and in return to receive a significantly lighter sentence. If judges accepted the defendant's sentence as honest and full, they could reduce his or her sentence by up to one-half, with the remaining time to be served doing community service work (TIG). Time already served counted toward the imposed sentence. Most who confessed could therefore be released immediately. Inyangamugayo often played an active role directing conversations and lecturing participants, using language explicitly drawing on mediation principles, such as reminding participants: "We need the truth in order to build unity and reconciliation."[8] They urged people to make sacrifices, set aside grievances, and rebuild relationships. As I discuss more in chapter 6, most inyangamugayo did not limit their interactions to the evidentiary facts participants contributed to the proceedings, they also interceded to address broader social concerns, such as to resolve conflict between two victims who disagreed, or to counsel feuding witnesses to come to agreement.

Authorities and inyangamugayo justified gacaca and its processual, mediation-based approach as a part of Rwandans' authentic cultural heritage. Educational materials, articles in the pro-government newspaper the *New Times,* radio broadcasts, and even promotional materials surrounding Rwanda's growing tourism industry described gacaca courts as "traditional community courts"[9] based on "the inspiration of the traditional context of conflict resolution."[10] They contended that as a part of Rwanda's past cultural traditions, gacaca was ideally suited to resolving the dilemmas of post-genocide justice and social repairs. As the National Service of Gacaca Jurisdictions proclaimed, gacaca was intended "to prove that the Rwandan society has the capacity to solve its own problems through a system of justice based on the Rwandan custom."[11] The emphasis on unity was two-fold: Rwandans should embrace gacaca because they were unified by sharing the ancestral tradition; also, by participating in the process itself, they would further restore harmony.

Yet, the pervasive threat of punishment was a crucial component of how people experienced gacaca. Every Rwandan with whom I interacted recognized that gacaca courts were criminal courts in which the state brought charges against accused defendants. In addition to sentencing defendants to prison, community service, or financial penalties, inyanga-mugayo could bring charges against case participants for refusing to testify, for perjury, for blackmail, or for coercion (Organic Law N.16/2004, Articles 29, 30). They could issue subpoenas to forcibly summon people to testify, and could arrest people who still resisted. Police, prison guards, and even soldiers served as a constant physical reminder of the role of forceful retribution and incarceration. Participation was mandatory for all Rwandans, and local leaders stamped people's identity cards after each session as proof of attendance. Authorities regularly threatened to impose fines on individuals who did not attend. Thus, even as national authorities encouraged mediation principles and expressed an optimistic view of social harmony, they always kept the idea of punishment through forceful enforcement of judgments at the forefront of people's minds.

Gacaca's Contextualized Conversations

I suggest that gacaca sessions like Claude's with which I began this chapter had an impact on people's social renegotiations (though rarely in precisely the ways the government intended) because they were contextualized and embedded in daily life: they were physically proximate, public, routine, participatory, and based on oral testimony. Ndora residents who sat together in gacaca one day a week saw one another the rest of the week, as they lived in mutual interdependence in a densely populated area. Sessions were episodes in a set of debates and knowledge claims that had started earlier, and would continue afterward. Participants bought goods from each other at the market or tilled their adjacent fields. For example, one inyangamu-gayo preached on Sundays before his congregation at a local Pentecostal church, and several released prisoners shuttled people to and from the nearest town on their bicycles or moto-taxis. Participants were members of the

Figure 4. Gacaca in Nyanza, 2007 (photo by author).

same business cooperatives, financial associations, and women's groups, or taught one another's children in school, or repaired clothes or bicycles for one another. The social connections were perhaps less dense in Nyanza or Nyamirambo, but nonetheless overlapping and interconnected. Even people who did not attend heard about the week's proceedings, as discussions spilled over the boundaries of the proceedings into other moments and conversations, over cooking fires or homebrewed banana beer. These discussions outside gacaca ultimately fed information back into the process, over the many years it was ongoing. By the time trials were under way in 2006, people knew the bulk of the charges and allegations against each other (based on the information provided during the documentation phase), and these had all been much discussed outside gacaca.

The law regulating gacaca procedures, Organic Law N.16/2004, laid out a general approach to trial sessions that fostered comparatively open-ended conversations. It provided the order in which participants should take turns providing their version of events, ensuring that the defendant had the opportunity to reply to all charges and testimony against him or her. The law allowed "any interested person" to "testify in favor or against the defendant" (Article 64). This broad inclusiveness was based on the idea that communal participation in gacaca was an antidote to the communal participation in the genocide. People testifying had to take an oath to tell the truth (Article 64). Participants were required to be calm and polite to the inyangamugayo, and to testify about crimes under the temporal and subject matter jurisdiction of the court—that is, genocide crimes from October 1, 1990, through December 31, 1994, that had occurred in the administrative unit of the court (Articles 3, 4, 71).

Other than these general guidelines, the law included no other specific regulations on what could be provided as evidence. This wide latitude for evidence was consistent with other justice systems that sought to address a breach of deeply embedded relationships and practices rather than a narrowly defined point of law (Colson 1974:73). There were no rigid constraints on the form or content of what people said, and no limitations on what was considered relevant or irrelevant. Testimony was typically open-ended and unstructured, especially given that there were no lawyers present. A person could testify on what "he or she knows or witnessed" (Organic Law N.16/2004, Article 64), so people testified about things they saw with their own eyes (that is, as eyewitness), as well as things they had heard about from other people (that is, hearsay).

Discussions should not be romanticized as being fully open; security forces and local elected authorities representing the regime monitored the process, in some contexts "not so active[ly]" (Ingelaere 2008:49) but in others "'controll[ing]'" the process (Thomson and Nagy 2011:23). At the same time, in the absence of lawyers and intervening technologies, during trials people directly and publicly confronted one another. They asked, for example, in a case in Ndora in September 2007, "Are you the one who killed my son and wrapped his body in a blanket, then showed it to his sister?" Or demanded in a case in Ndora in November 2007, "Explain your responsibility or show the good things you did." The immediacy often heightened the adversarial nature of sessions.

The evidence presented in gacaca sessions was what people said aloud, based on memories strengthened or diluted with the passage of time. Cases were thus weekly public debates in which people discussed death in meticulous detail, accused or defended one another, and provided names. Stories did not come out in an organized, linear narrative but rather in fits and starts, with sidetracks, extraneous details, and accidental omissions. People returned to details, jumped forward, and circled back again. Judges and people in the general assembly asked clarifying questions and added their own input or corrections when they agreed or disagreed with others' testimony. Often testimony was confusing, and everyone present had to work together to figure out how it related to the charges at hand. There remained ongoing uncertainty about which charges stemmed from which particular incident, and even the precise identity of specific victims, because of the logistics of how defendants' dossiers had been compiled.

In these public conversations, people discussed death in meticulous, graphic, personal detail. They accused or defended one another and named names. They talked not about what happened in aggregate to anonymous, faceless Rwandans but about what happened to people they knew (or knew of), and about things that they saw or did. As the following quotes show, discussions involved eyewitness testimony and hearsay from witnesses, victims, and co-perpetrators: "I saw François hit the girl with a club, then Espèrance continued dragging her while blood oozed out of her head."[12] "Vincent killed Béatrice, who was pregnant and carried a baby on her back. Then Innocent and others split open her womb to kill even the unborn baby."[13] "Gakwaya told me he was no longer afraid of killing, because he had just killed Kalisa, cut off his hands, and dumped him down a latrine."[14] "Emmanueli came to the roadblock with an old man, and asked us to kill him. Fidelis hit the old man with a club, and he died."[15] "Alfred grabbed and beat me, then took my child from my arms and threw him down the latrine to die."[16] "I heard that the killers blocked the door to the house where my father was hiding, and set it on fire. When it was burning, he ran out, and then they killed him."[17] These detailed, vivid, painful observations, occurring in weekly unavoidable public conversations, emblazoned the past onto the present.

In addition to death, in gacaca sessions people discussed property that had been stolen during the genocide. Discussions about property were in some ways even more contentious than murder charges because victims sought specific reparations for items that had been taken or destroyed. At the time of my fieldwork, approximately 54 percent of total nationwide gacaca cases were Category Three disputes over property, heard before cell-level courts.[18] Discussions about property permeated Category Two murder cases, too. There were often extended debates over destroyed houses, cows, fields, cups of beans, individual items of clothing, and kitchen utensils. Sometimes people used these debates in an effort to seek reparations for the property taken. Other times, they used the discussion about material items as part of their evidence in support of or against the defendant. For example, a widow might claim that she saw the defendant later wearing the pair of trousers that her husband was wearing when he was killed.

These specific acts of theft or killing were embedded in broader stories that provided context about other dynamics of the period. People testified about making lists of Tutsi to be killed and checking them against survivors, and described revealing people's identities as Tutsi. They talked about manning roadblocks, demanding identity cards, and detaining or killing people who passed by. People talked about how they managed to survive: they sought refuge among dead bodies or in pit latrines, or hid for days in banana plantations in driving rain, or sought refuge in home after home, only to continue to be pursued by different groups of killers. People also described everyday details of the period—drinking homebrew, slaughtering cows to eat at roadblocks, harvesting crops, trying to get medicines for sick relatives.

Because of the widespread destruction of physical property during the violence, people could not rely on documentary evidence or paper trails to substantiate or refute alibis or allegations. No one could, for example, show a photo of the crime scene with the defendant's footprints or clothing visible. Murder weapons were long gone or too ubiquitous to prove anything—for example, everyone owned a panga, a common farming machete. The exception was when testimony led to the recovery of physical remains of victims, who by this point had been missing for more than a decade. But unlike at some other notorious massacre sites, such as Srebrenica in Bosnia (e.g., Wagner 2008), there was no scientific technology provided to identify remains, so physical remains if found often provided inconsistent corroboration of other, oral testimony, and could serve as additional fodder for debate.

Gacaca sessions therefore emphasized oral testimony as evidence, and as the only form of corroboration to assess validity and credibility of other evidence. The emphasis on oral evidence, with its inherent malleability, meant that discussions turned into performances in which people positioned themselves, agreeing or disagreeing with one another's versions of the past, as when Claude's two sisters and neighbor spoke out to reinforce their version of what had occurred. Defendants needed others to attest to whether or not their alibis were legitimate, such as, "I was out grazing my cattle," "The property was gone when I got there," "Someone else took that cow," and "A different guy killed that person." Similarly, witnesses and victims needed confirmation from others about their statements, either that people had seen similar things or that the statements were plausible—that yard was visible from that doorway, or it was reasonable to graze cattle at that time of day—or that the speaker was credible.

As important as what people said before gacaca was what they did *not* say. A frequent testifier in Ndora described a common view: "People are still not revealing the whole truth about what happened. There are still some things they keep secret."[19] I regularly heard witnesses or defendants claim, "There is nothing I can say about that," or, "I know nothing about what he did during the genocide." Often the inyangamugayo asked people in the general assembly to chime in about a contested point, and no one spoke. These intentional silences or moments of "chosen amnesia" (Buckley-Zistel 2006:131), prevalent in everyday life in postgenocide Rwanda, were both a culturally appropriate coping mechanism and one that was often founded on fear (Burnet 2012:esp. 110–127). We can see silences in gacaca as another form of testimony (see also Burnet 2010:102), which also served as a form of alliance building (see, e.g., Rettig 2011:201–202; Reyntjens and Vandeginste 2005). These "strategic moments of silence" within gacaca can also be understood as what Thomson calls "withdrawn muteness," a form of everyday resistance to state power in Rwanda (Thomson 2011b:453; see also Thomson and Nagy 2011:25).

Discussions within gacaca sessions maintained a complicated relationship with truth, as no one I spoke with believed that the oral testimony provided was inherently factual.[20] In trials I attended, people constantly accused one another of speaking falsely, either through misremembering or deliberate lying. They used the term *Arabeshya!* translated as both "He [or she] is lying!" and "He [or she] is mistaken!" Concerns about testimony being fabricated for strategic reasons came from people on all sides of the process, and fit into a wider context of beliefs among Rwandans that their countrymen, from elite politicians to ordinary people, had a predilection to manipulate evidence and misrepresent the truth for personal gain (De Lame 2005:14–15; Ingelaere 2009:54, 2010a; Waldorf 2006:70). The official narrative identified the "institutionalization of lies," cultivated by the colonizers and the genocidal regime, as one of the "causes of disunity" among Rwandans (Rutayisira 2004:34). For example, a government-issued primary-school civics textbook, which had been revised after the genocide as part of a new history curriculum, captured the prevailing perception by teaching children that in the years leading up to the genocide, "Rwandans developed the practice of lying on an individual scale. It became a virtue and anyone who could lie without being discovered was praised as being more intelligent than others" (Rutayisira 2004:34). As one university law student earnestly explained to me, "Rwandans are good at lying and making false claims."[21] To be clear, the truth or falsity of claims about Rwandans' inherent deceptiveness is not what is at issue in my analysis. What is at issue is that many people *believed* this stereotype about one another. Ndora and Nyanza residents often told me that threats, blackmail, and bribes commonly influenced people's testimony on all sides of the process, and they saw people's choices about how to testify as directly linked to one another's efforts to improve their own economic and social positions or to settle scores. All testimony was open to interpretation and subject to allegiances and factions.

Though the gacaca process produced a paper trail accessible to government officials and inyangamugayo, most participants did not have access to the written documents. The transcribed proceedings were not comprehensive and not easily accessible. Though the gacaca law stipulated that a trial transcript be read aloud at the end of each case hearing, in many cases, including Claude's, this procedure was not followed (Organic Law N.16/2004, Articles 64, 65). Overall, with the exception of inyangamugayo who consulted the transcripts during deliberations, virtually everyone relied on the oral testimony, and word of mouth that revisited it, in their interpretations of what had occurred.

Social Maneuvering During Gacaca

The kind of conversations occurring daily across Rwanda during the days of gacaca were in stark contrast to prior years, when there was an unspoken convention not to discuss specific details of people's experiences with the recent violence except in private, intimate settings (Burnet 2005:215). Public mention of past violence prior to gacaca was dominated by the official

Figure 5. Gacaca in Ndora, 2007 (photo by author).

narrative, which included macro-level events that addressed the wide sweep of the genocide, supplemented by witness testimonials. Amid the nation-wide sensitization to the start of gacaca in 2003–2005, people continually talked to me about how this new legal process would force the genocide to become front and center. Some told me they were anxious, noting that it was traumatic enough to live through, so they did not want to revisit it. Many preferred not to know what their colleagues or neighbors had actually done during that time. Others were more positive, saying they were eager for a forum specifically designed to ask about details that had long been left unspoken, perhaps speculated about but not confirmed. They wanted to have a chance to explain their actions or exonerate themselves, or were impatient to learn long-sought-after information, such as how a certain relative had died or where someone had been buried.

Once gacaca began, testimony brought the past to life weekly in public settings, so it infused daily life in concrete ways. Information circulated and insinuated itself into close relationships and routine encounters. An elderly

Ndora resident whom I call Agathe, who testified in Claude's case as well as many others, explained to me how gacaca raised the stakes in how people considered one another in relation to the genocide period. She said:

> I had an old friend, we used to talk about everything. But there was something she kept a secret until recently. During gacaca, she testified that my second born was taken by the killers from her house. I was not even at gacaca that day, but some neighbors came to tell me. The whole time, my friend and I had continued socializing, but she never told me about the fate of my son. I wondered, why hadn't she told me? Maybe she feared if she revealed it they would hold her responsible for having handed over the child to be killed, or people would think it was her husband who killed him.[22]

Agathe's experience was a microcosm of events occurring across the country. Gacaca provided a forum in which people provided information they had withheld or spoke publicly of things that had previously only been discussed privately. Suddenly, people had no choice but to consider their friends and neighbors based on how they acted in the past and how they positioned themselves in relation to the present legal process of reckoning with the past. What had they done during the genocide? How did they explain or justify their actions? Were they cooperative and forthcoming with information or resistant and reticent in gacaca? Did they try to implicate or exonerate other family, neighbors, and acquaintances? People had to reevaluate their relationships, considering, as Agathe did, how her friend could or should have acted differently during the genocide, what it meant that she acted as she did, and what it meant that she was now providing information. Agathe had to decide if she thought her friend was guilty, or a bystander, or herself a victim.

People like Agathe could not passively absorb information but had to act in ways that impacted others. Agathe had to make a choice about how to respond, which would influence how her friend would be treated in gacaca. Would Agathe pursue additional allegations against her or her husband for complicity? Would she provide information in support of her friend or information that cast doubt on her motives? If someone else spoke up against her friend, would Agathe defend her or remain silent? Similarly, in Claude's case, we can understand the choices his sisters, neighbor, and other participants made as having equivalently weighty implications.

Encounters such as those between Agathe and her friend took on added significance, given that they were situated within a nationwide legal process that established criminal accountability for genocide, so there were high stakes in how people confronted the past. Gacaca was not just about providing information and speaking the truth, as in the model of truth commissions that offer amnesty to perpetrators. A neighbor's version of the past could imprison a loved one for up to thirty years, or allow him to have his sentence be commuted to community service work, or let him come home. Or it could require a neighbor to repay looted items.

In this situation, Agathe's friend came to her after testifying, and asked her forgiveness. She explained that she did not mention this information earlier because she feared it would cause Agathe pain and was better left unsaid. Now, with gacaca under way, Agathe's friend felt obligated to cooperate and speak of what she knew rather than withhold information. No charges were filed against the friend or her husband. Agathe ultimately forgave her, and during later trials, she interjected in support of her friend's positive motivations.

Similarly, in Claude's case, as in others, participants were very clear that how they publicly remembered the past had stakes for the present, in a state-backed legal forum with power to reallocate goods or exonerate defendants. Ndora residents were politically savvy and, unlike "casual observers," did not mistake their neighbors' participation in gacaca as signaling conformity (Thomson 2011b:451–456). They recognized the "dialectical relationship" between truth and lies (Ingelaere 2010a:54) within their own language, and were well aware that what Moore described as the "micropolitics of local social standing" shaped people's testimony in court proceedings (1992:42). People saw false accusations as directly linked to one another's efforts to improve their own economic and social positions or to settle scores. In one case in Ndora, for example, a young man was acquitted after it became clear through the trial testimony that the key witness, his mother's co-wife, only accused him as a strategy to prevent him from inheriting family land.[23] People claimed that threats, blackmail, and bribes commonly influenced people's testimony. It was quite common after a judgment for anyone who disagreed with it to offhandedly note, "They must have bribed the inyangamugayo," or, "He must have paid the witnesses." Other researchers of gacaca have made similar observations: Rwandans were equally, if not more, concerned with demonstrating loyalty as with truth telling (Waldorf 2010:195), people's performances in gacaca could be used to settle family disputes and seek other gains (Burnet 2010:113; Rettig 2011:201), and how people testified "depend[ed] upon the relations" among them (Ingelaere 2009:520).

My point here is that rather than focus on how partial truths, strategic testimony, and silences illustrate that gacaca sessions were not working in a normative legal sense, we can instead recognize the patterns of storytelling and language use in gacaca sessions as an extension of everyday communicative practices, and examine more fully how Rwandans used gacaca sessions instrumentally as part of ongoing debates. In what follows, I turn to exploring the work that people did within gacaca, which I suggest was one piece of negotiating social relations and collective belonging through disputes over the genocide.

Negotiating the Micropolitics of Reconciliation: Genocide Citizenship and Material Loyalty

I suggest we understand contextualized conversations in sessions as parts of efforts to "reconstruct moral orders" in a "micropolitics of reconciliation," as Theidon has described with respect to postwar Peru (2006:436). Discussions in case sessions were extensions of ongoing debates I heard outside gacaca about how people understood collective belonging: the meaning of social relationships and obligations in the past, and by extension how people understood those relationships in the present, and the current basis for unity, if any. People differentiated kinds and levels of guilt, discussed circumstances and motivations of their actions, and debated how ideas of protecting others or suffering fit with dominant understandings of how blame should be apportioned.

Gacaca was implemented consistent with the official narrative, defining the violence of the early 1990s as state-sponsored genocide by the majority Hutu population against innocent Tutsi victims, perpetrated by ordinary civilians brainwashed by genocidal ideology. Accordingly, gacaca contributed to formalizing the social categories of victim and perpetrator that emerged in the master narrative as legal citizenship categories.[24] Specifically, I suggest that gacaca helped reify "genocide citizenship" in Rwanda, similar to how Petryna (2002) has described citizenship status in the Ukraine becoming linked to formal designations of suffering in relation to the Chernobyl disaster.[25] In Rwanda, people designated as victims had access to special benefits such as scholarships or housing, while those defined as perpetrators were saddled with prison sentences or community service work, alongside other more informal restrictions. This genocide citizenship heavily shaped individual citizens' relationships to the state, in which one's relationship to the genocide heavily determined access to resources and opportunities.

Yet, if we understand gacaca sessions merely as predetermined performances scripted by ethnicity, we miss the more creative and varied ways people engaged with the process. Gacaca testimony revealed the complexity of creating a balance sheet of positive and negative actions that had occurred in morally ambiguous and constantly shifting situations, showing Rwandans recognized the complexity of the "gray zone" of violence (Levi 1988), as do people experiencing and recovering from political violence in other regions.[26] People in Ndora and Nyanza used gacaca sessions not simply to place one another in predetermined groups of guilt or innocence but also to debate the categories of victim and perpetrator themselves, arguing for richer understandings of guilt and innocence in relation to situated versions of the past. This was a way of debating genocide citizenship. As I indicate below, people challenged the omissions in the official version of the genocide and argued for more nuanced versions of the position of Hutu, including broadening the definition of victim and arguing for a category of innocent Hutu. The latter idea perhaps fit most uneasily within the official narrative, and therefore perhaps was the most destabilizing aspect of the narrative.

Because gacaca courts could incarcerate and redistribute resources, discussions there required people to confront head-on what Theidon calls the "economics of memory": how in an industry of truth telling and postconflict justice, people instrumentally "narrated with new possibilities and aspirations in mind," including "hope for some economic relief" (Theidon 2012:109). That is, people were debating over access to resources, to be sure, but also over the social meanings and relational obligations that came with that access. They attended to what Bolten has described in Sierra Leone as the concept of "material loyalty: relationships forged and sustained in complex, often compassionate acts of resource exchange" (Bolten 2012:3), which she suggests is crucial to understanding how people maneuvered during violence as well as how they rebuilt social networks after war. Christy Schuetze (2010) has similarly drawn attention to the importance women in postwar Mozambique placed on recreating networks of financial

and material support, which they did in part through participation in Pentecostal churches and spirit mediumship. I suggest here that people used gacaca
sessions to create pragmatic social alliances that attended to the material realities of daily life under conditions of extreme poverty, working out local power
conflicts (Burnet 2012:195). I do not suggest that these networks were harmonious, pure, or necessarily enduring; rather, attention to negotiations in
gacaca underscores how networks could be evanescent and instrumental,
could often include inequalities, and regularly intertwined divisions with alliances. This was the complex tapestry being both knit and torn through the
years of gacaca days, both within and outside sessions.

Perpetrators and Guilt

Consider, by way of example, a later portion of the previously mentioned case against Claude, where he was accused of being an accomplice
in killing a woman named Mukamurara, who was the godmother of one of
his children. A young woman with a baby swaddled on her back testified
that she was with Mukamurara, her maternal uncle's wife, during the genocide, and she asked Claude to explain his actions surrounding Mukamurara's death. Claude explained how Mukamurara came to his place with
several children seeking safety, and he agreed to protect them and gave
them food. Then the next morning a group of killers came to his father's
place, which was adjacent to his own. His father authorized them to search,
and soon the killers came to Claude's house. They kicked down the door
and searched the house, where they found Mukamurara and the children.
The killers, including Alphonse,[27] beat up Claude and his wife, and then
took Mukamurara outside. Claude said that he was too afraid to protest.
Alphonse asked him who had authorized him to hide, rather than kill,
Tutsis. The killers demanded money from Claude, threatening to turn him
over to the authorities if he did not pay. They demanded Frw 10,000, but he
bargained them down to Frw 3,000. When Claude handed over the money,
Alphonse told him that they would let him live because they had gotten the
person they wanted. The killers left with Mukamurara.

The young woman with the baby said that Claude's story was not completely true. She agreed that Mukamurara and the other children came from
the bush to seek refuge at Claude's house, but added that he gave them
work to do, insisting that they grind sorghum. She suggested this might
mean Claude had bad intentions and maybe was in league with the killers.

Another woman then stood up to testify that Claude left shortly after Mukamurara arrived, and therefore perhaps he was the one who called the killers. Claude's niece then testified, agreeing that Claude asked the refugees to grind sorghum but also adding that he was trying to protect so many people hiding at his house at that time.[28]

I suggest we must attend to how case discussions like this were not only about evaluating probative facts and determining guilt or innocence in relation to the stated legal charges but also involved contestation over the *meaning* of guilt and innocence. What did it mean that Claude accepted refugees into his home but then asked them to grind sorghum? What did it mean that he turned Mukamurara over to the killers but protected others, such as the victim who survived to testify with the baby on her back? As in the example with Agathe, should her friend be responsible for not having successfully protected the child when the killers came?

In gacaca sessions, people offered interpretations of cause and culpability that were alternatives to the master narrative, thus voicing the ways the predetermined categories of victim and perpetrator—designations defined by the state based on the genocide, which led to access to state resources or restrictions on certain rights—did not capture the nuances of local dynamics. The official charges against defendants classified in Category Two were: (a) killing; (b) going in groups; (c) going "to work" at roadblocks; (d) intending to kill even if killing was not carried out; (e) doing other bad acts even without the intention to kill; and (f) other.[29] People's testimony involved extended discussions about the circumstances and motivations of their actions, which sought more specific differences than these designations. Through the specific allegations people made in their testimony, distinctions emerged—for example, between refusing refuge to someone, versus failing to successfully protect someone when the killers came, versus actively flushing people out of their hiding places or sounding an alarm, versus overtly turning people over to the killers. Rwandan law had provisions that allowed for criminal penalties for failing to protect people, which was particularly controversial. Even some genocide survivors were conflicted about whether prison sentences should be issued for refusing shelter to someone. As one genocide survivor who had lost his wife and children told me, "I would have done the same thing. If someone had come, I would have said, I'm sorry, I'm protecting my wife and children."[30]

In areas where government soldiers with modern weapons committed most of the killings, cases involved particularly intricate discussions around distinctions of complicity for local people. For example, in Butare, a month-long case about genocide in the town hospital involved debates over what standard of care doctors and nurses should have provided to victims during the genocide.[31] Hospital staff members repeatedly explained how they did their best with what little medication or supplies they had at the time, even as victims were seized by the soldiers and killed overnight. In another example, in a typical case in Kigali alleging that a woman failed to protect a neighbor's baby, discussion centered on whether the defendant should have reasonably been expected to help someone on the path in front of her house, eliciting a detailed discussion of local understandings of private and public space.[32] Overall, these portrayals differed vastly from those commonly depicted in the national narrative, for example in President Kagame's speech at the ten-year anniversary of the genocide in April 2004, in which he said that perpetrators "chose to do evil because they were swayed by hate or hope of profit," killed "without remorse, and inflicted pain and agony and enjoyed doing so" (see Chapter 1).

Claude's case showed that many discussions in gacaca involved people debating how widely the net of guilt and liability should spread, to which people, and for what actions. Claude clearly sought to differentiate between himself and his father, noting that the killers came first to his father's house, suggesting that his father, not he, was the one who authorized them to search. Attempts to avoid collective guilt and liability often led people not only to disconnect themselves from close family and friends but also to seek alliances across ethnic lines. For example, Claude's sisters testified against him, positioning themselves as aligned with Mukatagazwa, the victim. In the same case against Claude, his brother, who was also a defendant before gacaca, testified against Claude, aligning with his goddaughter, a victim who made property claims against Claude.

Further, Claude's case revealed how in their testimony people sought to open up an idea of victimhood among Hutu perpetrators, using the same verb "victimization" from which the category "victim" in gacaca derived (*abahohotewe, guterwa*). For example, Claude claimed that he felt victimized at times by killers such as Alphonse, who harassed him verbally, threatened to turn him over to higher authorities, and took money from him. This was typical of testimony by other defendants and witnesses, who described their own fear at the time, as, in an often-repeated explanation, "The world went crazy, and people ran around killing." People explained how they had been forced to kill or had to pay money to be allowed to go free. Claude and other participants provided clear examples of how Hutu had suffered during the genocide. Defendants and witnesses in Ndora's court, as elsewhere, regularly described how they were required to go to roadblocks by men wielding guns or pangas but how they themselves did their best to avoid actively killing. In one typical example, a witness testified that the defendant forced him to kill his Tutsi father-in-law, and pulled at his T-shirt to show the wound on his shoulder caused by the defendant. Hutu women talked about how they had cowered together at night, sleeping in groups for safety, only returning hurriedly to their homes during the day. Some defendants dared to mention their own fear of the RPA, such as one man who explained, "I was fleeing the Tutsi who were persecuting us. I was running like everyone was running" (see also Clark 2010:211; Waldorf 2006:77). Perhaps the willingness to discuss RPA crimes was more prevalent (though still infrequent) in 2007–2008 than in earlier stages, since other researchers have suggested that "the idea that Tutsi might be guilty of serious crimes against Hutu" is "something that is rarely discussed among Rwandans in private, let alone in a public space like *gacaca*" (Thomson 2011a:384), or that these ideas are "not expressible" (Ingelaere 2008:56).

Claude's example further showed how people used case sessions to explain how they had tried to protect people. Claude's niece underscored that even if Mukamurara had been taken away, many others had not, and Claude spent several portions of his case discussing other people he had tried to protect, including a child he claimed to have hidden for days in a storeroom. These kinds of assertions were routine. As one defendant claimed, "I'm not saying I rescued her, but I did an act that contributed to her survival," or as another explained, "We couldn't have saved all of [town], we knew well that people were dying nearby but we couldn't provide reason for the *Interahamwe* to come in and kill more people, because we had so many Tutsi inside." During another trial in Ndora, for example, after the defendant confessed to participating in dozens of murders, many of the victims made positive comments about things he had done during the genocide, such as: "He got people from pit latrines and took them to the hospital," "He brought antibiotics to treat injured people," and "He even saved a person from being raped."

I draw attention to these portions of testimony because the constant voicing of these details, in case after case, week after week, illustrated the broadly existing disagreement with the master narrative and its classifications in Ndora and Nyanza, and the fact that the gacaca process did not fully silence it.[33] People challenged it without simply negating genocide or denying the basic premise of the violence but instead by providing detailed counterexamples to back up their claims. The variations people spoke of were not necessarily included in the written transcripts. The details did not necessarily lead to exoneration or to softened views of former adversaries, nor did they alter government policy. But it is important not to discount the fact that during gacaca days, in Ndora and Nyanza and perhaps on other hillsides across Rwanda, people regularly voiced these views.

Victimhood and Innocence

Discussions in gacaca occurred against a backdrop of broader nationwide contention about the meaning and political economy of victimhood. In Rwanda victimhood was politicized, as in other contexts of political violence, and much discursive and practical work had to be proactively done to maintain the category of victim as morally pure.[34] The master narrative claimed that "the victims were all innocent" (see Chapter 1), with the implicit corollaries that all Tutsi were innocent, and that all the innocent (Tutsi) were victims. Being designated a victim (*rescapé*) brought access to resources that, though minimal and not enough to make someone wealthy, were nonetheless heavily sought after given the poverty in which most survivors (and rural Rwandans more broadly) lived. Genoude survivors could be beneficiaries of national funds and programs to support victims, such as the Fonds National pour l'Assistance aux Rescapés du Génocide (FARG), or could benefit from convicted perpetrators' community service work, such as having their homes rebuilt. They could bury their loved ones in genocide memorials, which saved them burial costs and symbolically recognized their suffering.

Both within and outside gacaca sessions, rumors abounded about who had access to victim-designated funds, and who did not, generating jealousy, competition, and debates over who were the rightful victims and how the government should be supporting them. There was confusion over what the reality was, as well as what it should be. Consider Mukatagazwa's quote from the Claude case, that Claude thought the government would give Mukatagazwa cows if he confessed to killing her children. This kind of misguided belief was common. In another example, a genocide victim told me that he heard that Tutsi widows whose husbands had been Hutu were ineligible for the government support fund for survivors, because of the assumption that their husbands had been perpetrators.[35] Similarly, many claimed that children of Hutu killed during the genocide were not eligible for FARG, since they were not seen as proper victims.[36] Gacaca sessions occurred in a wider context of discussion and confusion over perceived government favoritism for survivors, and who was eligible for what resources, based on being afforded victim status.

An example from a gacaca session in Nyanza illustrates how people contested the notion of victimhood, and further shows how discussions of the past shaped social dynamics in the present. The defendant, Jean, a medical technician, was charged with being involved in actions leading to the death of a man called Sebijisho at the Nyanza hospital. A doctor from the hospital implicated Jean, saying they were together when Sebijisho was taken to be killed. Jean denied the charges, claiming that he was at the hospital with his family seeking refuge from the killings, since he was among those being targeted, and was merely trying to help people and stay alive. Toward the end of the trial, Jean's son Serge testified, explaining how his family suffered so much and barely survived during the genocide. Serge argued that people should not be accused just because they survived. He explained that his family was facing aggression from neighbors because of the allegations, and people had even thrown stones at their house the previous week.

The final testimony was from Sebijisho's mother, Jean's neighbor. She said that during another trial, her son's killer confessed and said that he was with Jean when Sebijisho died. She asked why people protected Jean from being killed but not Sebijisho? She said she believed that Jean should have done something to protect her son. She suggested that Serge was being dishonest, saying that although she was their neighbor, she had not heard anything about stones being thrown at their house. She asked, should the ones (like herself) with no families who survived become victims again, as those who were guilty were not punished?[37]

Though only a small percentage of cases I attended were against Tutsi defendants, this example is illustrative of wider-reaching dissent over victimhood and who deserved its designation. Sebijisho's mother's testimony revealed broader-reaching disagreements about who were the rightful "victims," reflecting a wider debate over who had suffered most and therefore who was most deserving of support. She claimed that her rights to victimhood were higher than Jean's, since she was the one who really lost her family, while Jean and his wife and sons had survived. Furthermore, Sebijisho's mother's testimony claimed that Jean also might be complicit in genocide, since if Jean and Sebijisho had been together and Jean had survived while Sebijisho had not, that must mean Jean had been complicit in the latter's death. Jean's son's testimony voiced anger, felt by his mother and siblings as well, over the allegations of complicity and the dismissal of the family's suffering, underscoring the deep rifts between these families of victims.

Jean defended his own position as a victim, claiming he spent the genocide desperately trying to survive, and lost his entire extended family. In his testimony, he explained that he fled with his wife and children to the hospital where he worked. In the ensuing weeks, he did his best to take care of people in hopes that his medical services would make him valuable, and therefore that the killers would be less likely to target him. He explained that he tried to help victims such as Sebijisho along with his own family but could not protect everyone. He believed the accusations against him were in retaliation for his testifying in other trials. In an interview eight months after his trial, Jean said: "I was in many, many, many gacaca sessions to speak the truth and to counter people's lies. I myself accused the one who killed Sebijisho, and then that one turned around and said that I was with him, as if we were accomplices, even though in reality, he also wanted to kill me. So the accusation was to distort facts and humiliate me."[38]

Jean was deeply embarrassed by being accused before gacaca, and he found the trial extremely stressful, even though he was ultimately exonerated. Months later, he still showed visible signs of anxiety and shame when talking about the case, and he feared that many still perceived him as complicit in genocide.

More broadly, gacaca discussions showed that the category "victim" on which the whole idea of gacaca was based was subject to debate, as people sought to maintain or trouble the notion of morally pure victimhood. Tutsi survivors were not immune to allegations of complicity, and concerns of guilt by association could pervade victims' families and neighbors. People contested who deserved to be considered a victim, and with what effects. Again, the sum of these discussions meant that people challenged the view of victims in the government narrative as all being innocent and equally deserving of support from government programs and perpetrators' repayments and labor. Further, these dissents came not only from convicted perpetrators but from a range of participants.

Economics of Memory and the Meaning of Exchange

Though much attention on gacaca focuses on murder cases, property cases were equally problematic (see also Clark 2010:126). Discussions about property were at the heart of several questions relevant to collective belonging more widely: What kind of treatment and resources did people deserve in the present? How deep were perpetrator's obligations to victims as individuals and as a category? How should obligations be shared among perpetrators with varying degrees of guilt and complicity? What were the enduring alliance effects, if any, of exchanging goods or labor? These questions and discussions, I suggest, were ways of debating the social and moral implications of relationships among people whom government interventions were intending to shape into a "community."

By mid-2008, as the gacaca process was drawing to a close, Category Three property cases made up 80 percent of all remaining cases.[39] More than 90 percent of the total property cases had already been judged, but very few had been enforced. Property cases proved particularly thorny to resolve because compromise involved redistribution of material goods, while most of the people who had looted more than a decade ago were too poor to repay items they had since consumed or lost. Authorities regularly lectured Rwandans on the mediation-based ethos of compromise about property issues in a way that they hoped would help restore harmony. An excerpt from comments at a community meeting by Albert, a staff member of the National Service of Gacaca Jurisdictions, in December 2007 provides a telling example:

> In solving property problems, there should be understanding between all of you. Be considerate, come together, and give the real value of things that were destroyed. Usually in the normal courts, you would be held liable for interest. If you took a cow, now, thirteen years after genocide, the regular court would come and take a cow, two calves, milk, and add punitive and moral damages. Gacaca says only "give back what was destroyed," if it was a pen, then give a pen, if it was a cow, then give a cow. So, the law is being lenient here, and people who don't want to pay are creating unnecessary complications. If you are going to require force, it will be a problem. We ask you to work hard so that we can finish these cases. Let's

move to justice, and prepare a future for the next generation. People should come forward and ask for forgiveness. If someone comes forward and tells you his economic status and mode of payment, then you can understand. People need each other and therefore should find ways to pay and accept compromise. If someone owes you Frw 500 and he gave you Frw 200 and can't afford the rest, know that he will find a way to help you later, like work for you, or take you to the hospital. I'm not saying he shouldn't pay, but people can find compromises.[40]

Authorities explicitly advocated for mutual understanding, forgiveness, and unity, and underscored the importance of collective cohesion, rather than emphasizing individual rights. They juxtaposed gacaca and its emphasis on social harmony with the punitive emphasis of the Western court system by reminding people that gacaca rejected punitive damages or interest. They pushed people accused of looting to find creative ways to reimburse victims, even if they did not have the money to do so. They urged victims to be reasonable and to accept social support and cooperation in lieu of money.

Property claims prompted particularly heated efforts for people to separate themselves from accused perpetrators, because guilt in property cases was more expansive than in murder cases, and repayment was a heavy burden in the context of rural poverty. For example, if a man was found guilty of murder, his children would not have to go to prison on his behalf, but they would be liable to repay his debts, on the premise that the children had benefited from the stolen goods. People redoubled their efforts to demarcate lines between themselves and guilty parties after the government further broadened the designation of perpetrator by implementing a new provision in 2008 intended to resolve property claims in which no one admitted liability. If, for example, a victim's house had been destroyed and no one admitted to looting it, then everyone who was living in the adjacent area at the time would now be required to share in the repayment.[41] The law pulled more and more people into the category of perpetrator, expanding the net beyond people currently detained to include their families and neighbors. On the other hand, many of those who were convicted were glad others were being forced to bear some of the guilt. Alphonse, who implicated Claude in several counts of looting but exonerated him in others, stated: "The individual people who are being asked to repay aren't the only ones who looted the property. At the time, so many people died, everyone took things. If a person didn't take a tile, he took a chicken, or at least he ate some of the meat. Everyone took things that belonged to someone else, or purchased property that had been stolen, such as blankets or saucepans or beer or rice. So everyone participated somehow."[42]

Given the economic struggles and pervasive poverty facing the majority of Rwandans, the redistribution required by property case judgments was contested and difficult to enforce. As Agathe, who was an inyangamugayo at the cell level, said, "When we finish the cases, we have not really come up with a solution. Of the over 200 cases our cell has decided, I can think of only one or two where people have actually paid back. We wonder how this will work out."[43]

For example, in another portion of the case against Claude, a young woman in her early twenties made a claim against Claude for taking her family's cow and its calf. Claude claimed he knew nothing about her charges, and no witnesses provided testimony about the allegation. The judges and assembled crowd nonetheless devoted nearly an hour to understanding the young woman's social position and circumstances, more than just trying to identify Claude's guilt or innocence. People discussed her mentally ill mother, her parents' divorce, her new stepmother, and how after her father's death in the genocide, the stepmother had left her with nothing. Claude seemed to think this information was irrelevant and that he was not responsible for her well-being, while others seemed to think that given the victim's poor living conditions, it was particularly important that she be reimbursed for her cow.

Exchanges and transactions, long identified as a tool of social integration in Rwanda (De Lame 2005:15, 105, 305), were at the core of Rwanda's legal forums—murder cases were predicated on the exchange of forgiveness for confessions and the exchange of community service work for prison time, and property case judgments involved exchange of goods, cash, or work—even as the social meaning of exchange was unresolved. For example, the pervasive debates about cattle in gacaca sessions have to be understood against a backdrop in which the exchange of cattle historically carried the weight of cementing alliances, whether among families in marriage or between patrons and clients (De Lame 2005:341–384; Maquet 1961; C. Newbury 1988:98, 118; Vansina 2004:32–33, 47). People invoked this idea regularly in gacaca testimony, for example using proof that "our fathers exchanged cows" as evidence of long-standing relationships between families. To repay a cow, therefore, was not merely about repaying a looting debt in order to provide closure on a past wound. It could carry a legacy of future-oriented obligations between giver and receiver, with potential power inequalities, about which the participants were ambivalent.

The meaning of exchange of labor was similarly charged. The common suggestion that perpetrators could repay debts through work, whether directly for a neighbor whose items they looted or for society more broadly through community service work, must be understood in a deeper historical context of mandated labor. Clients historically labored for patrons. Peasants were required to supply labor for their chiefs and the king. Most specifically, the practice of uburetwa, a form of mandatory unpaid labor performed for a chief as payment for occupation of the land, in the late 1800s through the 1940s differed according to ethnicity and class, and it contributed to forming an ethnicized political consciousness among Hutu, based on a "cohesion of oppression" (C. Newbury 1980, 1988; Vansina 2004:134–139). While the practices of uburetwa and community service work (TIG) were not linked in the dominant narrative, the idea of having to work for free for the benefit of a category of people (mostly victims) that overlapped with Tutsi remained linked in many people's minds (see also Waldorf 2006:59). Ultimately, exchanges in the aftermath of genocide had the possibility of being understood as creating enduring and repaired relationships and therefore as contributing to social cohesion, but they also risked carrying forward unequal or exclusionary meanings from the past. Debates over exchanges were a part of reconstructing moral orders in the present and imagining alternative futures.

Conclusions

To be clear, I do not want to overstate the flexibility of law here or to uncritically celebrate the emancipatory potential of agency, especially in a context like Rwanda with an increasingly authoritarian regime that perpetuates structural and physical violence. As late as 2014, President Kagame claimed that the gacaca process "allowed the nation of Rwanda to heal" (Kagame 2014), even as many researchers disagreed, claiming, as Bert Ingeleare did, that "everybody who has spent a significant amount of time in the rural areas of Rwanda has to conclude that nobody likes gacaca, it is not working very well, and it is bringing neither reconciliation nor justice"

(2010a:44).[44] While in theory gacaca had the possibility to promote reconciliation through a culturally sensitive process (Clark 2010; Clark and Kaufman 2009; Longman 2006; Venter 2006), in reality researchers found limited examples of the process contributing to restoring harmonious social dynamics in the short term (Burnet 2012:211; Rettig 2011:195). Much critical research agreed that gacaca was an "imposition of the central government on local communities" (Burnet 2012:212), in which the "near-total state control" (Thomson 2011a:373; see also Chakravarty 2015; Thomson and Nagy 2011:13) and pursuit of victor's justice (Reyntjens and Vandeginste 2005:111; Waldorf 2006:9, 29, 65, 81–85) often reinforced ethnic divides (Burnet 2010:114; Thomson and Nagy 2011:29). A growing body of work has illustrated how most Rwandans' lives were heavily constrained by gacaca, and how people often felt silenced, fearful, and insecure as a result. Analyzing gacaca as a form of government through community is one way to underscore the constant involvement of state governance in its operation.

Yet, if we attend only to the coercive elements in gacaca, then we risk overlooking the ways people found to work within its structures, which strips ordinary Rwandans of precisely the political acumen and voice that scholars have so thoughtfully sought to demonstrate empirically (Thomson 2011b).[45] Over time, Rwandans have expressed alternative views in public under coercive regimes, even while the stakes were high in challenging the historical interpretations of power holders (Longman 2000; D. Newbury and C. Newbury 2000:857, 872), and have used even highly centralized institutions for public healing, such as *ngoma* drumming (Janzen 1992). In the same vein, it is important not to write out of the scholarship on Rwanda and gacaca the ways that people could and sometimes did speak out against the grain within tightly constrained legal forums, and how they used these forums to negotiate their own micropolitics of reconciliation.

Further, though many researchers have noted how gacaca courts "reified ethnic identity" (Thomson and Nagy 2011:29) and "deepened cleavages between Hutu and Tutsi" (Burnet 2010:114; see also Longman 2010), detailed attention to negotiations within sessions shows more complex lines of alliance and division. Attention only to conflict between Hutu and Tutsi erases understandings of conflicts and differences *within* these groups and of conflicts across lines of political and economic power, both of which have been crucial to fueling instability in Rwanda over time

(C. Newbury and D. Newbury 1999; D. Newbury 1997:213, 1998:89; Vansina 2004:163). As the preceding examples showed, gacaca sessions revealed a more complex character of social fractures and connections than those that mimicked the lines demarcated by the conflict between Hutu and Tutsi.

Chapter 4

Comite y'Abunzi: Politics and Poetics of the Ordinary

In early 2008, a man I call Prosper came before a comite y'abunzi, or mediation committee, in Ndora with a case against a man called Alexis. Prosper claimed that he bought a piece of land in Kabuye from Alexis, but Alexis refused to register the land transference with the local authorities. Alexis admitted to having received money from Prosper and argued that he could not finalize the sale because his family said he did not have the right to sell the land. Several additional members of the plaintiff's and defendant's families were drawn in, including Prosper's father, Alexis's aunt Mukandaga, and his cousin Agathe. (Agathe was the cell-level inyangamugayo whom I introduced in chapter 3, who discussed learning news of her son's death from a friend's testimony before gacaca.) Thus, what began as a dispute between two men over a breach of contract over land actually rested on a dispute between a man and his own aunt over succession.

The sale's legitimacy hinged on whether Alexis owned the land individually or whether the parcel was part of jointly owned family land, as his aunt Mukandaga had claimed since 2004. The key issue came down to how Alexis's father, Sayinzoga, had acquired the land parcel. Alexis believed that his father purchased the land individually, and therefore Alexis was the sole inheritor and could do with it as he wished. Mukandaga claimed that in fact Sayinzoga inherited the land from their mother (Alexis's grandmother), and it was therefore shared ancestral land, which required her permission to sell, as she also had rights to it. As in many cases, discussion quickly turned to details and consequences of the past political violence, since confusion about land ownership was directly linked to migrations and deaths during upheavals. Mukandaga had fled Rwanda for Burundi in 1959, during the violence around independence. She had returned immediately after the genocide, though all but a few members of her extended family had been killed. Alexis too grew up outside Ndora, but he returned after the genocide because his family had been killed and he needed a place to start afresh. Most of the family members living in Ndora had been killed, with Agathe among the few survivors.

In the absence of any documentation—contracts, wills, or photographs—the entire case came down to oral testimony from the parties and witnesses, including elderly men who lived around the contested piece of land. Witnesses presented their versions of who bought the land, how he or she earned the money to do so, how the land was partitioned, and who farmed it and lived on it. Participants on all sides challenged the credibility and motivation of the various witnesses and pointed out contradictions in testimony. For example, Mukandaga and Agathe claimed that the people who really knew the truth were deceased and that those testifying had recently returned from living in exile and were ill informed, or even had been bribed. Prosper, in turn, accused Alexis's family of refusing to accept the truth, in an effort to steal land that he had rightfully purchased.

In this chapter, I turn to the politics and poetics of ordinary disputes within mediation committees, comite y'abunzi, in order to explore how law-based mediation operated with respect to the mundane. I use the term "poetics" here to gesture toward the ethics and aesthetics of disputation, to attend to the performative, ritualized, creative, emotive, and nondiscursive dimensions of disputes that shaped social engagements.[1] I examine mediation committee cases as sites of government through community, illustrating how harmony and punishment were intertwined in framing and practice there. Comite y'abunzi was designed in deliberate opposition to legal forums that applied established law in a codified way to settle disputes. Mediators (abunzi) valued custom (umuco) as well as written law, and they sought creative compromise more than objective application of preexisting principles. These elements contributed to an environment in which people did not simply present evidence but advocated for what they thought the evidence meant, and what the implications should be. This invited intense, contentious negotiation over social values, mutual obligations, and appropriate behaviors. As the example of Prosper and Alexis illustrates, many disputes before comite y'abunzi centered on land, which participants saw as crucial to daily needs. Discussions were intimately intertwined with the economics of memory and exchange in relation to social networks, both within and between families.

Thus, I show that, like gacaca, comite y'abunzi sessions were contextualized and contentious conversations in which people negotiated the micropolitics of reconciliation, specifically in relation to the meanings and ideologies of "family" and "community," which I explore in later sections of this chapter. Throughout the chapter, I trace the ambivalent effects of gendered mediation in which women were framed in conservative, essentialized ways related to their inherent nature—which they contested—even as this framing could sometimes increase their access to legal rights. Succession cases and women's efforts to seek property titles presented an opportunity for negotiation, performance, and social change, even as Rwandan women faced "uncertainties" in access to justice, as Sindiso Mnisi Weeks has explored in similar institutions in South Africa (Weeks 2011, 2013). The cases thus show both how discussions in legal forums could perpetuate inequalities as well as how they could create space for negotiating new possibilities.

Further, the case between Prosper and Alexis that I explore in more detail below draws attention to how people contested authority within the shifting postgenocide legal landscape, and illuminates how cases were situated within a wider system of dispute resolution. That is, the newly created state-backed legal forums, including comite y'abunzi, did not have immediate de facto legitimacy; rather, the nature and location of legitimate authority—as to which forms of evidence, which people, and at what levels of scale—remained a point of contention. Finally, these cases show the overlaps between genocide-related disputes and quotidian disputes in the aftermath of genocide, complicating our assumptions about among whom and about what "reconciliation" needed to occur in postgenocide Rwanda.

Harmony and Punishment in Comite y'Abunzi

In 2004, at the time that gacaca was being modified and launched, the Rwandan legislature passed a law creating comite y'abunzi, or mediation committees, as a first step for resolving civil and criminal disputes based on a "framework of obligatory mediation" before locally elected mediators at the cell level (Organic Law N.31/2006, Articles 3, 20). The premise

behind comite y'abunzi was that mediators would resolve low-level disputes, primarily within families and among neighbors, through a forum
that emphasized conciliation (Constitution of the Republic of Rwanda
2003, Article 159; Organic Law N.31/2006). Cases over which comite
y'abunzi had jurisdiction—civil and criminal cases whose value did not
exceed three million Rwandan francs, including damage to land, livestock
or property, theft, insult, or minor assault (Organic Law N.31/2006, Articles
8, 9)—were required to be heard before abunzi before they could be filed
in ordinary courts. Mediation committees were implemented based on the
same principles undergirding gacaca, intended to serve as ongoing forums
for public, participatory, grassroots justice. Comite y'abunzi were not a
separate court system as gacaca courts were but were maintained by the
Ministry of Justice.

The comite y'abunzi process had a discontinuous start. It was initially
launched in 2004, with the first elections of abunzi in July (Munyaneza
2004). The new abunzi attended trainings after election, prior to beginning
to hear cases. For parts of 2005 and 2006, comite y'abunzi proceedings were
briefly put on hiatus as the law was revised. The new law was launched in
August 2006, and proceedings began to start up again across the country.
Mediators in both Ndora and Nyanza said they began regularly hearing
cases at the beginning of 2007.

Rwandan leaders justified and legitimized comite y'abunzi as being part
of Rwandan cultural practices, as they did with gacaca, suggesting people
should accept the process because it was part of their natural cultural heritage. Authorities at the National Unity and Reconciliation Commission, for
example, described abunzi alongside gacaca as a "home-grown reconciliation approach." The emphasis on cultural practices was explicitly written
into the comite y'abunzi law, which drew a distinction between culture
(custom) and law, emphasizing culture as more desirable. Abunzi were formally instructed to take custom into account, both in evaluating testimony
and making decisions. In the event of "nonconciliation," the mediators
were to make a decision "in all honesty and in accordance with the laws
and *place's customs*, provided it is not contrary to the written law" (Organic
Law N.31/2006, Article 21, my emphasis). Because of the emphasis on culture, abunzi's local knowledge was privileged over objective knowledge of
legal procedures. For example, one mediator in Ndora told me that he was
selected not only because people knew that he would be impartial and consider evidence carefully but also because they valued the fact that given his

age, he was "familiar with the culture" and "knew how things were done in the past."[2]

During case sessions, mediators regularly invoked principles of unity and harmony and aimed to find compromise solutions with which parties would voluntarily comply. In the case of Beata and Joselyne, which I discussed in the Introduction, the mediators explicitly reminded the participants that their goal was not to punish but to reconcile. In Prosper and Alexis's case, the abunzi proposed several compromise solutions, including the proposal that Alexis's aunt could keep a small portion of the land while Alexis sold the rest of it or that the family could return the money to Prosper and keep the land.

Harmony and punishment were inextricable before comite y'abunzi, just as they were before gacaca. The threat of binding state-backed punishment was written into the law instantiating the mediation committees. When the guilty party "does not conform to the decision of the Mediation Committee or shows a delay in the execution, *the victim may seize the Judicial Police for pursuing his or her case*" (Organic Law N.31/2006, Article 24, my emphasis). "Forced execution" (that is, enforcement) could be carried out if anyone obstructed implementation (Organic Law N.31/2006, Article 24). Based on comite y'abunzi judgments, authorities could seize land, livestock, crops, and other personal property. If either party to the case was not satisfied with the mediators' verdict, he or she could, within thirty days of judgment, file a new case in the lowest level of the ordinary courts at the sector level (Organic Law N.31/2006, Articles 25, 26). When one side resisted complying with an abunzi settlement, the other side typically demanded help enforcing the judgment rather than trying to come to a new compromise. Often people participated only because they felt they had to, and they protested losing land or property in judgments. The threat of state-backed punishment was crucial to why plaintiffs brought their cases to abunzi. People like Joselyne often filed cases with comite y'abunzi not because they wanted help repairing their social relationships but because they hoped a third party authority would compel their adversary to do something.[3]

Ordinary Disputes: "This Is Land We Are Talking About"

"Ninety-eight percent of our cases are about land," the president of the mediators in Ndora informed me during one of my initial visits to his comite y'abunzi session.[4] While my data later suggested it was closer to 50 to 70 percent, his hyperbole captured the overwhelming predominance of land cases.[5] Even cases about crops, cattle or other livestock, or houses (other kinds of personal property) were intimately tied to the land on which people grew, grazed, or built them. These cases shed light on how land disputes were intimately tied up with people's efforts to reconstruct moral orders and negotiate the economics of memory.

Land disputes have long been identified as both contributors to and consequences of violence in Rwanda, and access to land continued to be a source of struggle in Rwanda more than a decade after the genocide (Ansoms and Hilhorst 2014; Ansoms and Marysse 2005:80–87; Gasarasi and Musahara 2004; Pottier 2006:510; Vansina 2004:40–41). The stakes around land were high, in a country with among the highest population density in continental Africa and a nationwide reliance on subsistence agriculture. For example, in 2000, the average distribution of arable land was nine people per hectare (2.47 acres), and most rural families owned less than one hectare, too little to earn a living (Ministry of Finance 2000:7).

The national government was aware of what it described as the "acute land shortage" (Ministry of Finance 2000:15) and sought a variety of legislative remedies over the years, which generated intense debate and were closely followed by Kinyarwanda- and English-language newspapers and radio programs. For example, during 2007 and 2008, Rwandans closely followed debates about a change in land tenure limiting the amount of land a single person could own to twenty-five hectares, with the aim of a more equitable distribution. They questioned whether wealthy landowners (including government elites) would comply with the new rules and why certain groups, such as *repatriés* (repatriated Tutsi refugees) or soldiers, were slated to benefit over others (Kimenyi and Ntagungira 2008; Musoni 2008a).

The intense human need for land in Rwanda was marked on the physical landscape itself. Virtually every square inch of hillside was cultivated, except those areas too steep to hold crops. The hillsides and valleys were divided into small plots, each cultivated by hand, forming a sweeping patchwork quilt of alternating squares across the country. Even in cities, vegetable gardens grew in small clumps along fences and road corners. Cows and goats grazed in the areas without crops, and disputes over livestock damaging gardens were common. Lawns and unplanted brush were extremely rare, even remarkable.

The notable exceptions were the three protected national parks. Volcanoes National Park in the north and Nyungwe National Park in the southwest were home to globally valued endangered mountain gorillas and chimpanzees. Akagera National Park was a savannah game reserve in the east, roamed by standard African game. The borders of the parks were under constant dispute, demonstrating that they were susceptible to national land pressures. For example, in 1997 nearly two-thirds of Akagera's land was turned over to the state to redistribute to the population, especially for grazing. All of the parks faced continual pressure at their borders by, for example, people hunting, grazing animals, planting, and felling trees. In efforts to balance tourism and environmental goals with people's very real needs for access to land, the national government, tourism office, and international and national NGOs pursued specific community development programs working with people living in the park's "buffer zones," attempting to redirect their land-based subsistence activities.[6] These exceptions attest to the intense interest and attention paid to managing land access in Rwanda, at international and national levels, and to the competing demands on land access stemming from these different levels of scale.

Land was important to people's being able to provide for their families, for growing food, grazing livestock, or building a house, and it was significant more broadly for acquiring and conveying status. People therefore disputed ownership of, use of, and access to land. They filed cases, for example, if someone moved a property boundary demarcation; if someone damaged land that had been tilled for planting; or if they felt they were given a plot that was too small or too infertile during land partitioning. They filed cases accusing others of trying to inherit leased land, of harvesting trees off their property, or of wrongly terminating a long-term lease. Cases over breach of contract, inheritance, theft, leasing, or unauthorized sale of property could all relate to land.

The central role of land in providing sustenance for families was enshrined in national law, in which land was treated differently from other kinds of property. Land transferred across generations was considered a shared family asset and therefore could not be sold without the "prior consent of all other members of the family" (Organic Law N.8/2005, Articles 35–38). This derived from a patrilineal system in which patrilineages, tracing agnatic ties back three to six generations, held common rights over land and cattle (d'Hertefelt 1971; C. Newbury 1988). Even ordinary Rwandans who did not know the more intricate legislative details understood this key distinction. As one woman remarked, "This is land we are talking about, it is not just like potatoes you go and carry to the market and sell away. These are things that require consensus."[7]

In land cases, the law itself recognized equal validity in land rights acquired through written law versus custom.[8] The abunzi and the participants were put in the position of debating what the balance should be between custom and law, since the two often varied (Gahamanyi 2003:266). For example, "custom" typically implied corporate lineage-based ownership (Vansina 2004:40), while "modern" law increasingly prioritized "freedom of exchange" (Ministry of Finance 2000:16) through individual ownership rights (Reyntjens 2009). This generated particularly heated exchanges, especially over land, as I discuss more below.

Confusion over land ownership was directly related to the migrations, exoduses, forced removals, dispossessions, and deaths caused by political violence. This began most noticeably with the violence around independence and the exodus of many Tutsi to neighboring countries, and continued through various waves of violence and political instability, including the exodus of Hutu who fled as refugees during and after the genocide and subsequent wars, as well as the ongoing return of prisoners released after gacaca trials. Cases reflected the reality that people were constantly returning to rural Rwanda and seeking access to land.

Comite y'abunzi cases also reflected a rising trend of women seeking access to land. This was spurred by changes to the inheritance law in 1999 that allowed women, who formerly had no clearly defined rights to land within a patriarchal system as they could not inherit directly from their fathers or brothers (Jefremovas 2002:98–99; D. Newbury 1998:92), to be counted in family succession (Organic Law N.22/99, Article 43). There remained confusion and lack of clear information among most rural Rwandans (including abunzi) over the precise laws and their implementation (Rose 2004). In general, women now had the idea that they had rights to land and were more likely to try to exercise them.

The other disputes making up the vast majority of cases before comite y'abunzi involved other items of personal property—similar to the debates in Category Three gacaca cases over trousers, sacks of beans, roof tiles, or cattle, as I discussed in Chapter 3. Items under debate in abunzi cases typically reflected the rhythm and business of everyday life—a sack of homemade charcoal, a weighing scale used by a woman to sell flour and sugar, ten dollars' worth of chipped glass soda bottles, a cell phone, a pig, a bicycle,

Figure 6. Ndora comite y'abunzi waiting for session to begin, 2007 (photo by author).

or parts of a house. In the context of economic scarcity, it was often worth fighting for a single animal or a few dollars. Cases thus related explicitly to material loyalty and the economics of memory, in people's negotiation of the micropolitics of reconciliation.

Contextualized Conversations

Comite y'abunzi cases must be understood, like gacaca sessions, as contested, contextualized conversations. In determining judgments, abunzi aimed to "conciliate" the parties, rather than simply to apply predetermined legal guidelines to their evaluation of the testimony (Organic Law N.31/2006, Article 21), which meant that participants had to debate the very rules by which their social interactions should be guided. The ambivalent emphasis on custom and written law meant that there was not one clear yardstick against which to measure whether evidence was sufficient to meet the burden of proof, or whether proposed solutions were legitimate. Discussions therefore existed in an often adversarial, messy gray area, as I demonstrate in more detail through a specific example in the next section.

Knowing that proposed resolutions were suggestive rather than mandatory often caused people to contest them even more. Ultimately, the emphasis on compromise solutions that valued both custom and law meant that the comite y'abunzi process inherently involved negotiation and contestation, over the details of evidence, truth about the past, and access to resources, as well as over the social norms governing solutions, relationships, and authority.

Like gacaca, comite y'abunzi sessions involved an open back-and-forth of contested narratives among people with tight interconnections. In an absence of other corroborating evidence, people used their own oral testimony to support or refute one another's versions of truth about the past and present. Evidence was typically open-ended, polysemous, and subject to multiple interpretations. The named parties had to convince friends, neighbors, or family members to come and speak for them, and so broader groups of people were drawn in, voluntarily or involuntarily. Abunzi did not remain above the debates but joined in, presenting their own stories and counterexamples as they advocated for proposed solutions and tried to convince parties of what they should do.

Comite y'abunzi sessions were open to the public, though participation of the general population was not mandatory (Organic Law N.31/2006, Article 20). The parties convened weekly, in spaces contiguous with ordinary life and easily accessible, typically in the center of town, near markets, schools, central thoroughfares, and administrative buildings, within walking distance from locations and items under dispute. The mediators presiding over the case, as well as witnesses, were drawn from the local population. Case parties were typically acquaintances or family. Discussions typically extended beyond the plaintiff-defendant dyad to include broader groups of participants. In Ndora, where I attended most often, the size of the assembled crowd typically ranged from ten to forty people. Most people attended only if they had an interest in a case being heard that day, though sometimes people dropped in if they were nearby. For example, there were typically a few women who sat in on sessions while waiting to visit their husbands in the jail, located in a facing building. Inyangamugayo often wandered through, if they were nearby for gacaca business. School children might drop in during their lunch break.

Oral testimony was the primary form of evidence in comite y'abunzi cases, as we saw in the case of Alexis and Prosper, and as before gacaca courts. The only guidance provided in the law instantiating comite y'abunzi was that abunzi should hear from "each of the parties in conflict and from witnesses if any" as well as from "any person who [could] shed light on the matter" (Organic Law N.31/2006, Article 20). As in gacaca, this wide allowing of evidence was consistent with the restorative-justice focus on relationships, not a specific point of law (Colson 1974:73). Without attorneys, disputing parties and witnesses directed their own testimony, with frequent interjections by abunzi to clarify questions or minimize digressions.

It was rare that people could produce documentation, such as a contract of sale, and yet the absence of documents did not mean the alleged contract or transfer did not exist. There were often plausible reasons that documents would have been lost or destroyed, related to the destruction, displacement, and chaos of the waves of political violence and genocide. Further, documents were not necessarily required when people claimed customary ownership (Organic Law N.8/2005, Article 7). When participants could in fact produce documents, others typically raised questions about authenticity and forgery, and therefore documents themselves were imbued with controversy.

Without consistent documentary evidence, then, the primary form of corroborating evidence was other people's oral testimony. Like gacaca sessions, comite y'abunzi discussions unfolded as heated volleys of competing versions of events. In the face of contradictory evidence, people frequently accused one another of speaking falsely or misremembering. They challenged one another's motivations for testifying, arguing that bias could cloud someone's honesty or capacity to accurately interpret and analyze evidence. Case discussions included debates over people's credibility, character, and motivations as much as the specific details of the property and ownership under dispute.

Evidence before comite y'abunzi was inherently open-ended, as cases usually hinged on long-standing issues of ownership and transfer (often rooted in customary practices rather than in official written laws), intentions, and character, which developed over years or decades. People often justified their actions and evidence in relation to traditional practices and norms, which changed over time. For example, abunzi had to decide whether, when a man partitioned his deceased brother's land, he accidentally or deliberately omitted to give his niece *umunani*—the small plot of land customarily provided to sons at marriage, enough for a small house, distinct from the rest of the cultivable fields (De Lame 2005:126; Vansina 2004:130), sometimes also given to an unmarried daughter. Testimony was rarely clear-cut; instead, it included assertions based on witnesses' own inferences. A man might claim he knew a land parcel had been given, not leased, because he had heard the old men talking about it when he was a child. Or a witness might argue that she knew the plaintiff's request for unpaid debt was fabricated because the plaintiff had not made her claim at the debtor's funeral, as was typical. In an effort to maximize precision, abunzi sometimes asked witnesses to specify how they knew what they were saying; that is, asked them to clarify if they were testifying about things that they knew for a fact, versus hearsay. Many witnesses resisted this differentiation, asking, "What is the difference? What I heard is what I know."[9] This epistemological discussion got at the heart of the nature of comite y'abunzi testimony: it was complex, contingent, contested, and open to interpretation. Tanya Murray Li has similarly argued that in land disputes among highlanders in Indonesia in the 1990s, custom did not stand outside the process as a stable point of reference but was selectively revised through words and deeds (2014: 85, 114).

Because of the emphasis on oral evidence, people were put in the position of taking sides in a forum that was both public and connected with daily life. Thus, by agreeing or disagreeing with one another's versions of truth, they created alliances and divisions. Particularly in land disputes, this meant that people used their versions of the past to shape social relationships in the present. The social connections and rifts performed in comite y'abunzi sessions were not one-off but rather were embedded in ongoing dynamics of relationships and contesting authority, as I explore in the following section.

The seemingly distinct cases before gacaca courts and comite y'abunzi were actually closely intertwined and transgressed institutional boundaries in a shared social field. Both sessions emphasized oral testimony, with lay judges, in public, and without attorneys, based on mediation principles. Sessions were held in either the same or nearby spaces. Many of the people who testified or adjudicated one attended the other later in the week, or vice versa. People moved between the institutions, in the course of everyday life. For example, the conclusion of a defendant's gacaca case and his or her release from prison often did not provide closure, instead opening a new but related set of concerns, which he pursued first through the local authorities and then before comite y'abunzi. People might testify one day before gacaca, and perhaps the next before abunzi. Some alliances and identifications carried over between the two. In general, people's socialization into how to participate in gacaca courts shaped how they engaged with comite y'abunzi, and therefore how the institution developed. For example, people became accustomed to taking the oath before providing witness testimony in gacaca courts, and therefore often voluntarily did so, without prompting, before comite y'abunzi sessions.

As the case of Prosper and Alexis showed, where the dispute began with migration during violence, the consequences of genocide and political violence continued to shape people's lives, and people confronted the details of the past in ordinary disputes. They brought the past into the present by, for example, framing their complaint in relation to the genocide, or by punctuating their testimony with political history. Cases often were complicated by someone's death or disappearance in the genocide or its aftermath, or imprisonment. The presence of history in the public domain, for example in adjudicating disputes over boundaries between fields, is continuous with earlier periods in Rwanda (D. Newbury and C. Newbury 2000:855). Cases thus blurred a clear distinction between genocide-related disputes and ordinary disputes in a legally plural environment.

Ambivalent Authority: Resolving a Problem or Creating More Conflicts?

The case between Alexis and Prosper was typical of how comite y'abunzi was one among several levels of administrative hierarchy for dispute resolution. This is crucial for understanding how mediation efforts in harmony legal forums were situated within a broader system of dispute resolution efforts, in which people contested the authority of mediated solutions and state representatives at multiple levels of scale. Cases brought before abunzi had typically already appeared before other local authorities, and might continue into the ordinary courts. Comite y'abunzi proceedings were episodes in ongoing social disputes and interactions that occurred in other institutional spaces. Sessions served as another public performance of positions in a longer-standing dispute. The hearings before each level of authority could become additional fodder for parties' disagreements, and participants contested both the content of the dispute and the legitimacy of different levels of authority. As I indicate below, people contested levels of authority (from the most localized to national officials) as well as debated

Figure 7. Participants waiting for abunzi to begin hearing cases, 2007 (photo by author).

the comparative degree of legitimate authority of forms of evidence, whether paper, spoken, or otherwise.

The disputants in this case had taken their dispute to previous levels before coming before abunzi. Everyone agreed that Alexis accepted money from Prosper in 2004, without the knowledge of his wife or the rest of his family. When his wife learned of it, she alerted Mukandaga, who immediately complained to the local authorities. Parties had different perspectives on what occurred next. What could have been a straightforward chronology—recounting which levels of authority heard the dispute, when, and to what effect—was in itself contested, made more so by the he said, she said nature of oral testimony, with a lack of precision on dates and no documents presented as corroboration. The previous levels of attempted resolutions themselves got folded into the dispute.

Prosper described how he felt he had been cheated out of receiving land for which he had legitimately paid:

> When I first paid Alexis for the land, there was a local authority around, so it was official. But then Alexis learned there was a problem with the land that he had to clear up with his relatives. We went before the abunzi to get it resolved. They investigated in Kabuye and found that Alexis's father had bought the land, so Alexis was allowed to sell it. The second time I paid, the case had already been decided so there was nothing illegal. There was an agreement between the two of us, and even an authorized witness. I have a judgment from abunzi to prove that Alexis sold me the land. Yet now they are saying I bought stolen land.[10]

Alexis explained how he was caught between his family and Prosper:

> I had to sell the land because I had two children who died suddenly. I needed money, I was so desperate. When I first took money from Prosper, there happened to be local authorities in the bar, but not in their official capacity. Then, after my auntie and family started complaining, Prosper and I went together to a committee at the sector. Prosper is not speaking truthfully about taking the case to the abunzi. Then Mukandaga took the case up to the District level. Meanwhile, Prosper wanted to take the land and kept giving me money but I told him I still had failed to get the land from my family. Then one morning the Executive Secretary of the cell came to my house and said that the people at the District decided I should sign the contract. I said finally, it's up to my family to decide, if they return the money and take back the land, or leave the money and let Prosper have the land.

Agathe challenged Prosper's version of events, and tried to justify her family's ownership of the land:

> Alexis and Prosper never pleaded before the abunzi, that decision is fraudulent. They went to a committee at the sector level, where Prosper bribed witnesses and tried to trick Mukandaga into taking a smaller portion of land. Then we took the case to the district

administrators, and they decided that the land was supposed to be returned to the family. That was in 2004. In 2007, Prosper started cutting down trees on the land and employed people to cultivate. Mukandaga went to the Executive Secretary at the cell level, but he told her she did not have rights over that land. Then we went to the Executive Secretary of the sector, and he wrote a note ordering Prosper to stop carrying out any activities on the land. When Prosper realized this, he decided to file a case before abunzi.[11]

This case shows how participants debated over not only land or property ownership but also over the nature of authority itself in a shifting legal and governmental landscape. The contestation in this case encompassed virtually everything—the provenance of the land, the authenticity of documents, the levels of the previous disputes, and whether people could in fact have certain knowledge. There were accusations of lying, bribery, and forging documents.

Alexis and Prosper's case showed how there was confusion over which levels of authority had jurisdiction over what. This kind of confusion was common, given the periodic restructurings of administrative levels and government positions, with the multiyear implementation of nationwide decentralization programs that shifted who was responsible for what. As in this case, people often tried to "forum shop," taking their disputes to different authorities, depending on who they thought would be most sympathetic to their claims. Some people began by consulting pastors or family elders, or asking for help at the legal aid clinic or at a specialized NGO (for genocide widow's issues or specializing in protection of children, for example). Some people went directly to the governmental administrative hierarchy, which had a prescribed path for complaints, beginning at the *umudugudu* (the smallest administrative unit, a grouping of ten houses), then moving to the executive secretary of the cell, then to the sector, then to the district. At any of these levels, people might be referred to abunzi.

People saw comite y'abunzi as in an ambivalent relationship to the other local government authorities who heard their complaints. Some participants felt that abunzi themselves were easily controlled by local authorities, and that sessions therefore were pro forma rather than real hearings. Some complained that abunzi were unprofessional and their decisions ungrounded in law. Others thought abunzi were more authoritative than other administrators, because they were more tightly rooted in local social and knowledge networks, and therefore could make more accurate assessments and provide more feasible solutions than distant officials at the sector or district level. Abunzi and local authorities sometimes reinforced, at other times overrode, one another's judgments. In general, the legitimacy and authority of comite y'abunzi, both in terms of the forum and the judgments, were works in progress. This was particularly true because the system was new and experienced typical institutional growing pains.

In the case between Alexis and Prosper, after hearing the case in three sessions over three months, the mediators decided that Alexis should sign the contract of sale to give Prosper possession of the land. The motivating logic for their decision was that Alexis was at fault for selling land without ensuring it was his to sell, and that Prosper should not suffer as a result of confusion among Alexis and Mukandaga; instead, Alexis's family should bear the burden of his debt. This decision, then, suggested that maintaining the integrity of business transactions between two men should take precedence over intrafamily ownership disputes, and emphasized individual rights to land over corporate (that is, shared and enduring) ownership. The mediators noted that though Alexis had been with his wife for more than a decade, they only officially married in 2006, two years after the initial sale to Prosper, and therefore she had no rights to the land. They may have seen this as the less contentious decision, implying that Alexis's family was robust enough to absorb the internal dispute.

On the surface, the comite y'abunzi process seemed to work. A local authority in Ndora told me that he estimated that 70 percent of cases closed at the comite y'abunzi level, which was consistent with the Ministry of Justice's claim that mediation should, and did, work to resolve local disputes.[12] For example, even if Beata and Joselyne did not become friends as a result of the mediation, conflict did not escalate further between them. In other cases, similar abunzi verdicts successfully halted rising tensions or even restored civility among participants, including between a man and his neighbor whose son had allegedly stolen his pig, and between a man and a woman who claimed he had given her poor-quality charcoal to sell at the market. In many cases, people came to accept the judgment, whether openly or reluctantly. The decisions often helped to avoid escalation, by eschewing punitive damages. Even when people left disgruntled, they often accepted the solution. In many cases, people grudgingly agreed to share land or take responsibility for debt after repeated refusals. The many stages of attempted administrative and legal solutions directed the vast majority of cases away from the ordinary courts, with their more expensive, time-consuming, and adversarial process.

Yet, we cannot understand the existence of mediated judgments, or people's compliance with them, as transparently reflecting restored relationships. As I walked around Ndora, participants whose cases I attended would routinely stop me to complain about verdicts that had gone against them. Even if they did not ultimately contest the judgment, people publicly expressed dissatisfaction and claimed the process was not fair. Often people did not escalate to ordinary courts because they did not have faith in the system or simply because they missed the deadline to do so.

In the case of Prosper and Alexis, while Prosper was delighted at the result and immediately made plans to cultivate his land, Alexis seemed resigned to the decision and exhausted by the process. Alexis's cousin and wife, by contrast, were angry and said they planned to file the case in the ordinary courts. Agathe and Mukandaga claimed the judgment document omitted comments they made challenging Prosper's version of events, and therefore did not include grounds for their appeal. This was typical of how the documents containing the decisions were controversial, which underscored both the lack of consensus at the formal conclusion of a given case and the uncertainty surrounding written documents. The judgments included the parties' identifying information, the nature of the disputes, and minutes of the testimony heard, based on the secretary's longhand transcription during sessions (Organic Law N.31/2006, Article 22). Judgments were formalized with the signatures (or thumbprints) of the three abunzi who decided the case and the named disputants, and stamped with the mediators' seal. Parties used the signed, stamped judgment to convince the relevant authorities to enforce the mediators' decision or to appeal the case to the ordinary courts. People routinely complained that the judgments did not accurately summarize testimony or even omitted key details entirely. For example, often abunzi did not include in the transcript comments from people in the general assembly, while participants might see some of these comments as crucial evidence supporting their side of the case. The documents were an effort to introduce more professionalism, transparency, and efficiency through generating a clear paper trail, but they remained a point of debate.

A few days after this case decision, Agathe expressed her frustration. She asked, "How could they make such a decision? They're not resolving a problem but creating more conflicts!"[13]

Micropolitics of Reconciliation: "Family" and "Community"

In this section, I draw attention to people's involvement with comite y'abunzi sessions as part of their ongoing processes of reconstructing moral orders. People disputed over not simply circumstances of disputes but also the micropolitics of reconciliation across a range of dispute types. These debates hinged on the economics of memory and material loyalty, as I discussed with respect to gacaca: who had access to what resources, when, and how. I illustrate here that comite y'abunzi served as one site in which people negotiated the meaning of, and membership in, "family" and "community," which were seen as the basic building blocks in the architecture of social repair, natural bases for Rwandans' shared cultural identity. The framers of comite y'abunzi intentionally designed it to help revitalize these local forms of belonging, on the premise that disputes among people who had preexisting relationships and lived in mutual interdependence would be open to being resolved amicably, through mediation principles, by local mediators. These strengthened families and communities would accumulate across the nation to create a stronger social fabric and a harmonious Rwandan nation.

As the case of Alexis and Prosper showed, heavy burdens were placed on these localized forms of belonging, and people's allegiance to them was not preordained. There were as many cases within families as between neighbors, suggesting the family was not a stable, homogeneous group. For example, in comite y'abunzi cases I attended in Ndora, seven were within a family, ten outside family, and three unspecified. In cases that people brought to the legal aid clinic after taking them to comite y'abunzi, seventy-five were within a family, forty-four outside, and fifty-five unspecified. This is consistent with other periods in Rwanda's history, where conflict was as often *within* groups as between them (D. Newbury 1997:213). Cases illustrated the tangible, practical debates people engaged in as they tried to restore what it meant to be part of a family or community. As I discuss below, my goal is not to render fixed the precise meanings of these forms of social belonging but rather to foreground meaningful forms of collective belonging other than ethnicity.

Family Belonging

The case of Prosper and Alexis, and others like it, showed that the idea of "close family relations" did not mean an absence of conflict; families were not stable or uncontested. Collective belonging at even this intimate level was shaped by contestation of what material rights and responsibilities came along with being a member of a family. People typically came before the comite y'abunzi when it became a question of access to resources—inheritance, partitioning of land and property, selling family land, or child support—because legal forums could reify membership or exclusion and formalize distribution. In case after case, people contested who counted as family, trying to demarcate lines between who was in and who was out. They also debated what it meant to belong, and how much responsibility they had for one another.

Family, or *umuryango*, was considered the most basic, universal level of collective belonging for Rwandans, their primary social security net and often their most salient form of identity (De Lame 2005; C. Newbury 1978:18, 1988:114; Ntampaka 1997), even as the definition of what counted as family was in flux, both legally and in ordinary usage. Norms of daily life reflected these assumptions of mutual support and responsibility. For example, people identified themselves to one another by their family, both legally and socially, and sought to identify others the same way ("son of X," "wife of X," "mother of X"). They were constantly aware of their own obligations to their kin, sharing the burden of school fees, medical expenses, celebrations, and funerals. They shared living space, took care of their own widows and orphans, found one another spouses. They bore responsibility for relatives' debts and transgressions. Scholars of Rwanda have translated umuryango as lineage, a social institution with a deep history, characterized by patrilineal descendent and internal corporate responsibilities (C. C. Newbury 1978; D. Newbury 2009; Vansina 2004).[14] Property rights were traditionally vested in umuryango, which contributed to internal cohesion (Vansina 2004:40). There were changes in the responsibilities of umuryango over time, for example, in relation to taxation (C. Newbury 1988:111). Scholars differentiated umuryango from *inzu,* or house, to refer to the family unit of residence, a localized, exogamous patrilineage (Vansina 2004:30).

Rwandan government documents, including land laws, translated umuryango not as lineage but as family, which they typically defined as "spouses legally married," and children, both minor and of majority age (Organic Law N.8/2005, Article 36)[15]—thus reflecting a more Western, Christian view of the nuclear family. Yet, even while marking a clear shift away from lineage as an organizing principle, the land law: (a) continued to prioritize family as the basic decision-making unit, (b) stipulated that others beyond the nuclear family might have rights to family land, and (c) included several provisions about customary (that is, corporate) access to land, all of which reflected the assumption that extended families had shared identity, collective responsibilities, and vestiges of corporate status. In everyday usage of the term "umuryango," most Rwandans similarly blurred the distinction between lineage, family of residence, or something in between. Overall, the definition of what family meant was shifting, both in legal and in ordinary usage, influenced by a variety of factors, including economic pressures; Western-derived ideologies about nuclear families, monogamy, and family planning; and legal definitions.

I use the term "family" here, as most Rwandans do, to point to a broadly inclusive, but imprecise and not universally agreed upon, group of relatives, with shared responsibility for one another. In Kinyarwanda, people also referred to family as *abavandimwe* (relatives), or *abacu* (our people). The loose term "family," then, captures the adaptive, contested definitions of kinship, rather than the more ascribed, specific definition associated with lineage (recognizing of course that lineages have always had flexibility to creatively include and exclude people). The term "family" itself meant different things to different people, as it did over time, and that is part of what participants were working out in comite y'abunzi cases.

Comite y'abunzi cases show that even though family was considered a basic, universal level of belonging, the urgent realities of survival placed tensions and burdens on this level of belonging, pushing people to negotiate who was in (abacu) and out, and to try to negotiate what it meant to belong, in terms of what were their presumed obligations to one another. Cases showed how people tried to gain access to, or prevent others from having access to, specific resources, such as land, houses, and other property. This reflected a tension between collective versus individual interests within families. This occurred both among victims and among perpetrators.

Disputes among family members before comite y'abunzi often involved debates over who was legitimately a member of the family—that is, the disputes involved contesting the boundaries of belonging. Technically, comite y'abunzi did not have jurisdiction to recognize paternity, marriage, or death—those were matters for ordinary courts (Organic Law N.31/2006, Article 8). But often during a case before comite y'abunzi one of the parties would assert that the person claiming to be a sister, or son, or wife was in fact not a member of the family/lineage. The abunzi would often hear brief evidence about the nature of the relationships and try to counsel people toward more inclusive rather than less inclusive definitions of family, consistent with mediation principles. Some mediators chose to rule as if they could determine family lines conclusively, while others referred the cases to the ordinary courts. So abunzi cases revealed, or brought to a head, people's questions of who belonged in their family and who did not, and caused people to take sides in public performances. Cases also showed how family belonging was complicated in relation to the magnified absences of dead kinsfolk, who were still connected to ideas of belonging in the present, as commentators have shown (Burnet 2012; Eramian 2014b).

Knowing who did or did not count as family was complicated by pervasive informal family practices that did not align with formal legal definitions. People often cohabitated as husband and wife for years, perhaps with a church ceremony but without ever formally marrying in a process recognized by the state. Some men practiced polygamy, though with only one legal marriage according to state law, and had children with each of several informal wives. Many a widow married her late husband's younger brother, in traditional levirate practices, typically without a formal marriage. Adults often raised children who were not biologically theirs—perhaps nieces or nephews whose parents could not provide for them, or the child of a friend—without formalizing the relationship through legal adoption. These types of family relationships were common and were not always solidified in law. The waves of political violence affected these shifting family relationships, as parents died, disappeared, or went to prison, which led people to take responsibility for extended family members and neighbors in response to material needs, and to adapt their families in creative and shifting ways. These informal practices all left space for questions regarding for which child or woman a man was responsible, having to pay school fees or medical bills, and who could inherit from him after his death.

The case between Alexis and Prosper involved a typical example of contention over who qualified as family. Prior to Alexis's controversial sale of the land, there had been a question of whether or not he belonged to Mukandaga's family at all. Alexis grew up outside Kabuye, in the eastern part of Rwanda, with his mother and his maternal uncle. As a child, Alexis's mother brought him to Kabuye claiming that he was a child of Mukandaga's brother, Sayinzoga, and that he should therefore have access to land on which Sayinzoga was living. Sayinzoga refused to recognize Alexis as his child, saying he had divorced Alexis's mother before they had any children.

But Sayinzoga's mother insisted that Alexis did belong to the family because Alexis's mother was in her third trimester of pregnancy when she left. Later, after losing most of his relatives during the genocide, Alexis returned to Kabuye and settled on the piece of land from his now-deceased father. Agathe, who had lived her entire life in Kabuye, described the family's willingness to let Alexis settle on the family land, noting, "We said fine, let's let him enjoy the fruits of that land because he belongs to the family."

From Mukandaga's perspective, after she and her mother embraced Alexis and drew him into the family, he repaid them by selling land—which he claimed to have inherited from a father who denied him—that belonged to the family, in an effort to benefit individually at the expense of others. From Alexis's perspective, he believed he owned the land individually, having inherited it solely after the death of his father, stepmother, and half siblings. His own children were deceased, and he was not formally married, so he believed he could sell it as he wished.

This case shows how, even among a family of genocide survivors, there were debates about who belonged and how to look after one another. On one hand, in the wake of the massive extermination faced by Tutsi families, many genocide survivors embraced inclusive interpretations of family and lineage, reestablishing connections with distant cousins as close kin. They recreated complex genealogies to determine who was related and how, and sought out information by word of mouth on who had survived. In the years after the genocide, people would travel for days to show up on the doorstep of someone they heard was a surviving relative, even if they had only the vaguest prior notion of having been members of the same "family." In the wake of such widespread killing, people clung tightly to, and tried to reconstitute, a sense of family and lineage. At the same time, given the destitution faced by most rural genocide survivors, competition over resource allocation among families could be particularly fraught, increasing divisiveness.

Families of alleged and convicted perpetrators confronted similar disputes about who belonged, and to what that meant they were entitled or for what they were responsible. This was exacerbated by gacaca property cases, as I noted in Chapter 3, where people had to bear responsibility for their father's, husband's, or son's looting debts. The return of prisoners to their families associated with the gacaca process intensified many of these concerns. Men returned home to find that their families had taken over their land, or sold off portions of it, in their absence. Many found that their wives had had children with other men or had taken in orphans. Men who fled genocide prosecution returned to find that their house, land, or property had been sold. As one Rwandan woman who served as a counselor in her village explained, "People need to identify these issues among prisoners' families as equally important [as issues between perpetrators and survivors] so these problems can be resolved. If it is not seen as a real concern, then it will cause additional problems."[16] Many women who came before abunzi were wives, daughters, or sisters of men in prison for genocide crimes, who sought to gain access to means to support their children. Many lived through the genocide, then fled into exile in the neighboring DRC or Burundi, before returning home to Rwanda. Their husbands often were either dead or in prison for genocide crimes. The women had to bring food to jail for brothers or fathers or husbands and participate once a week in gacaca sessions while trying to support their children. They brought cases against their husbands' brothers over land, or their brothers' wives. Or they filed cases to protect their own children's inheritance from illegitimate children their husbands fathered while in exile.

A typical example illustrates what cases within families of accused perpetrators could look like. A man called Aloys, in his early forties, brought a case before the mediators in Ndora against his own brothers and sisters-in-law, hoping the mediators would compel them to give him access to a house or piece of land.[17] He had spent twelve years in prison for genocide crimes. Following his gacaca trial in 2005 he was acquitted and released. Now out of prison, he was forced to rent a small room in the center of town because he could not live on his family's land. He had built his own house, but while he was incarcerated, the wife of his elder brother (who was also in jail for genocide crimes, serving a thirty-year gacaca sentence) were living on the land, and, on the advice of the brothers, tore down his house to build another. He explained that, from his perspective, "the bigger problems facing communities are not between the ones they consider victims and the ones accused, but it is mainly among families of people who were convicted or people who were suspected of genocide crimes. Because if you come and find out that the kin you left in charge of your property has sold it off, that's a problem."[18] He explained that he felt frustrated that the authorities could not help him to resolve his problem with his own siblings, since they kept telling him that his sister-in-law in fact had rights to her husband's house and did not have to give him access to it.[19]

Alexis's case and Aloys's case both point to the gender dynamics that suffused comite y'abunzi cases and reveal that while the genocide and post-genocide periods shaped gender roles, relations, and ideologies they did so unevenly, opening up some new spaces while also reproducing prior inequalities.[20] Cases reflected women's efforts to obtain rights and advocate for themselves, even as calls for unity in law-based mediation were often built on restrictive, subordinate roles for women, frequently drawing on their naturalized role as mothers.[21] In Alexis and Prosper's case, both Agathe and Alexis's wife described feeling disenfranchised by the case proceedings and the judgment, consistent with evidence that despite strides in gender equality at the national level, women remained structurally vulnerable in postgenocide Rwanda (Burnet 2012). Agathe was frustrated at the final decision that she had to lose access to the land and bear the burden of Alexis's debt simply because "he belongs to us," even though she had not seen any of the money from the sale. Alexis's wife was equally dissatisfied with the outcome. She had explained to the abunzi her outrage that Alexis had sold land without her knowledge, only to be told that she had no claim to the land or its sale because although she had been Alexis's common law wife for many years, they had only legally formalized their marriage recently. Both women felt their rights were subordinated to the actions of a man in their family, actions they considered both morally wrong and illegal. In their case, the abunzi's judgment emphasized the unity of the family as *a priori* natural, assuming it could bear the weight of the internal dispute. This is consistent with how justifying practices as collectively beneficial in the name of a naturalized group—whether "indigenous rights" or, here, family—can disempower, oppress, or coerce members of those groups, particularly with respect to gender and age (Gahamanyi 2003:267; Merry 2006; Speed 2008).

But to suggest that mediation cases typically involved men coercing lower-status women would be reductive. In Aloys's case, the abunzi did not compel his sister-in-law to give him access to the house and land on which she was living. Neither Alexis nor Prosper had the status of Alexis's cousin Agathe, who was herself an inyangamugayo, hearing cases on property at the cell level. I saw her provide damning testimony in murder cases that influenced inyangamugayo in determining confessions, and also heard her raise frequent property claims against defendants, even while she advocated unity and compromise in other property cases. By contrast, no one contested Alexis's self-description as poor and desperate (*umukene*). He had barely survived the genocide, and had returned to Ndora to reconnect with his few remaining relatives. He said he had only decided to sell the land in question after two of his children died suddenly. Some suggested Prosper had pressured Alexis into selling land that he had no right to sell. I suggest that we can see these cases as examples of how some women, such as Agathe, used law-based mediation as a forum for the work of reimagining women's roles and rights, refiguring how responsible they were for men's actions, and how much access they should have to previously collectively owned property.

This negotiation of family belonging appears to be an extension of historically deep processes in Rwanda from precolonial times through the present, in which people have negotiated membership in social institutions of collective belonging—whether clan, ethnic group, or lineage—over time and in relation to state expansion and shifting economic circumstances (d'Hertefelt 1971; C. Newbury 1988; C. Newbury and D. Newbury 1999; D. Newbury 2009; Vansina 2004). I do not aim here to delineate how precisely lineage, clan, and ethnicity operate and interrelate in contemporary Rwanda. Rather, I want to move beyond an exclusive focus on Hutu and Tutsi as the key dimensions of allegiance that needed to be addressed and redefined. I underscore the creative potential of family as a form of belonging in Rwanda as well as the pressures it faced, and show the role that legal institutions such as comite y'abunzi served as sites for negotiating these tensions and adaptive possibilities.

Community

The case between Alexis and Prosper also showed that people were negotiating what it meant to live together in tight economic, physical, and social proximity and interdependence, whether in disputes over land, contracts, or defamation. People negotiated over the rules of interaction, what they owed one another and could expect in return, in disputes scripted not only by the former lines of political violence. This was a means of determining what kind of moral order existed among the people with whom they interacted on a daily basis, and what responsibilities and privileges went along with the shared social networks of which they were a part.

Like the imprecision around the term "umuryango," there was not one agreed-upon term for describing Rwandans' local "community." While people agreed that the term "village" did not accurately describe the physical and economic networks in which Rwandans lived—partly due to the continuity of settlement across the country—there was debate over which term did. For most rural Rwandans, the hill *(umusozi)* was historically the fundamental unit of settlement (De Lame 2005:112–115; D. Newbury 2009:300; Vansina 2004:15, 39). Scholars and government officials referred alternately to the grouping as communities, hillsides *(imisozi)*, housing settlements *(imidugudu)*, or cells *(akagare)* (e.g., Ministry of Local Government 2008a; van Leeuwen 2001). The terms meant different things to different people, and brought different assumptions about the nature of this unit in terms of its size, scale, and reason for connection.

I use the term "community"—which was used by the government, international donors, and national and international NGOs, particularly in reference to the decentralized legal institutions—to refer to the groupings of people who were linked together by function of location, shared economic networks, and face-to-face social interactions. I use this term to capture the fact that this unit was the site of extensive top-down community-building efforts (government through community), all aiming to engender the sense of group identity and shared mutual responsibility and duty associated with collective belonging (Ministry of Local Government 2008a, 2008b). The government's community development policy was aimed at the umudugudu, the smallest administrative unit, as the "core formal community" and the focus of the policy (Ministry of Local Government 2008a:3). Rural Rwandans' local community thus involved people with whom they lived in close proximity, and with whom they chose to participate in shared networks, such as voluntary associations (for example, churches or financial associations), as well as people to whom they were indifferent, or whom they preferred to avoid.

Cases before comite y'abunzi in Ndora, and in Nyanza to a slightly lesser degree, demonstrated the mutual interdependence and tight interconnections of people in rural areas. The predominance of breach of contract cases showed that there were, in fact, prior agreements with varying degrees of formality between people, and therefore prior relationships. Pooling resources with neighbors to build a house, sharing land to graze livestock, or selling goods on credit was normal. Comite y'abunzi cases were a means of discussing when transgressions occurred and how they should be resolved. Thus, in cases before comite y'abunzi, people debated the moral and economic duties associated with living together, whether or not they felt a sense of shared identity.

In case after case, people negotiated what responsibilities neighbors had to one another. For example, should Prosper have had a duty to Alexis's wife to ensure she knew about the sale of the land, and therefore to ensure it was a legitimate transaction? Although Prosper was the plaintiff, he quickly came on the defensive, needing to show that he did not knowingly purchase stolen property. How honest did people need to be about the quality of products they sold to neighbors, whether charcoal or used cell phones? And what were the appropriate sanctions for transgressions? When mediators tried to restore property without assessing damages or interest, in the interest of limiting escalation, some feared this created a climate of impunity about harming people.

The case of Beata and Joselyne I discussed in the Introduction illustrated how the mix of harmony principles and punishment in comite y'abunzi confronted contesting views on how to reconstruct moral orders, engaging ideas of fairness, justice, redress, and appropriate ethical behavior. It further revealed gendered dimensions to the renegotiation of community, including assumptions about what issues constituted "women's disputes," which could be resolved through reconciliation efforts outside legal forums, versus disputes warranting law-based mediation, and how normative gender roles permeated mediation sessions.

The original defamation case was about an insult rife with sexual innuendo. Joselyne explained that she was seated in her yard one day cooking dinner, when Beata passed by, joining a group of people who were talking about a child who had just had a seizure. Beata, Joselyne claimed, asserted that Joselyne must have caused the boy to fall because she always caused passing men to ejaculate (*gusohora*). Beata objected, saying that was not how she had said it. She explained that she had only been expressing surprise that Joselyne had not come out of her compound to help the boy as he was having a seizure, saying she had merely replied that that's why you would think she was the one to cause the boy to fall. She went on to say that she had heard people gossiping that Joselyne would wait for men when they would go on "short calls" (to urinate). An elderly female mediator (*umukecuru*) interrupted to ask Beata what, precisely, it would mean for Joselyne to be waiting for men when they went on short calls, asking her to make explicit the insult. Beata did not respond but stated that Joselyne had gone to the women's committee with her complaint, which had fined Beata three thousand Rwandan francs. Beata said that she could not afford to pay but instead went to Joselyne to ask forgiveness, and asked if she could pay her by cultivating for her. She said she went to work once, then fell sick.

Joselyne spoke out to argue against Beata's claims, saying that she had never agreed to forgive Beata individually, that she had never agreed that Beata could dig for her, and that Beata had never even come to begin her punishment. Agathe, who was one of the members of the women's committee that had heard the case, spoke up to provide further detail and corroborate some of Joselyne's claims, including saying that Beata's claim that she had gone to work for Joselyne was not true. Agathe explained that the women's committee had attempted to reconcile Joselyne and Beata, asking Joselyne to forgive her—underscoring that this case had already been heard before another level of dispute resolution, one that had also attempted mediation. The women's committee had determined that the fine paid by Beata should go not simply to Joselyne but to the committee itself because the slander insulted *all* women. This decision illustrated the principles of unity and collective over individual good, where the collective was defined as "women." Yet, in both the initial mediation efforts before the women's committee and before comite y'abunzi, Joselyne and Beata were disinclined to accept unity merely on the grounds of being women. Beata had resisted even coming before comite y'abunzi—she ignored the summons on multiple occasions. This underscores that while mediation rested on gendered assumptions about women's roles in family and as a group that asked women to prioritize collective good and harmony, they were not necessarily more interested in being mediated.

An elderly male mediator (*umusaza*) then spoke to Beata, saying that she had accepted her guilt before the women's committee, so the remaining issue must be the unpaid fine. He and the other male mediator clearly decided that the sexual insult was an issue for the "women" to decide "among themselves" (the lone elderly female mediator hearing the case, *umukecuru*, was the one willing to ask about details of the initial allegation, while the men did not engage with it), while the two men would handle the unpaid fine. This reflected naturalized but perhaps unexamined ideas of women as a category with particular roles. The elderly man asked her why she had not gone back to finish digging for Joselyne after she got well. Beata explained that after she recovered, her child fell sick for nearly two months, and meanwhile her husband was doing twice-weekly community service work as a result of his gacaca sentence. The mediator lectured her sternly that it was her responsibility to have completed her payment to Joselyne. His tone with her followed consistent norms in which men, particularly older men, had higher status than women and could speak down to them while women listened quietly without objecting.

The mediators proposed a compromise that Beata should simply pay the original fine, to which Beata agreed, even though she defended herself by saying that she had in fact fetched water and tilled Joselyne's garden. Joselyne, by contrast, insisted that this compromise was insufficient, given the nature of the insult, the contempt Beata had shown, and her disrespect. "I want you to punish her," Joselyne insisted, in an explicit repudiation of the mediation principles. As I described in the Introduction, the abunzi used a variety of strategies to try to convince Joselyne to forgive Beata, all consistent with her essentialized role as a woman and mother. The elderly woman mediator was the one who pointed out to Joselyne that she could always file the case in the ordinary courts if she did not like the decision—underscoring the "out" she had, in relation to harmony principles. In contesting their cases, Joselyne and Beata pushed against the ethos of mediation and the idea that they should subordinate their own rights or wants in the name of collective unity.

Obligations among neighbors came up in relation to land cases when people returning from exile tried to reclaim land on which others were living. What was the responsibility of the person who was living on the land to the person from whom it was taken decades earlier, especially in the absence of clear documents to trace ownership or land transference? Land issues among "old-caseload" refugees (repatriés), that is, Tutsi returnees who fled beginning at independence through the 1980s and returned after the RPF took power in 1995, raised this question particularly clearly and frequently (Burnet 2010:113; Prunier 2009:5).

These returnee land cases could be particularly contentious and often carried over the divisions from the political conflict, showing how comite y'abunzi cases confronted genocide citizenship. For example, in one typical comite y'abunzi case, a man who fled with his family in the 1970s returned in 2002 to find another family on his land. He brought a claim against the woman who was the head of the household, claiming that she had obtained the land illegally, because her husband was friends with the commune leader, and therefore the transaction should not stand. She claimed that her family bought the land in 1980 from the commune leader at the time, and the paperwork was lost during the war. This kind of dispute was common. Returning refugees needed access to land and wanted to resettle where their family lived originally. Meanwhile, the family who paid for the land and used it for decades typically resisted losing it. The land law left this open, saying only that the state had responsibility to give land to persons who were denied their rights of ownership, which could include the "sharing of owned land" (Organic Law N.8/2005, Article 87). In comite y'abunzi sessions, then, people debated the gray area between custom and law to determine how the land should be reallocated.

The harmony emphasis combined with the warning of formal punishment could make people feel coerced into land judgments they did not support, or which they felt were legally invalid. In a typical example, a man from Ruhengeri told me that he had recently purchased land in the north of the country, but then a family of repatriés returned and claimed that the land was in fact their great-grandfather's, though they had no documentation or other proof. He explained, "You are asked to give up land that you have purchased. You need to do so because there is an understanding that you are supposed to, for the benefit of the country. And the local authorities are on the side of the people making the claim. You just have to say okay. You don't have a choice."[22]

Comite y'abunzi cases shed light on the kinds of practical negotiations that went into reconstructing moral orders among people who lived in close proximity, both in regulating access to land and property and in regulating appropriate behavior and ethics. They showed the complex intertwining of family, community, gender, economic status, and genocide citizenship.

Conclusion

Comite y'abunzi was in its early stage during the period this book covers. Many people did not engage with it, or did so only tangentially. But those with disputes aiming for the courts had to. Perhaps with the conclusion of the gacaca process, comite y'abunzi may become a more robust institution as people channel their familiarity with regular engagement in grassroots courts into this ongoing forum. Regardless, I suggest that while the vast majority of discussion about "culture-based" justice in Rwanda is focused on gacaca, it is crucial to see that the mediation principles also operated here, and to examine the effects of law-backed harmony. Cases before comite y'abunzi underscored three final key points.

First, they showed that disputes were not just predetermined by the lines of the conflict. People who were positioned very differently with regard to the genocide and to the state faced similar concerns, largely linked to their shared structural position with respect to economic and political power, as in earlier periods (see also C. Newbury 1978:25, 1988:208). Families of survivors and families of convicted perpetrators engaged in many of the same disputes. People coming home after a long time away, whether old-caseload refugees (repatriated Tutsi), new-caseload refugees (Hutu who fled during or after the genocide), or prisoners (Hutu defendants or convicted perpetrators) confronted similar problems when they returned home, trying to fit back into family, find networks of support, and earn a living.

Second, comite y'abunzi reinforced the broader practice where systems based on mediation were used for rural and less-educated people, while systems based on Western law were used for urban political and economic elites, reinforcing class divisions. This resonates with Obarrio's analysis of how a restrictive kind of "customary citizenship" in Mozambique is produced through subjecting citizens in particular places to traditional, customary authority, through "an entanglement of orality and writing" (2014:150) that requires "blending of customary law, kinship norms, and official law by the community court" (2014:15). Though comite y'abunzi was intended to exist nationwide, in practice it was unevenly implemented, primarily used for farmers and land disputes, which increased its potentially coercive impact. Comite y'abunzi sessions occurred most regularly in rural communities across Rwanda, and less so in larger towns and cities. While mediators met regularly in Ndora, I went to Nyanza for planned comite y'abunzi sessions for months only to find they had been canceled or postponed for a variety of reasons. Educated elites in Kigali and Butare told me they were skeptical about comite y'abunzi. If someone stole their car, for example, they were much more inclined to use the police and lawyers to solve disputes in courts, and used comite y'abunzi only as a last resort.[23]

Last, while I have underscored overlaps between gacaca and comite y'abunzi, there were of course distinctions between the two forums, which meant overall that law-based mediation before comite y'abunzi was experienced as less punitive or persecuting than gacaca. In gacaca sessions, the state was clearly the plaintiff, bringing criminal charges against individuals related to actions during the genocide. By contrast, comite y'abunzi involved civil disputes brought by other parties, not by the state, so it was not seen as targeting one group for criminal prosecution. Further, while gacaca sessions demanded mandatory participation, comite y'abunzi drew in a smaller group of participants for any given case. Comite y'abunzi seemed to be more flexible for participants, as they could appeal decisions to the ordinary court system, while by contrast inyangamugayo justified their sentences based on specific legal sentencing guidelines, and appeals were directed to other levels of gacaca. Sessions were markedly more relaxed than gacaca sessions. There was no police presence at comite y'abunzi sessions, no weapons, no prison uniforms, and no public examples of detaining citizens. Defendants and key witnesses often ignored summonses multiple times, with impunity. People who disagreed with the comite y'abunzi judgment regularly stalled before complying, typically because they elicited few sanctions in doing so. The government seemed to relegate enforcement of comite y'abunzi regulations to a low priority status, particularly as compared with gacaca. Overall, people saw comite y'abunzi as a more innocuous institution, while many saw gacaca courts as tightly linked to the national government's political use of genocide. There was, accordingly, arguably more room for social maneuvering and challenging authority before comite y'abunzi, even as it served as a technique of government through community that often reinforced genocide citizenship.

Chapter 5

The Legal Aid Clinic: Mediation as Thick Description

In May 2008, a twenty-year-old woman I call Yvette came to the legal aid clinic to ask the staff's help in securing paternal recognition for her baby, who was swaddled to her back with a bright kitenge cloth. In a meandering narrative, she explained that she had come to Cyarwa, adjacent to Butare, from her nearby home village and had been working at the local factory. She had begun dating a man I call Lucian, who worked in the university hospital lab and was the head of umudugudu.[1] She explained that nearly a year earlier she had feared she was pregnant and told Lucian, who had taken her urine sample to the lab for confirmation. She explained that he had become angry and had pressured her to get an abortion, and then had even accused her of infecting him with HIV, demanding a blood sample and beating her when she refused to give him one. She said she had told him that he was the father and that she would take him to court; he had responded that the only proof would be his own admission, which he would never give. When the baby was born, Yvette explained, Lucian had named him—a father's role—and had purchased health insurance for Yvette, though in an individualized plan for her, rather than listing her or the child as a beneficiary on his plan.

In the midst of her narration, the students helping Yvette at the clinic interrupted to ask her to simplify her story and get to the point. She said that she wanted their help getting Lucian to formally recognize the baby, in order that the child could have access to the rights he deserved. The students asked what evidence she had that Lucian had claimed responsibility for or accepted the child as his own, as she maintained. While her baby cooed and periodically nursed, Yvette noted that while there was no written evidence—no love letters or photographs, no joint insurance, no proof that he had taken in the urine sample—people had seen them together, had seen him visiting her, and vice versa, and had seen her on the day that he had beaten her. The students pointed out that in a court proceeding, to prove paternity she would need to have concrete evidence. Yvette lamented that she had nothing written and pointed out that Lucian was just using her because he was so much older, and that this was a pattern for him as he had done this before with another woman. She pointed out that her child took after Lucian. One of the students noted that he knew Lucian and confirmed to me in a whispered aside that, indeed, the baby looked just like him. The students continued to discuss with Yvette a possible paper trail. They noted that Lucian was indeed named as the father on the baby's birth certificate, but that this would not be probative in court, as the mother could list it herself.

The clinic director then joined the discussion and agreed that they should begin by summoning Lucian for mediation. Yvette scoffed that he was unlikely to change his mind, since he had shown his lack of responsibility from the beginning. Yvette explained that she had already taken the case to other levels of authority, but Lucian had repeatedly denied fathering the child. She said that while she was still pregnant she first went to Haguruka, an NGO that supports women and children, but was told that she did not have evidence. She described how she went to the village level, but since Lucian was among the leaders, she felt he was too influential and that this was why she had not prevailed. The local authorities sent the case to the cell level, where he had also denied it. The clinic director explained to Yvette that if mediation did not work, the students would talk to the witnesses she claimed could speak on her behalf, and with the help of the executive secretary of the cell, they could prepare a written statement that could be used in court. After nearly an hour of discussion, Yvette left, planning to return the following week.

In this chapter, I examine the Legal Aid Clinic of the National University of Rwanda in Butare as another forum in which the typical clients—poor, minimally educated, rural farmers like Yvette—were more likely to be subjected to mediation than to be guided into adversarial disputes in the ordinary courts. Cases such as Yvette's emphasize the fallacy of seeing mediation and unity principles as limited to the so-called customary-style processes of gacaca and comite y'abunzi I discussed in the previous two chapters. The legal aid clinic's staff explicitly emphasized resolving clients' disputes through compromise and negotiation with the goal of avoiding the courts whenever possible, consistent with the ethos of alternative dispute resolution. At the same time, threat of force or punishment directed towards those who did not comply, both symbolic and physical, were crucial to this approach.

I contend that it is only by acknowledging the prevalence of mediation-like efforts at the legal aid clinic that we can accurately capture how Rwandans experienced mediation as a mode of power across a broad landscape of dispute resolution. To be sure, the mixture of harmony and punishment varied across the three forums and diverse types of disputes I explore in this book, and I do not suggest that these jurisdictions were identical. Yet, I want to take seriously the fact that when Yvette took her search for paternal recognition of her baby to the legal aid clinic after already consulting a Rwandan NGO and local authorities, the staff started with efforts at mediation, rather than beginning to gather evidence and file a case for her in the courts. How can we understand the prevalence of the mediation approach across a range of disputes within this more universalized legal form, and what was at stake in it?

The examples I explore in this chapter show how deeply contextualized the legal aid clinic was and how people used it to negotiate the micropolitics of reconciliation—as the previous two chapters illustrated with gacaca and comite y'abunzi—not always in relation to identities defined by the political conflict, but in a context shaped by it. The examples here illustrate again how people used a law-based forum as one space in which to shape moral orders and attend to localized dynamics of power, resources, and loyalty, often in relation to gendered notions of roles, belonging, and hierarchy. Sharon Abramowitz has similarly shown how in postwar Liberia, "Discussions of human rights, like discussions of violence, trauma, and social reintegration, became a site for contesting norms over social roles, political rights, and economic institutions that mattered in Liberians' everyday lives" (2014:191). She described a workshop led by a human rights trainer and showed how "his human rights training gave him the authority to address—often without challenge—some of the most foundational moral problems of social and community life, which have long been relegated to the domain of tradition" (2014:199). In mediations at the legal aid clinic, people negotiated the socially embedded nature of their rights—that is, the ways that their rights were accessible in and through particular, often gendered, social roles. In particular, I show here how, as we saw in previous chapters, mediation rested on essentialized assumptions of Rwandan women as mothers and wives, and as people who preferred peace over conflict, even as women themselves used the process of mediation to carve out different possibilities, reimagining moral orders and alternative futures through contesting the meanings of these relational identities.[2]

The legal aid clinic highlights particularly clearly the ambivalent position of mediation approaches within the broader push to rule of law in Rwanda. Even as Rwandans were being taught to be legal subjects through attention to documentation, standardization, and regulation, they were routinely guided through dispute resolution efforts that relied on conversation, exhortations to custom and community, and compromise. Juan Obarrio has argued, based on ethnographic work in peri-urban and rural Mozambique, that this dynamic is pervasive in Africa, where "despite the wave of democratization and liberalization that has occurred over the last two decades, currently the African state juridically enforces a type of restricted citizenship, linked to the reappraisal of precolonial customary formations" (2014:6). He described this "customary citizenship" as "blending national belonging, official rights, and local norms and claims, encompassing vast sectors of the population within a process of inclusive exclusion" (2014:6). Obarrio's characterization of how reliance on customary-style law creates differentiated forms of citizenship is consistent with how, as I described in the Introduction, law-backed mediation in Rwanda could reinforce divides between elite and rural Rwandans, particularly risking disenfranchising the majority rural Hutu population.

Through examination of law-backed mediation at the legal aid clinic, in this chapter I build on Obarrio's notion of customary citizenship in two ways. First, examples from the legal aid clinic show how customary citizenship could be produced not only within explicitly "customary"-style forums such as gacaca and comite y'abunzi but also within Western-style legal forums built on universal human rights that were at once separate from but proximate to state power. Mediation at the legal aid clinic existed as a discretionary approach outside the formal state, enacted and perpetuated by people with formal training in "modern" Western-style law, and with a commitment to universal human rights. I thus suggest that what Obarrio calls customary citizenship might be better conceptualized, in Rwanda and perhaps elsewhere, as mediation-based citizenship, and linked more broadly to global trends in alternative dispute resolution both within and outside Africa. Second, the legal aid clinic examples provide more detail on the *nature* of the restrictions associated with what Obarrio calls customary citizenship, and, conversely, the new spaces and opportunities opened up through processes of social negotiation. I emphasize not just the ways that law-backed mediation creates a class of subjects differentially placed in relation to the state, as the idea of customary citizenship emphasizes, but also how people negotiate among themselves within this legal logic. That is, the examples below provide additional detail on the complex dynamics among those emplaced as customary citizens.

I suggest that mediation was a form of thick description that was, as anthropologist Clifford Geertz described in relation to the work of the ethnographer, an interpretive, micro-focused attempt to render fixed the flow of social discourse and practice in search of clearer understanding (Geertz 1973:20) and, in the context of legal forums, clear solutions. Specifically, I suggest that the interpretive practice of mediation served in part as a strategy for clinic staff members to manage inconsistencies and uncertainties in evidence and shifting legal norms with clients who were being newly inculcated as legal subjects, including the fetishization of documents and entextualization that is part of cultures of legality and bureaucratization (Gupta 2012, Hull 2012). Mediation was a way for both clients and staff to navigate thin documentation and incomplete paper trails through thick oral description of dense social facts. Attending to the thick description of law-backed mediation shows the multilayered dynamics within mediation that often reproduced existing power hierarchies but could also invert the status quo in specific relationships.

Harmony and Punishment at the Legal Aid Clinic

The Faculty of Law at the National University of Rwanda in Butare launched the legal aid clinic in 2001. The clinic's aim was to provide legal services to underserved populations who could not afford lawyers and had limited knowledge of their rights and the law. Its goal was, as the director described to me, to "promote human rights," specifically to "help the population know their rights, claim them and to facilitate them to easily access justice."[3] It was funded by international government donors and U.N. agencies. The clinic's goals were consistent with the overall decentralization process, which sought to remove obstacles of cost, distance, and time and to bring government services, including justice institutions, closer to the people. A clinic staff member explained to me that the legal aid clinic, like the Ministry of Justice, was working to help "bring law closer to people on the ground."[4]

In 2001, fifty-two cases were registered by the legal aid clinic, while the yearly total of cases handled rose to nearly two thousand by 2008. The Butare clinic was part of a nationwide Legal Aid Forum organized in 2006, which included other national and international NGOs that provided more targeted legal services, such as Haguruka, for women's and children's rights, Avega, which targeted genocide widows, and Liprodhor (Ligue Rwandaise pour la promotion et la défense des droits de l'homme), which focused on human rights violations. The Butare clinic also provided the model for three subsequent university legal aid clinics, which opened in 2006 and 2007, at Kigali Independent University campuses in Gisenyi and Kigali and at the Independent Institute of Lay Adventists of Kigali. The university legal aid clinics were distinct from the NGOs because the legal aid clinic served a wide range of clients and cases.

Every Thursday around noon, in a grassy field behind a multipurpose building on the main road through Butare, people began to gather to wait for staff of the legal aid clinic to arrive. At least a hundred clients came each week, rain or shine. The clinic was less deeply contextualized than gacaca and comite y'abunzi, insofar as it was in one central location, rather than embedded within local communities. Yet, clients perceived it as more accessible and open than the ordinary courts. They waited patiently, tightly pressed on rows of wooden benches arranged under an overhang, many clutching a few papers, carefully folded and wrapped in plastic. By about 2 P.M., clinic staff—a few lecturers at the university law school and a rotating group of approximately twenty students from the undergraduate law program who worked at the clinic as part of a mandatory third-year course—began consultations with each client. They gathered in pairs or small groups across the grass. Staff would collect information about the client's case in extended conversations, then would conduct follow-up work throughout the week, including visiting rural cell offices to talk to local authorities and involved parties, or visiting clients in prison.

Cases regularly included contract disputes, paternal affiliation or child support, divorce, disputes over inheritance of land and other property, and concerns about criminal cases and prison issues. Many of the cases were appeals of comite y'abunzi judgments or questions related to gacaca. Other cases addressed issues handled exclusively by the ordinary courts, such as insurance claims and employment disputes. Students on the clinic staff did not provide direct representation for clients in court but helped them understand their legal rights, wrote legal briefs clients could use to represent themselves, and advocated for them with government officials or other relevant parties, including going on site to talk with witnesses or local authorities. The university lecturers who oversaw the clinic and the students' work had been admitted to the Bar and occasionally represented cases. The clinic staff and lecturers were not located in the clients' social and knowledge networks in the same ways that abunzi and inyangamugayo tended to be, as I explore in more detail in the next chapter. As academics and students, not elected officials or state representatives, they were ambiguously and variously placed in relation to the state. As Yvette's case showed, they sometimes knew some of the case participants, as acquaintances or colleagues.

In the months that I spent attending weekly public sessions at the legal aid clinic, I observed that typically when clients came to the clinic requesting help with filing a case or defending themselves against a claim, they ended up participating in a mediation, rather than being directed to the Western-style courts. Whether it was a divorce, land dispute, breach of contract, or insurance claim, staff would usually begin by getting the details of the complaint and then would try to bring the parties together—either on site at the clinic or visiting the parties where they lived—to work out their differences, sitting with them for hours over repeated visits. As the head of the legal aid clinic told me, "Very often clients are advised about the option of mediation and when both parties agree with the idea then it is the privilege of the legal clinic to reestablish the broken social fabric." Some staff members described the work they did as "social work" as much as giving legal advice, and I heard the clinic director reminding the students that they had "to help the client feel content," no matter what the decision about the dispute might be. In typical cases, staff members aimed to mediate solutions that did not escalate the charges but solved them to the satisfaction of both parties, and to determine solutions with which parties would voluntarily comply.

Supervising faculty explicitly taught the law students who worked at the clinic about the importance of the mediation approach. They claimed it produced better outcomes for clients—saving them time and money by comparison to the ordinary courts. Mediation, they claimed, would help most clients achieve a better final solution than if they (typically poor,

Figure 8. Groups of staff/client consultations at the legal aid clinic, 2008 (photo by author).

semiliterate farmers) tried to negotiate the often winner-take-all, adversarial legal system on their own, without legal representation, especially against more powerful opponents. The lecturers saw the conventional courts as a last resort. This justificatory language was consistent with the framing of alternative dispute resolution globally, which emphasizes efficiency, access to justice, and avoidance of adversarial disputing. The clinic specifically saw its mission as helping "indigents," or the "vulnerable population," to have more access to justice, which meant that when clients came to the clinic needing help with a problem with someone more powerful, the staff did not hesitate to call the other party for mediation, whether he or she was a local authority, businessperson, or university employee. We can see this voluntary embrace of mediation principles at the legal aid clinic as a way in which staff took on the government-through-community approach at a wider level of scale, self-regulating according to mediation principles as they advocated unity among peers in a community of Rwandans, even across power differentials.

Unlike gacaca and comite y'abunzi, the legal aid clinic was explicitly modeled not on restorative justice principles and customary law, which emphasized the collective, but on universal legal principles and human rights discourses that foreground the individual. The cultural justification for mediation was prevalent, though less pervasive than in the other courts. The legal aid clinic staff often used the idea of participants' preexisting shared culture to justify the basis for unity and compromise in the mediation discourse. Staff members routinely talked to clients about Rwandan customs and norms, saying that in "our" culture, people were supposed to act in certain ways. For example, marriages should stay together, men should accept paternity, and families should not seek to benefit financially at the expense of extended kin, because of how Rwandans valued "strong family ties." Neighbors should forgive each other's transgressions or accept the sharing of land because that was the Rwandan way, and how it was done in the past.

The legal aid clinic was not a state-backed "commanding institution," and staff members did not have police or military authority to enforce their negotiated settlements or sanctions. Nonetheless, several symbolic dimensions conveyed the idea of state power and punishment that, as the director explained, "remind[ed] [people] of what they [we]re required to do by the law." Clinic staff members had high social and cultural capital, indicated by their style of dress, fluency in English and French, and access to material possessions, such as laptop computers and cars. The clinic's affiliation with the National University of Rwanda reflected proximity to state power, since, for example, many current and rising members of the national government graduated from the university. Clinic staff members therefore communicated power and authority that often appeared indistinguishable from state-backed government, such that the symbolic power to punish actually eclipsed the legal jurisdiction to do so. The clients who sought the clinic's help did so because they thought the clinic carried legal authority to enforce sanctions, and they and their disputing parties typically complied with judgments. People explained to me that they believed the staff could enforce judgments or, if not, could turn them over to other authorities who would.

Legal aid as mediation was more discretionary than in the other forums I have examined: that is, unlike the more consistently mediation-based procedures before gacaca and comite y'abunzi, the procedures at the legal aid clinic were decided by staff members; they chose when to mediate or otherwise to negotiate outside the formal legal system, versus when to provide paperwork for the client to support himself or herself in court, or when to say they could not in fact help the client. The choice to mediate was often linked to national policy: for example, staff typically pursued mediation in divorce cases on the logic that judges also mediated before granting divorce, and they typically pursued mediation in land resettlement cases, consistent with national policy around old- and new-caseload refugees (discussed in more detail in Chapter 4). But as the following examples illustrate, mediation efforts were not reducible to implementing national policy, and not best understood as a straightforward privatization of state law. Rather, the examples show the ways the thick description generated through mediation could open up space for social renegotiation while also reinforcing existing hierarchies.

In the following examples, I further show how mediation at the legal aid clinic combined coercion with resistance, as before gacaca and comite y'abunzi. The existing literature on legal aid clinics in Africa is consistent with Laura Nader's (1990) critiques of alternative dispute resolution and how mandatory mediation is a form of coercive harmony. Harri Englund (2006) has demonstrated how legal aid as mediation in Malawi, because of conditions of resource scarcity, served as a technique of governance and did not challenge the status quo. He has shown how legal aid as mediation undermined legal aid officers' passion for justice and, when operating in conditions of inequality across vast power differentials, further disempowered already vulnerable clients. Legal aid as mediation was predominantly a "crime of exploitation" (Englund 2006:123–169) against structurally vulnerable people. This example is suggestive for Rwanda, as I have argued throughout this book that the dangers of coercion in legalized mediation in Rwanda are high. Yet by looking not only at employment disputes but also at family, land, and other business disputes, we see that while mediation could indeed serve as harmony-based pacification, it could also sometimes challenge or even invert the status quo.

Consider the next step of the dispute between Yvette and Lucian, with which I began this chapter. In the days after Yvette had come to the legal

Figure 9. Clients awaiting consultations at the legal aid clinic, 2008 (photo by author).

aid clinic, one of the clinic staff members repeatedly phoned Lucian to ask him to come in to talk with them. Lucian finally agreed, and he arrived with several witnesses. He claimed that he did in fact have unprotected sex with Yvette, but that it was just once, and that she was a prostitute and was living with another man at the time. The staff members had asked Lucian to return and sit down with Yvette. He grudgingly agreed—in no small part because he knew they would continue to badger him until he came.

The next week, a law professor who worked with the clinic took Yvette, Lucian, and the friends each of them had brought into one of the open-air, round, thatch-roof *bandas* that dotted the field behind the town meeting hall in sight of the other clients and students. Over the next hour and a half the professor, wearing a pants suit that differentiated her from the kitenge-clad women, leaned on the low brick wall of the banda, alternately listening to, cajoling, and lecturing Lucian. A male clinic staff member joined them periodically. The professor began gently, suggesting that it was Lucian's duty as a Rwandan father and man to take responsibility for his child. During the discussion, Lucian again admitted to having sex with Yvette but said that he had paid her two thousand Rwandan francs for it and that when he left, she had done the same with four other men. Yvette retorted that he kept changing his story, saying that when they had disputed their case before the local authorities he had claimed she had had ten customers that night. The clinic staff pressured Lucian to ask why Yvette would be consistently claiming that he was the father if there were other men equally or more wealthy than him. Ultimately, the staff suggested they would pursue paternity tests if necessary.

At that, Lucian relented and agreed to accept that he was the father of the child. He put it in writing before the clinic staff and agreed to go to the Chargé d'État Civil to formally register the child, on the condition that Yvette would not brag about the result, since, as one of the law professors told me, "It is demeaning for a man, to be beaten by a woman like this."[5] I am uncertain what specific factors caused Lucian to concede to the pressure of the mediation, as he was not interested in speaking to me about it. He was clear in his conversations with staff members that his acceptance of paternity was not an admission of guilt or a contrite recognition of an earlier incorrect position.

It may seem a stretch to call this mediation, since the staff members seemed to be advocating primarily for Yvette with the goal of compelling Lucian to do what he felt was the right thing and accept paternity, rather than serving as impartial mediators aiming to find a compromise solution. Yet, they themselves called it mediation and explained to me that their goal was to avoid court. Consistent with mediation in other contexts, they combined rhetoric of harmony, in terms of family obligation and collective responsibility, with threat of force. The threat of punishment in this case was the added cost of a paternity test and potential litigation, as well as the social embarrassment of public discussion of the case if it was not quickly resolved. The staff members clearly emphasized relationships and compromise, including extra-legal dimensions such as asking Yvette not to gloat.

Yvette's case is a clear example of the staff members thinking that their mediation helped their client achieve a fair solution that she would not have obtained in ordinary court, thus providing justice to the less powerful. Lucian's allegations against Yvette followed long-standing patterns in Rwanda of slandering or stigmatizing "loose women" as dangerous and in violation of their preferred roles of "virtuous wives, exemplary widows, and dutiful daughters" (Jefremovas 1991). Yet, Yvette ultimately prevailed, even though she inhabited a precarious position in the sociocultural imaginary, as a young, unmarried mother. Many clients like Yvette welcomed how mediation at the legal aid clinic could transcend common power dynamics, providing more favorable solutions for low-status people, often poor rural women, while the people likely to feel coerced or punished by the mediation discourse were actually people who were more powerful, such as Lucian, or male local authorities with comparatively high economic, social, and political capital. Word of mouth spread that the clinic could help people obtain solutions like Yvette's, and many of the clients were women who wanted help with paternity or inheritance cases. Thus, we see in the legal aid clinic how mediation linking harmony with punishment occurred not only in ways that were uniformly coercive.

This case further illustrates, as I examine in more detail below, how this conversation served as a debate over idealized gender roles, sexuality, financial and social responsibility, moral behavior, and family. The micropolitics of reconciliation here were not explicitly along the lines of the conflict (victim versus perpetrator) but rather were influenced by other dynamics of local social standing and networks. I explore a variety of examples in order to consider how mediation operated across different kinds of case examples, and what was at stake in the push for it and in people's contestation during it. I begin with cases about land and ownership, then consider cases foregrounding family and divorce, and end with analysis of business and contract cases.

Land and Ownership

Like those before comite y'abunzi, many of the cases that arose before the legal aid clinic related to land disputes. In the cases I attended and those in the six months of registry logs that I analyzed, clinic staff members were more likely to pursue mediation in land cases that related to resettlement with respect to political violence, as compared to issues among families (which had typically already been heard before comite y'abunzi).[6] The dynamics of coercion in resettlement cases, which intertwined land access, genocide citizenship, family, and inheritance, were complex. On one hand, the negotiated compromises often helped less wealthy people, particularly women, obtain land currently held by men, who were often more promi-nent landowners. On the other hand, people who felt they had legally acquired land, often at considerable cost, routinely feel coerced into sharing it against their financial or perhaps even legal interests.

Land ownership cases revealed particularly clearly the fetishization of documents within legal approaches, and within neoliberal governance more broadly (see, e.g., Abramowitz 2014:194), and how mediation as thick description could be a way to work within and against the emphasis on documentation. The emphasis on written documents and paper trails within legal processes was a means of conjuring official power, as "the state [is] constituted through writing" (Gupta 2012:143), and producing fixed truths. Yet, the quotidian details of everyday life in postgenocide Rwanda belied easy documentation, as documents often did not exist, or when they did, they were improperly created or people could not read them. For example, many people could not access or read the shifting national laws. Up against the push to entextualization and documentation of law, legal aid clinic mediation elicited thick description from clients, in which they voiced their own interpretations of the micropolitics of disputes in which they were engaged. Land cases showed particularly clearly how mediation could be invoked as a strategy to circumvent documentation problems. Ultimately, these cases reveal again how people negotiated the micropolitics of reconciliation, in relation to genocide citizenship and within families, and how they debated the meaning of exchange of land.

In a typical example, in February 2008, a fifty-two-year-old woman named Jeanne came before the legal aid clinic. She lived in Kigali but had traveled to the clinic in order to ask its advice about land nearby. Her family had fled Rwanda in 1959, leaving behind her father's land, banana trees, and house. Jeanne had returned to Rwanda the previous year and had learned that the house was still standing, but that someone else had pur-chased the land in her family's absence. She had documents proving her father had bought the land and built the house, and she was hoping to gain access to the plot. She had taken her case before comite y'abunzi three months prior (in November 2007), but the mediators had ruled just a week before that they did not have jurisdiction because the value of the house and land exceeded three million Rwandan francs.

The clinic head, David, told Jeanne that they would try to pursue the case without litigation. He explained repeatedly that as a first step they needed to ascertain if this man had obtained the land legally from the district authorities. He said that if he had not, then she could file a case against him, and would likely be successful. But if the man had papers to show that he had obtained the land legally—and this is what David presumed was probably the case in this situation, as he knew this man was a "big man" who owned a lot of properties—then she would bring her case against the district authorities. But, David explained, it would probably not be in Jeanne's best interests to go to court, as it was likely the man would produce the papers, and she would just have lost time and money and have caused herself distress. Instead, she would be better off meeting with the man and the local authorities and asking for a portion of the land to use.

The emphasis on state-backed harmony pervaded the approach to resolving land disputes. David went on to explain, to me and to Jeanne, "The government addressed the land issues politically and administratively more so than legally. Usually what happens when people get resettled after being refugees is that people go to local authorities, and the authorities ask people currently staying on the land to give a portion of it back to the person who has returned. This is equally true of 1959 refugees (old-caseload refugees) and people who were refugees in 1994 and are coming back now (new-caseload refugees). People have been sensitized to share the land that way."[7] David said it would be more efficacious to approach the district authorities, explaining to them that this woman had come back after being a refugee for many years and needed to be resettled.

As part of his strategy to negotiate on Jeanne's behalf, David also emphasized bringing her paper trail up to legal standards. This underscored how the comite y'abunzi judgments (here as in many other cases) were imperfectly inserted into a regime of paper documentation that came with widespread legalization, and how the legal aid clinic staff members often found themselves in the midst of this ambiguity. Jeanne had come to the clinic the previous week with no papers and had then gone to search for the documents at the staff's urging. David now looked through her documentation and determined that she was missing the first page—since the first paper she had said "page 2." He showed her a copy of the abunzi guidebook and illustrated what needed to be provided for a ruling. He explained that the decision documentation was flawed, and therefore would be found faulty if she took it to court, because it was missing (a) a date, (b) the defendant's signature (or an explanation of why he hadn't signed it), and (c) an explanation as to why the parties did not agree. This is consistent with what David indicated was a widespread lack of attention to detail and standardization among abunzi verdicts, as the institution was still new. He saw a key part of his role and that of the clinic as helping teach abunzi and local officials how to better professionalize their documents, consistent with the growing necessity of having paperwork to support truth claims within the legal mode of dispute resolution. A colleague of David's similarly explained to me that while he felt rule of law was important, "it is difficult with an illiterate population that cannot even read and write."[8] This staff member saw his efforts as situated within broader institutional capacity-building efforts, including conducting trainings for local leaders and abunzi on how to write judgments and how to execute orders. He said that in 2003 the legal aid clinic provided training for local authorities on land succession laws and children's rights, and that the clinic staff then saw a reduction in intake cases on those issues. The staff members' decision to pursue mediation in a given case must be understood in relation to these problematics of documentation.

Jeanne's case was typical of other legal aid clinic cases in terms of the mediation approach, the proactive role staff members took in advocating with local authorities, and their efforts to find justice (as they saw it) for their clients. David took out his cell phone and called the appropriate person in the administrative sector in which Jeanne's case had been heard. He described the case and his questions, indicating who Jeanne and the defendant were, and explained the problem with the abunzi ruling. He further explained that he wanted to learn if the man had obtained the land legally. After this discussion, he told Jeanne that the sector authority had agreed to meet with her and the abunzi secretary the following morning to finalize the abunzi judgment, and that he would look into whether the man had appropriate documentation about ownership of the land. David asked Jeanne to come back after her meeting so that they could determine how to proceed. She left, promising to return the next day.

This case shows how the legal aid staff used mediation as a way of navigating among competing claims to land and instances of uncertain documentation. In this case, Jeanne was the beneficiary of the harmony-based mediation approach, though likely the man whose land she sought would not have seen the process as so benign. Further, by considering how the legal aid clinic staff used discretionary judgments to mediate or not in land cases, we can see how the limitations of mediation as advocacy in land cases were tied up with genocide citizenship—that is, here the advocacy supported old-caseload refugees, typically Tutsi and associated with victim-hood in the genocide, consistent with national policies.

Jeanne's case and the next case I discuss were both exemplary of how most of the land cases that came before the legal aid clinic had already come before comite y'abunzi, showing that contestation often did not stop with the judgment; rather, disputes moved among multiple regimes of attempted resolution. In bringing the following case, the clients disagreed with and attempted to bypass the comite y'abunzi verdict already rendered. In this example, clients made a claim for legal rights through custom in a family dispute over land, which was typical of intrafamily disputes of suc-cession and inheritance and reflected common uncertainties around chang-ing land laws. This case shows how people used the legal aid clinic as another space in which to negotiate the meaning of Rwandan custom and culture, and the role the clinic played in shaping norms of belonging, responsibility, and access to resources in the present. The contestation shows the fallacy of the idea of "agreement" over Rwandan culture, as well as the differential application of mediation and legal aid.

In May 2008, a sixty-one-year-old woman I call Clementine came to the legal aid clinic with a question about land and family inheritance. She was from Nyanza, the sector where I attended gacaca sessions. She and her younger sister were in dispute over her father's land with her relatives, includ-ing her half brother's son (her nephew) and her sister-in-law (the wife of another half brother). She explained that her father had died in 1971. He had had four wives, so she and her brothers had different mothers. Her nephew's father (her brother) had died in 1972, and the sister-in-law's husband (her other brother) had died in 2006. She explained that she had already taken the case before comite y'abunzi and said that she had lost, handing the staff a judgment dated April 22, 2005. The staff looked over her judgment briefly, then explained to Clementine that neither she nor her sister-in-law (her half-brother's wife) could inherit the land because at the time of the father's death (1971), women were not allowed to inherit land.

At that point, Clementine's younger sister came over to join the conversa-tion from where she had been waiting on a bench with the other clients. As the women spoke, they clarified their request. Though the initial case before comite y'abunzi had been about inheriting the rightful piece of land, having learned that the law did not allow for that inheritance, they now wanted the legal aid clinic's help to request *umunani*, a small piece of land often given at the owner's discretion to unmarried or divorced daughters or sisters, on which to build a house.[9] Clementine and her sister explained that her father had not partitioned his land before his death, and so his brother (their uncle) had been the one who partitioned it, and he had only divided it among the sons, without allotting any discretionary portion to the daughters.

At this point, Clementine's husband arrived, an older man in a suit and hat, walking slowly with a staff. One of the clinic staff members commented to me in an aside that this was the hardest part of their job, explaining to people that the law did not provide any rights for them. The students at the clinic explained that since the giving of umunani is at the father's discretion, as a gift, if it was not provided at the time by him or by the person representing him, then his daughters had no legal claim to get it now. Clementine angrily explained that it was not fair, since her nephew was not even using the land but had sold it and moved to Kigali. She handed the students a letter, which she said indicated that the cell-level authorities had told her nephew that he could not sell land while it was being contested. Upon reading it, the students told her that in fact the letter said that the women did not have rights to the nephew's land. The students kept explaining why the women had no legal claim. Clementine's husband—who had married her after the father's death—leaned in and explained to them that usually when a man marries into a family, the family gives him something in recognition. He said that the client's father had died before he could give anything (land, cows, and so on), and that he had thought that the small parcel of land could stand in for that. The students again pointed out that the law does not provide for that as a requirement; it is just something done by tradition. They explained again that while it was unfortunate that the uncle had made an oversight in not giving something to the daughters after their father had died, they could not legally do anything about it now. Clementine's husband said that the law should give the women the right to inherit, but the students explained that the current inheritance law was not retroactive. The sisters listened with their arms crossed angrily on their chests. The staff again pointed out that the men who inherited the land could have chosen to spare land for the women but had no legal obligation to do so. After a few more minutes, the women left, seemingly frustrated, and the husband walked haltingly after them.

This time, the staff chose to tell the clients they did not have a case and decided not to help them further. This case is interesting because, in theory, the staff could have decided to pursue a mediation with the family and to advocate for the cultural claim to land—even if it had no grounding in law. We have seen other examples where clinic staff chose to use mediation as a tool to compel people to give resources even in the absence of a fully documented legal claim, often in cases deemed to be family disputes. Instead, here the staff members decided not to pursue any intervention. This suggests that they felt the customary claim to ownership was less valid than the claim held in written law—revealing contestation over the status of legitimate authority between custom and national law. By including this case as a counterexample to the prevailing examples of mediation, I want to emphasize the discretionary dimensions of mediation. That is, if we understand mediations as carrying potential for coercion or disenfranchisement, as I have discussed throughout the book, it is also important to recognize that in some situations people were excluded even from efforts at mediation. Though I did not have additional information about the clients, one suggestive interpretation is that the staff members perceived this to be a struggle among rural Hutu farmers with which they did not want to get involved, therefore linking their decision to genocide citizenship.

Divorce and Family

Disputes related to family issues such as divorce and paternity nearly always began with mediation, in part because family law required judges to attempt to reconcile a couple before granting divorce.[10] This has much in common with how mediation is emphasized in family disputes elsewhere, including in the United States.[11] In virtually all such cases that I attended, the client bringing the case was a woman, though the legal aid clinic registry included a roughly equal number of cases of men and women seeking divorce. The only divorce requests in which the clinic staff appear to have immediately filed legal briefs (bypassing mediation efforts) was in cases where the couple had already been separated for more than three years, or where one spouse had convincing physical evidence of abuse, thus meeting conditions in Article 237 of the 1988 Civil Code for situations in which immediate divorce could be accepted. The following cases show how clinic staff on one hand supported women in efforts to achieve their legal rights but simultaneously interpolated them into narrow categories defined by gender and family responsibility. This is consistent with how, as Burnet (2012) has shown, Rwandan women could access some new social positions in the altered postgenocide landscape, yet continued to be subject to circumscription by strong and long-standing normative gender roles in rural Rwanda, particularly in terms of access to resources (De Lame 2005; Jefremovas 1991). The thick description of mediation revealed contestation over, and the mutual imbrications of, gender, family, property rights, and genocide citizenship in a context of shifting laws.

In May 2008, a middle-aged woman I call Antoinette came to the legal aid clinic seeking a divorce from her husband, Patrice, on the grounds of adultery. Antoinette claimed that Patrice had cheated on her after they fled to the DRC in the wake of the genocide, and also after they returned home to Rwanda. The law students on the clinic staff advised Antoinette that she fulfilled the conditions for filing for divorce, but they thought it would be best not to rush into court but rather to try mediation with Patrice, who was currently serving his gacaca sentence in a nearby prison. They asked her to think it over and return the following week. When Antoinette returned to the clinic, she carried letters from Patrice in which he admitted his adultery, and she again reiterated her desire to file for divorce.

Examining the grounds on which the clinic staff spent the next several hours attempting to persuade Antoinette to agree to mediation underscores again how coercion and resistance were intertwined, and sheds light on what was at stake in debates over mediation principles in divorce cases. As the two young, unmarried male students lectured Antoinette (rather patronizingly) about the moral obligations of her marriage, she remained steadfast, having already endured exhortations to compromise for the collective good during Patrice's recent gacaca trial. She invoked principles of unity herself, explaining that she had already tried forgiving Patrice and reconciling with him, but she was convinced now that he had no remorse and would never change. She explained that she had been very patient and had suffered tremendously in supporting him. The students asked if she had taken the problem to other nonlegal avenues, like her family or her church. Antoinette said yes, but that none of them would help her end her marriage, which is why she came to the clinic. When the clinic director, David, joined the discussion, he lectured Antoinette for another hour about the need to maintain a strong family, stay together for the sake of her four children, and support her husband.

This case suggests with particular clarity how principles of national unity were implicitly built upon a naturalized definition of family (umuryango), and that this idea of family was connected to political definitions of guilt and innocence vis-à-vis the genocide. David explained to me later that he thought the real issue motivating Antoinette was not Patrice's infidelity but shame that she was associated with a genocide perpetrator. Further, David told me he thought Antoinette was motivated by a desire to be a good mother, which entailed protecting her children's inheritance over that of Patrice's illegitimate children, which she could do by divorcing Patrice. In David's view, for her to be a "good mother" meant, not maximizing her own children's future wealth, but considering her obligations to a broader network of children, including those fathered by her husband with other women. This emphasis on the needs of "all the children" (*abana bose*) identified youth as central to future-oriented conceptions of national unity. David remained confident that Antoinette's loyalties to family would win out over what he perceived as her narrower interests, explaining that once Antoinette went to the prison and saw the man she had been with for twenty-one years she would be open to his apology. David reiterated, "I know the mediation will be fruitful."[12]

This case discussion again shows how there were disagreements at the root of assumptions that family was a naturalized unit of belonging: what did a mother owe her children and her husband, how much should a woman bear for her family, how should loyalties to husband versus children be balanced in terms of present and future, how should guilt by association for genocide crimes be managed? We see how the meaning of family was bound up in people's minds with political categories, such that relatives of perpetrators carried the weight of association with them and bore specific obligations to support them now and upon their eventual release. These debates entailed people working to reconstruct moral orders through rene-gotiating social connections, as they imagined alternative futures. In debating mediation, people were contesting the very terms of moral community, including gendered notions of family, on which the government aimed to rebuild Rwanda.

What ultimately convinced Antoinette to agree to visit the prison was strategy rather than a change of heart: she wanted the written proof of attempted mediation that David eventually told her a judge would require, should she chose to go to court. Yet, the week following the mediation attempt, Antoinette returned to the legal aid clinic steadfast that she wanted to file for divorce, and two weeks later I saw the clinic staff helping her prepare the appropriate paperwork.

This case thus shows how the ideology of mediation was pervasive for students and other staff members attempting to resolve this dispute. Antoinette was not simply compelled into compliance, as she ultimately succeeded in getting their help to file for divorce. Mediation here perhaps can be understood as a mode through which people constructed new moral orders and sought instrumentally to achieve the futures they imagined for themselves. Yet, we cannot overlook the presence of coercion. Antoinette clearly was not interested in "being mediated" and perhaps felt she did not have any choice but to comply with mediation efforts, as a Hutu woman and farmer. Even when the staff members agreed to prepare her legal brief, they asserted that she must already have another man, which must be why she wanted a divorce. She denied it, and the student assisting her followed up, "I'll be here next year, I'll keep watching!" This suggestion of surveillance, moral judgment, and sexual indiscretion, especially directed from a younger man to an older woman, served to reaffirm Antoinette's lower social capital. It was consistent with the relationship focus of the legal aid clinic's efforts, rather than a narrow focus on legal claims.

Another example showed the prominence of mediation efforts in divorce cases, not only in cases concerning rural farmers but also in those concerning well-educated, middle-income Tutsi women. A woman named Tharcisse returned for her third visit to the legal aid clinic in February 2008. She was thirty-one years old and worked as a hostess at a hotel in town. She and her husband had been having marriage problems for several months, and she had moved out with her children. Her husband had two months previously retained a lawyer, who had prepared a legal brief that sought divorce on the grounds that she had abandoned her home and was not contributing to her family. A court date to handle the divorce before a judge had been set, but on the appointed day, when Tharcisse went to court, her husband and his lawyer did not appear. The judge had asked her how she wanted to proceed, so she asked for another court date, scheduled for the following month (March). Meanwhile, the clinic staff had been counseling Tharcisse and her husband for mediation across multiple visits since the initial missed court date, working with them separately. When the staff members had brought her husband to the legal aid clinic to talk with them, he said that he no longer wanted a divorce—though the couple had not yet reconciled. This case is exemplary of how legal aid clinic efforts were not one-off but typically played out over weeks and even months, and how the staff members (who ultimately served as mediators) came to know the parties well, even outside the clinic, and thus complicated a simplistic identification of their role as "outsider" mediators.

This week, Tharcisse had come to the clinic to ask for help preparing a brief that she could use to defend herself in court for the rapidly approaching new court date. The staff members again reiterated that they wanted to reconcile Tharcisse with her husband, rather than help them to get divorced. A female student emphasized that Tharcisse and her husband seemed to really love each other, and she pointed out that the couple had two small children both under the age of seven, so they should stay together for the sake of the kids. Tharcisse, unlike Antoinette, was open to these exhortations to stay together, and nodded willingly. Tharcisse said that her husband had recently told her that he did not in fact want a divorce, and she said that she would be happy to remain in the marriage but was not sure he would accept his mistakes and make it work; she feared he would go back on his word. The clinic staff urged her repeatedly to reconcile with him and try to win him back.

The staff members specifically invoked Rwandan culture to define what they saw as the remaining problem for Tharcisse and her husband: that she was hesitant to make the first move. They reminded her, "In our culture, the problem is that the woman is not supposed to come to a man to say that she loves him, or wants him back, the man has to come to her first, even if they are married."[13] Even as Tharcisse protested that because of this custom she did not think she could go to him and ask him to come back to her, they told her she had a role to play in convincing him to come back. One of the staff members pointed out to me that Tharcisse's husband had come to the clinic the previous week and had seemed "a bit shy, I couldn't picture him as someone who would make the first move." The clinic director said the husband had lamented that the problem was that Tharcisse did not respect him, and that she had publicly embarrassed him by moving out. All the clinic staff agreed that this was not a serious reason for divorce but a problem that could be fixed. One staff leader kept joking that the problem was the husband had a lawyer, whose only incentive was to go to court (to get paid), so the lawyer would not counsel his client to avoid divorce. This was consistent with how staff members often framed their mediation efforts as inherently superior to the adversarial approach, and to the instrumentality of lawyers. Their approach was a compelling example of how alternative dispute resolution "transforms facts and legal rights into feelings, relationships, and community writ small" (Nader 2002a:131). As in the case with Yvette and Lucian, the staff members paid attention in their mediation to helping the man "save face" in relation to normative notions of masculinity, and again used Rwandan culture to justify their claims.

Ultimately, the clinic director said that they would write the brief for Tharcisse so that if she and her husband could not reconcile, she would be prepared to go to court and defend herself properly. But, as in the case with Antoinette, he reiterated that even at the court level the judge would first try to reconcile them before ruling on the divorce, so he urged her, in the meantime, to meet directly with her husband and discuss how to proceed. Eventually Tharcisse left after exchanging cell phone numbers with one of the students so that she could phone him to discuss when she could pick up the brief, and she would report on how the meeting with her husband went. The clinic director admonished her to be sure they did not have discussions about anything else, so as to avoid giving their spouses cause for concern. At this parting remonstrance—reminiscent of the comment in Antoinette's case—Tharcisse blushed, displaying discomfort in stark contrast to the relaxed rapport she had had with the staff members during the previous hour's discussion.

In this case, punishment seemed to loom less heavily, as Tharcisse appeared open to mediation efforts and even actively sought them, unlike Antoinette, who resisted mediation. Tharcisse readily asked for advice on how to win back her husband—suggesting she wanted counseling as much as, or even more than, legal advice. When I subsequently ran into her in town in the coming months, she indicated that she and her husband were indeed still working things out. As with Antoinette's case, we see prevailing gendered assumptions about women's roles in keeping families together, attracting husbands, and caring for young children. We see people working out the meaning of marriage, in relation to the individuals but also linked to custom and country.

The following case reflected how clinic staff used mediation not only to help clients access their legal rights but also to negotiate complex demands of property ownership and moral obligations amid a shifting terrain of changing norms *and* changing laws about marriage and property rights. In this case, we again see how the staff first pursued goals of education and relationship-based mediation before moving the case to the courts. Mediation here confronted notions of family specifically in terms of access to resources.

In July 2008, a rural woman from Gisagara came to the clinic with a problem about marriage property. She and her husband, who was the head of umudugudu, had married in 1991 and had three children. They had a communal marriage in terms of sharing property ownership and had acquired property together. She explained that her husband had recently taken a second wife and fathered her child, whom he recognized and listed on his identity card. But, the client explained, her husband was now giving things of hers to the other woman to help support her and the child. The students at the clinic explained to her that her husband was indeed not allowed to do this, since in a communal marriage system the husband must get consent from his wife before disposing of any shared property. They suggested that perhaps the reason the husband and other woman thought this was acceptable was that the client had not yet objected to it, and perhaps the husband did not know the rules. They offered to talk to him. The client explained that she knew the rules and had stated them to her husband, but he was flouting the rules and taking the shared property anyway. She explained that she had already complained to the local authorities, who had written him a letter, which he ignored.

The students continued to suggest that they wanted to talk to her husband and her before moving forward to court, in order to ensure that he understood the rules and her rights as his wife. The client then said that she had heard as well that there is a law prohibiting a man from having two wives, so she wanted the clinic to tell her about that. They agreed with her, pointing out that yes, it is forbidden to be married to two women, and that if his behavior continued this way, she could ask for a divorce and then divide up the property. But, they emphasized, before getting to that they wanted to talk to her husband and discuss with him the marital contract and the rules regarding communal property. The client said that she would be willing to accept her husband back if he would change his behavior. She explained that her children were suffering because they did not have both parents. She lamented that it was not fair that he was making their children financially insecure by giving away items that she and he had worked for together. The students explained to her that they would write a letter for her to take to her husband, asking them both to come to the clinic the next Thursday for mediation.

I did not see the actual mediation between this woman and her husband, but I include this example to reiterate the typical decision by clinic staff to pursue mediation, even in a case that might be more efficiently directed to the courts, given that the client had already taken the case before the local authorities, who had agreed with her and censured her husband. Instead, efforts at harmony through mediation prevailed, including pressure on the client to be a dutiful wife and mother, consistent with the gendered dimensions of mediation I have noted above. I suggest here that the mediation efforts were a strategy for staff to better understand and interpret the specific situation in the absence of documentation, and to negotiate between the older normative order, in which women were beholden to men for access to resources even as men could have multiple wives, and the newer legal rights of women to own and inherit property.[14] It provides another example of how staff members seemed to be helping women overcome their precarious position, even as they simultaneously reinterpolated them within circumscribed roles.

Employment and Contracts

As the employment dispute I discussed in the Introduction showed, the clinic staff also mediated in nonfamily disputes. Mediation in contract or business disputes was perhaps better characterized as informal negotiation, yet the staff members typically called it mediation and made clear that their goals were to increase efficiency and to help clients avoid the courts. I mention these cases briefly below, including contractual disputes stemming from employment and insurance, to illustrate that mediation extended beyond family law or land ownership. These cases show how mediation could operate at the margins of the explicit goals of the "total environment" (Abramowitz 2014) of national unity and reconciliation, and its often pacifying effects (Thomson 2013). The cases show a shifting mix of harmony and punishment and help us to analyze the broader links with global trends such as alternative dispute resolution, challenging the emphasis on the "customary" in our understanding of the logics of mediation and informal dispute resolution.

In the case I described in the Introduction, Joseph, a former night watchman at a health center run by the Catholic Church nearby, sat through a mediation attempt with two of the head nuns. Joseph had come to the legal aid clinic claiming he had not received two months of severance pay when his contract was terminated. He wanted to bring a case against the nuns. The clinic director, David, told him that they should start with mediation, so he summoned the two sisters. They came, and told David that the reason they had fired the watchman was because he had stolen many blankets, "worth thousands and thousands." Apparently he had admitted it and written them an apology. They had not gone to the police about it, because they did not want to punish him beyond his employment termination. Joseph later realized that because they had not gone to the police, they owed him the money. In an explicit acknowledgment of the imbrications of Christianity with harmony ideology, he said he knew they were "Christians" and therefore would not want to take him to the courts. During the mediation, David had the nuns repay the two months' salary to Joseph, and they all signed papers to that effect, each side receiving copies.

This case is in part interesting because it highlights the separations and overlaps between legal aid mediation and the formal apparatus of the law. The participants' comments made explicit how mediation at the clinic was seen as explicitly extralegal, outside the law, and that this was part of its virtue. The disputants juxtaposed it with the police and the courts but also kept the threat of police involvement (and thus state-backed punitive intervention) as a looming presence in their discussions. As they signed the papers, David told the nuns it was up to them to take Joseph to the police for the blankets he stole, if they so chose. The nuns smiled and said that if he apologized, they would not need to take him to the police. They said that the church was having enough troubles with the courts, and they would prefer to resolve it among themselves. David told me later he thought they were referring to the Catholic Church's priest sex abuse cases. These comments serve as a powerful reminder of the ways these localized interpersonal mediations were situated within broader constellations of power that extended far beyond the situated interactions.

In this case, mediation seemed to serve to support a lower-status person, an unemployed man accused of theft, in obtaining money from representatives of a powerful institution, the Catholic Church. It further hints at the interplay of gender with other forms of institutions and positions, as the nuns magnified their ideal womanhood with religious authority. I suggest that, as we saw in other examples, the discussions here could serve as ongoing spaces for thick discussion of moral responsibility and relationships of care among people in ongoing relationships, including employment—even though I did not gain sufficient information about the participants to analyze this example in terms of the micropolitics of reconciliation. I witnessed many other cases like this where individuals brought disputes related to breach of contract and the clinic staff began with media-tion efforts. In one, for example, several men came to the clinic claiming that their employment had been unfairly terminated as security guards with a nationwide company Garsec, and the clinic staff began by reaching out to the company to negotiate.

The final case I examine is in some ways an outlier in several dimen-sions. First, it is between an individual and an institution, specifically a woman negotiating with an insurance company over the amount of a pay-ment. Without suggesting a false elision between this and other examples throughout the book, I include it because the staff members themselves saw their efforts across these disparate cases as linked, describing this as another example of counseling clients to reason with the other party, proposing compromises, and avoiding litigation. This example, typical of many other cases before the legal aid clinic, shows how the tentacles of mediation extended beyond interpersonal or familiar interactions. Second, this case involved a much richer amount of written documentation than most other examples I have considered thus far. Yet, even in the face of a comparatively clear paper trail, there remained space for interpretation and uncertainty. The case draws attention to the ways staff members helped people navigate through these standards when they had thin documentation but thick description of the social context and conditions, showing that it was not simply an either/or (mediation without documentation versus litigation with documentation). Third, this case was an example of negotiation across a steeper power differential than most of the previous examples, and is thus closer to the example Englund (2006) described in Malawi. Negotiation was the policy of the insurance company nationally, not just a strategy pursued by the legal aid clinic. Here, the staff members' efforts at negotiation were to help the client receive a higher (and, in their view, more fair) payment than she might on her own, suggesting the clinic mediation here was not simply exploitative.

A woman came to the clinic in July 2008 with an insurance case. She had been disputing with Cogear, a prominent insurance company, about a payment she was due after her brother was killed in a car accident. She explained that she had produced all the necessary paperwork and expenses to Cogear, and then she had refused their offered settlement (Frw 380,000) because she felt it was too low. The students explained to her that their role in insurance claims was to help the client develop her proposal for the insurance company and to aid in the negotiation between her and the company over a payment they could agree upon. The client withdrew a thick stack of papers from a brown envelope in her briefcase and handed the students copies of the documents she had submitted to the insurance company, as well as copies of receipts for costs she had incurred during the process. She also provided papers showing that she and her brother's son were the intended beneficiaries of the insurance policy, and papers showing that the police statement made it clear that the accident was indeed the driver's fault, so the insurance company was liable. The client clarified that she was seeking the payment as well as the expenses she had accrued in trying to get the payment, and expenses related to her brother's hospitalization, death, and burial.

In their discussions with the client, the students emphasized her legal rights and the formal documentation of her evidence (by asking her for copies of her receipts and helping her identify the amount of financial damages provided for in the law, depending on what kind of accident, and what kind of death or injury resulted), but the students simultaneously advocated compromise and counseled her to be reasonable in her demands. They reminded her that whatever amount they determined was fair would always seem small, because nothing can ever seem sufficient reparation for a loved one's death. Even in the face of her detailed documentation, the students pushed her to clarify why she did not have receipts for some of the expenses listed. She explained that for some, such as minibus rides, she was not given a receipt, and therefore she had simply made note of the expense. They again encouraged her to find a way to get the real receipts, not just a list that she had provided herself.

She put her hand on the side of her face as they said that, as if pondering the difficulty of doing such a thing. She sighed, then asked again whether, even if she could not get all the receipts, the students could at least help her to reach a compromise for a reasonable sum of money from the insurance company. The students again explained to her that they knew it had been a long time, and maybe she had lost the receipts, and they would still try to help her. When the supervising professor came over, he confirmed that the students should indeed develop a proposal and take it to the insurance company to discuss it with them, and only go to court if the mediation failed. But, he suggested, the insurance company would understand the implications of going to court if the negotiation failed (thus, seeing it as a punitive threat), since the courts usually found against the insurance companies in these cases, requiring them to pay higher amounts.

These cases thus serve to further remind us how people experienced the law-as-mediation approach in Rwanda across a broad range of disputes, including in relation to thin documentation. They connect trends in Rwanda to alternative dispute resolution more broadly and suggest that thus we must be careful of framing the forms of citizenship deriving from these processes as "customary" (qua Obarrio 2014) for fear of obscuring the global processes that inform them and the varied sites in which these regimes of power are deployed. For example, the nuns' decision to mediate with a fired night watchman was surely in part shaped by the postgenocide context, but it was also affected by a broader global context in which the Catholic Church was mired in litigation over priest sex abuse cases. Similarly, the woman's complaint with her insurance company was part of a broader mode of corporate capitalism, in which consumers around the world face negotiation and binding arbitration in efforts to make claims against companies (Mattei and Nader 2008). While mediation in employment disputes and with corporations seemed vastly different from interpersonal mediation over genocide disputes or land claims, by attending to the threads of similarity across examples, a clearer picture of the social force of law-backed mediation emerges.

Conclusion

Attention to the legal aid clinic's mediation efforts underscores the diversity of ways mediation was deployed in postgenocide Rwanda, by varied actors, with multiple effects. The legal aid clinic cases crucially demonstrate how law-backed mediation was not merely cultural or customary but was consistent with global trends in promoting rule of law. For example, the Africa Justice Foundation, a British NGO dedicated to developing "robust, stable and predictable legal systems" in sub-Saharan Africa, made this link explicit on its website in 2013, stating that "Alternative dispute resolution and mediation is becoming more and more important in Rwanda. Community based justice is seen as [sic] way to encourage non-adversarial processes."[15] By 2014, the Africa Justice Foundation provided training in mediation techniques to this clinic and other legal aid providers in Rwanda.[16]

These cases show how Rwandans' experiences of law-based reconciliation extended beyond, and were not reducible to, gacaca and even comite y'abunzi. People took their disputes to a variety of different people and spaces for resolution, such that disputes cannot be understood as one-off or easily bounded. Each legal forum was situated within a much broader system of dispute management, in which many of the other levels also emphasized mediation. In addition, the examples explored here bring to the fore the diverse nature of disputes and concerns people faced in the aftermath of genocide, and how they crosscut institutional boundaries, further underscoring the limitations of focusing exclusively on "genocide" crimes versus ordinary disputes, or on customary-style law versus Western law.

The legal aid clinic showed particularly clearly how mediation efforts coexisted with a broader push toward expanding rule of law across Rwanda, and how this bumped up against the paucity and tenuousness of written documentation. It was out of this context that mediation as thick description emerged, as participants sought to grasp and fix the shifting, contested social facts. Looking at the mediation principles here, in a legal space that looked different from the "customary" instantiations, revealed it as a broader tool of governance (and government through community) consistent with wider-reaching global mediation and arbitration approaches. On one hand, mediation could serve as a tool of advocacy, helping people who otherwise did not have access to adversarial justice to achieve their rights, to paternity or to land. On the other hand, this extralegal mediation was often applied with discretion and could be used consistent with broader landscapes of power and inequality across Rwanda, linked with genocide citizenship, whereby, for example, particularly in land or contract disputes, staff were more likely to mediate on behalf of Tutsi. I turn next to consider in more detail the sources and effects of some of the improvisation in which lay mediators engaged.

Chapter 6

Improvising Authority: Lay Judges as Intermediaries

Over the course of a week in December 2007, I attended three public meetings across my field sites in which government authorities informed people about the status of the gacaca process, specifically clarifying the procedures around the gacaca appeals phase and the lingering cases against property. These meetings were emblematic of how lay judges, the people at the center of these harmony-based legal models, were situated as intermediaries (Merry 2006) between the national government and the people bringing complaints. In this chapter, I turn our attention to these lay judges to examine the ambivalence of their positionality as intermediaries and what effects it had on their exercise of state power and their efforts to negotiate the micropolitics of reconciliation. Their insider status was crucial to the government-through-community approach, and to how law as mediation in harmony models was operationalized.

In Ndora, the gacaca meeting began midmorning in a field in the center of town, across the dirt road from the courtyard where gacaca and comite y'abunzi were held. Several local leaders sat in the front, while the inyangamugayo from the many cell- and sector-level courts sat together, filling a handful of benches. Over the next four hours, the crowd behind and around them thickened, to up to at least a thousand people.

In all three meetings, I quickly noted that the inyangamugayo positioned themselves as a group, allied against critiques from the national office staff members as well as from the general population. In each meeting, the national representative of the gacaca office, whom I call Patrick, explained that he had visited the nearby prison where most of the gacaca defendants from the area were being held. He described having spoken with prisoners to solicit their concerns about the gacaca process, and he made a show of holding up the spiral-bound notebook on which he had written his notes of those meetings. He then proceeded to go through the concerns one by one, calling upon the assembled crowd—which included the judges, family, neighbors, and witnesses who had participated in the trials—to help him understand the problem and the solution. For example, in Ndora, in one complaint, Patrick related that a prisoner alleged that he should get a retrial because the judges had heard testimony via cell phone. One inyangamugayo who had heard the case spoke up to explain that they had not heard actual testimony via cell phone, just an explanation from a witness of the written testimony he had submitted. People who had been in the general assembly during the case in question spoke up to disagree with this version of events and raise questions about the inyangamugayo's judgment. Patrick interjected to suggest alternative interpretations, and to suggest the inyangamugayo had not followed procedural rules. The panel of judges insisted that they had not used the phone information as evidence and that it had not influenced their judgment in the case. An inyangamugayo from another panel spoke up to say that given the difficulty of getting some witnesses to attend the trial, sometimes phone calls were necessary, and that in this case, since the witness in question had also submitted written testimony, the procedural norms had been followed.

In another case, Patrick related that a prisoner wanted an appeal because he had not been allowed to hear part of the case when it began raining and the judges moved the case inside but left him outside. Debate ensued about whether the prisoner had been excluded from the actual trial proceedings, as he claimed, or from the deliberations, as the judges claimed, with a detailed discussion about when, precisely, the rain had begun to fall that day. All the while, Patrick kept intervening, trying to keep the case focused on the point of law rather than going into the details of the case (a distinction that seemed quite important to him but either unclear, or unimportant, to the assembled crowd), and trying to present what the procedural solution should be, compliant with national policy. Patrick pushed heavily for the inyangamugayo to agree to rehear the cases. Throughout the discussions, inyangamugayo from other courts spoke up in support of each other, to defend or justify the inyangamugayo's actions in question.

While Patrick was the authority on official procedural issues, it quickly became clear that he did not know the situated details or practical dilemmas as well as the inyangamugayo did. In a particularly performative moment, Patrick interrupted everyone to ask where, precisely, was Kabuye Hill, the location about which everyone was speaking. Dozens of hands pointed purposively in the same direction—clarifying for everyone present the individuals in whom locally rooted knowledge and even authority were located. Patrick's normative claims about what the inyangamugayo should do were positioned among a multiplicity of competing truth claims about the process. The judges demonstrated precise, detailed knowledge of the cases and the process, and clearly argued that some of the procedures were impractical for the daily realities of their jobs, often pushing back against Patrick's implication that they had not followed procedure. My point with these examples is not to suggest that the inyangamugayo were indeed correct, but rather to show how they performed solidarity with one another, and differentiated themselves from the general assembly and the state representatives.

I refer to the people at the center of harmony legal models as lay judges here rather than as mediators to emphasize their simultaneous status as unprofessional (that is, not part of the professionalized judiciary) and as bearers of decisive state-backed power. By referring to lay judges as intermediaries, I build on Sally Engle Merry's call for detailed attention to the people who "work at various levels to negotiate between local, regional, national, and global systems of meaning" (Merry 2006:39), and follow Merry's emphasis on the dilemmas and vulnerabilities of their position. Lay judges' insider status, particularly in comparison with other judges and representatives of the state, illustrates the deep contextualization of these harmony models. Lay judges were embedded in local social and knowledge networks and had no formal training in law, as I illustrate in more detail below. At the same time, they served as representatives of the state with authoritative force to imprison people or remove their property, in a nationally driven, quickly changing process over which they had no formal control. Their intermediary structural position had correlates in other processes of postconflict reconstruction, and thus my analysis here is suggestive outside Rwanda. For example, Sharon Abramowitz has similarly described psychosocial trauma counselors in postwar Liberia as intermediaries who "were enmeshed in the same global project of radical social change and structural reconstruction as were the Liberians they counseled. In their lives and experiences, they often bridged the reality of existing as the objects of humanitarian aid and as the agent and purveyor of global therapies for local distress" (2014:234).

Attention to lay judges reveals the textured ways the government-through-community approach unfolded, in which local people, that is, "insiders," took on active self-management practices embodying mediation themselves and encouraging others to do so as well. I focus in particular on abunzi and inyangamugayo in this chapter, given the similarities in their structural position, and then consider how legal aid clinic staff members served also as intermediaries, though with some differences. Focusing on the lay judges in this example and in others I explore below shows that their self-regulation and subjectification through mediation were not seamless, and that to consider these Rwandans as proxies for uniformly exercised regime power is inaccurate and erases the complexity of how they exercised law-based mediation as a mode of power. I illustrate the ways that their status within local social and knowledge networks influenced their role, attentive to how it could feed instrumental and biased uses of law, while not reducing all of the effects of their role to corruption.

Specifically, I claim that lay judges showed a side of state power that was improvisational and ambiguous, which is crucial to understanding how people experienced variations in state power in Rwanda. I use improvisation here in the spirit of how Julie Livingston recently described health care providers in a Botswana oncology ward as "improvising medicine." She argues that "examining processes of making do, tinkering, and ad-libbing help us to better understand the nature of biomedicine in Africa and the work of African healthcare workers, for whom improvisation is inevitably the modus operandi" (Livingston 2012: 6). I suggest that improvisation is an equally pervasive modus operandi in legal as in medical realms in contemporary Africa, as I illustrate below. People tasked with implementing legal processes often faced structural conditions similar to those faced by health care providers: they were promoting a set of values that did not always dovetail with people's situated understandings of dispute resolution, and they conducted their work with minimal training, a paucity of supportive infrastructure, and heavy caseloads. Like Livingston, I suggest that lay judges' improvisation in part emerges out of resource-poor conditions but also, and equally important, was characterized by "innovation and care" (2012:21), forms of creativity and caretaking that I trace below.

The improvisation, I further argue, meant that state power could be experienced as ambiguous, contingent, or even arbitrary, and therefore as not monolithic. My position here is consistent with Akhil Gupta's argument that by analyzing how low-level bureaucrats provide services in India we see that "the entire process is shot through with contingency and barely controlled chaos" (Gupta 2012:14), a "production of arbitrariness" which is an inherent part of state bureaucracy, and which underscores the nonunitary nature of the state. I diverge from Gupta in emphasizing creativity rather than the depersonalization he suggests is part of bureaucratization in India. Gupta further argued that arbitrariness in the provision of care in India is "systematically produced by the very mechanisms that are meant to ameliorate social suffering" (2012:25)—which resonates with how in Rwanda lay judges worked in legal forums intended at face value to help rebuild the social fabric—and that this "production of arbitrariness" (2012:6) is a way the state actively produces structural violence. I suggest that similarly, even though we can see how the ways lay judges enacted state power through mediation in harmony legal models was not identical to top-level regime power, and even though it could at times be productive, its improvisational variation could nonetheless reproduce structural violence—particularly against people who were rendered more vulnerable by their genocide citizenship or other markers, such as gender and class.

Becoming Lay Judges: Elections and Trainings

My focus here on how inyangamugayo and abunzi (and to a lesser degree legal aid clinic staff) exercise state power is consistent with how anthropologists, sociologists, and political ethnographers have studied the state over the past decade, viewing the state not as a fixed object but as culturally constituted in everyday bureaucratic practice.[1] This work seeks to shed light on how states are complex constructs that must constantly legitimate and reinforce themselves in the face of contestation (see also Abrams 1988; Habermas 1979 [1976]). It does not view the state "as a given—a distinct, fixed, and unitary entity that defines the terrain in which other institutions function" but instead considers "the ideological and material aspects of state construction" (Sharma and Gupta 2006:8).

Legal forums are a key terrain for examining how people within them conjure and contest state power, especially in so-called postconflict contexts where the state's legitimacy and authority are intentionally being reimagined and reconstituted (Comaroff and Comaroff 2003; 2006; Mattei and Nader 2008; Obarrio 2014). Focusing on law as one dimension of state power from an anthropological, ethnographic perspective (as I do throughout this book) shifts focus from seeing legal institutions as a simple reflection of the state to instead exploring the following: (a) how the state is made, unmade, and imagined through legal institutions, (b) how legal institutions are used to "conduct the conduct" of citizens (Foucault 1991; Nader 2002; Rose 1999), and (c), how law is interconnected with power, politics, and instrumentality, and thus, how states are complicit in illegality (Comaroff and Comaroff 2006; Heyman and Smart 1999; Nordstrom 2007; Thomas and Galemba 2013). I use lay judges as a site for examining how "'the state' comes into being, how 'it' is differentiated from other institutional forms, and what effects this construction has on the operation and diffusion of power throughout society" (Sharma and Gupta 2006:8). While lay judges worked locally in areas across Rwanda, they were not at the state's margins but were the keystone of institutions that were central to how the Rwandan state legitimized itself. They are crucial to understanding how people exercised and experienced state power through harmony legal models.

People became inyangamugayo or abunzi through elections and training, thus taking on a dual community-state position.[2] The role of lay judges had several specific characteristics. They were residents of the local jurisdiction and were not professionals; they were untrained in formal law and unpaid. In addition, inyangamugayo and abunzi were inquisitorial judges. Unlike judges whose role is restricted to deciding issues of law and making decisions based on information presented in court, as is typically found in systems of common law, lay judges played an active role conducting investigations and questioning, during and outside trials, much as the prosecution, defense, or even police do in other legal systems (see, e.g., Terrio 2009:43–44).[3]

Rwandans selected their neighbors as inyangamugayo and abunzi in special elections that were organized by the National Service of Gacaca Jurisdictions and the National Electoral Commission, respectively. The legal requirements stipulated that the lay judges be residents in their jurisdiction, meaning they were embedded in local relationships and circuits of knowledge. The premise was that ordinary Rwandans identified by their neighbors inherently had the knowledge of local context and the ability to make reasoned decisions necessary to become capable adjudicators in gacaca courts and comite y'abunzi. The key requirements for eligibility for both positions were related to moral character—as "persons of integrity," "acknowledged for their mediating skills," "free from the spirit of sectarian-ism . . . of high morals and conduct . . . [and] characterized by a spirit of speech sharing"—rather than specific professional training. In an attempt to depoliticize the legal process and cement the judges' lay status, staff members of administrative entities or judicial organs were ineligible, including soldiers, policemen, career judges, and active political leaders (Organic Law N.16/ 2004, Articles 14, 15; Organic Law N.31/2006, Article 4).

Elections for both courts were based at the cell level. Protracted election campaigns and speeches were unnecessary, as the electors were supposed to know the nominees. These were people with whom their lives were intertwined—they lived near one another, shopped in the same markets, attended the same churches, walked the same paths to and from daily activ-ities. They were members of the same business cooperatives, women's groups, or financial institutions, and overlapped at weddings, funerals, har-vests, and other celebrations.

The elections of inyangamugayo and abunzi were intended to formalize the role of informal opinion leaders who were trusted by their peers and known to make carefully reasoned decisions. Of course, this was not always the case, as people strategically lobbied to elect their allies. Lay judges' expe-riences reflected the local social dynamics of livelihoods, education levels, and displacement caused by decades of recurring political violence, and as a group their experiences were expected to complement and balance one another. Inyangamugayo panels were made up of seven people, plus two substitutes, requiring a quorum of five to convene any session (Organic Law N.16/2004, Articles 8, 23). Abunzi panels were made up of twelve mediators plus three alternates, from whom participants would select three to preside over and deliberate on any given case (Organic Law N.31/2006, Articles 4, 18). Typically, as was the case in Ndora and Nyanza, panels included both men and women of a wide range of ages, some as young as twenty-one, others in their eighties. Abunzi panels were required to be 30 percent women (Organic Law N.31/2006, Article 4). Most rural judges were farmers, not educated beyond primary school. Urban judges were more likely to have been educated through some or all of secondary school, and to work for local businesses or in administrative or NGO offices.

Panels of inyangamugayo were sometimes heavily rescapé- or repatrié-dominated, as they were in Ndora, given that many Hutu were disqualified by accusations before gacaca.[4] Laurence, the presiding judge in Ndora, was a pastor in his early forties. He was born in Burundi and grew up there, and returned to Ndora in October 1994, resettling on land his family had abandoned decades earlier. He was educated through Primary Six. He engaged in small commerce for a living, to support his wife and eight children. Another judge on the same panel, whom I call Faustin, was in his mid-forties and had served as a soldier with the RPF from 1995 to 2003. His first wife died in the genocide. He remarried and lived with his wife and four children, farmed for a living, and was in charge of security for the commune. He was educated through Primary Four. Both Laurence and Faustin were elected at the beginning of the gacaca process. Vincent, in his early fifties, was elected as a judge in mid-2007, to replace a judge who had been dismissed. He was educated through Primary Six. He lived with his one son who had survived the genocide, and farmed. Another Ndora inyangamugayo was a repatrié who fled Rwanda in 1959 at the age of three and returned to Rwanda with her husband, who was originally from Ndora, in 1995. Another was a woman in her late twenties who had survived the genocide in Ndora.

On the other hand, some panels were more Hutu-dominated, particularly in areas where few Tutsi had survived. In Nyanza, the majority of the inyangamugayo were Hutu, including young women, older women, and middle-aged men. There was more experiential diversity among abunzi, because they were not barred from serving if they had been accused (and acquitted) of genocide.

Panels of judges were not static. Abunzi served for two-year terms, while inyangamugayo served for the duration of the gacaca process. Some judges had held other local positions before, for example as cell leaders or youth leaders, while for many this was their first elected leadership position. Some judges shifted roles between the courts, serving first as inyangamugayo and later as abunzi. Some of the original inyangamugayo were dismissed because they were accused of genocide or for misconduct, such as inconsistent attendance or revealing secrets of the court. New inyangamugayo were elected to replace people or to build new panels—for example, Ndora initially had only one sector-level court, but two more were quickly added to operate in parallel, in order to more efficiently try cases. Sometimes the composition of the panel changed from one week to the next as alternates sat in while inyangamugayo were absent, perhaps sick or testifying in a separate trial. Abunzi benches were comparatively consistent over the two-year period of election, but they shifted more between cases, because only three of the twelve presided over any given case. This meant that empanelled mediators changed during a given day's session.

Most lay judges elected were thrust into the judicial role in the newly formed legal institutions quite unexpectedly. They described approaching their selection with a combination of patriotism, humility, and uncertainty. They juggled their judicial responsibilities alongside however else they made a living, perhaps farming, running a business, or working in an office. This meant that some were doubly dedicated to the core mission of their task, while others were distracted, overworked, or more susceptible to monetary manipulation. Yet they typically did not see the position as one they could turn down. Many people selected as inyangamugayo were apprehensive about reentering the details of genocide and taking on such a weighty task. Others describe being eager to participate, framing their participation in terms of a desire to help rebuild Rwanda. In a comment echoed by many other lay judges in Ndora and consistent with the self-regulation of the government-through-community approach and the national unity and reconciliation agenda, one said, "I was glad to be elected, I had an obligation to serve my country."[5] Elaste, the presiding inyangamugayo in Nyanza, similarly reflected, "Given the magnitude of the situation in this country and the problems it created, I was glad to be among the people providing solutions."[6]

People selected as lay judges did not have training in law or analytic reasoning and had no professional adjudication experience, on the premise that knowledge of context and culture was paramount, and specifics of the legal process could be added once they were elected. Before beginning to fulfill their duties, lay judges participated in mandatory specialized trainings designed to familiarize them with the rules and procedures of the courts, and to prepare them to serve as representatives of the state. Staff members from the national gacaca office, the local gacaca coordinator, and sometimes staff members of international NGOs such as Human Rights Watch, led the trainings for inyangamugayo, which typically lasted three or four days. Representatives of the Ministry of Justice, and often teams from NGOs and the National University of Rwanda's Faculty of Law, held similar trainings for abunzi.

The trainings ostensibly transformed judges-elect from individual citizens with idiosyncratic allegiances into official representatives of the state. My purpose here is to underscore several key elements of the trainings in order to emphasize their ideological goal. First and foremost, these trainings instructed inyangamugayo and abunzi in the rules and procedures of the respective courts. They were taught to demarcate the boundaries of their authority by each court's geographic, temporal, and subject-matter jurisdictions. They were taught the technologies of organizing and recording information. For example, inyangamugayo were instructed in how to properly compile dossiers with charges and judgments, and abunzi were instructed in how to record proper minutes and write judgments.

Further, lay judges were trained in the regulations and guidelines on how to make decisions and allocate sentences in accordance with the law—that is, how to use their state-backed authority to punish and award damages. Inyangamugayo could impose prison sentences of up to thirty years, or alternatively, could release a prisoner immediately, based on sentencing regulations, and they could bring charges against participants for refusing to testify, for perjury, blackmail, or coercion (Organic Law N.16/2004, Articles 29, 30, 73). Abunzi could make legally binding judgments, which would be enforced by the local authorities or the judicial police (Organic Law N.31/2006, Articles 11, 14, 24). Since the gacaca process was under constant evaluation and modification, inyangamugayo attended other brief trainings whenever there was a subsequent amendment in the gacaca law—for example, on changing the way punishment would be served or how confessions should be handled.[7]

Even with the clear legal guidelines, judges had discretion, so trainings emphasized how the lay judges should consider these more subjective aspects of their role. For example, the inyangamugayo could accept a defendant's confession, in which case they could transmute half his or her sentence to community service work, or they could reject the confession as partial or dishonest, in which case the defendant would serve the full sentence in prison (Organic Law N.16/2004, Article 73). Abunzi had leeway to devise solutions not dictated by, though consistent with, formal law (Organic Law N.31/2006, Article 21). Deliberations over these flexible points were confidential; revealing information about them could be grounds for a judge's dismissal.

Equally important to procedures, as the trainings throughout underscored, was the philosophy of reconciliatory justice, consistent with mediation principles. This was at the heart of the government-through-community approach, which most mediators took on with aplomb. They presented themselves to me (an outside researcher) in particular as ideally self-regulating according to mediation principles. As one umwunzi remembered, "We were taught how we were supposed to help the population, to discourage tendencies of genocide ideology, and reminded that we should love our nation."[8] The trainings aimed to indoctrinate inyangamugayo and abunzi in values of unity and collective harmony, which they were supposed to model for, and pass on to, their neighbors through their judicial role.

Finally, trainings emphasized the need for lay judges to maintain integrity and impartiality, avoiding making decisions based on emotions or prior relationships. The gacaca law included a specific provision intended to keep this in check. Article 10 provided that judges should recuse themselves from any case involving a close family member, someone with whom they had a preexisting relationship (either positive or negative), or "any other relation considered incompatible with the honest persons independence." Of course, this was somewhat absurd in rural Rwanda, where people's lives were intertwined and many were related, even after the displacements of the genocide and surrounding violence. Judges were expected to read this at the beginning of each trial and ask the assembled witnesses, victims, and defendant if they knew of any concerns of partiality among the empaneled judges. Abunzi similarly were instructed to remain neutral, though there was not a corresponding article in the law. That is likely because, unlike in gacaca, where defendants had no choice as to which judges heard their trial, participants could select their mediators in comite y'abunzi, and they typically did not select mediators they feared would be partial. There was often vigorous debate about which mediators would hear a particular case.

Abunzi and inyangamugayo took an oath of office before beginning their work, underscoring their transition to becoming representatives of the state. The oath emphasized the rule of law and international language of human rights. It also emphasized impartiality and national unity, consistent with the mediation principles. As the oath demonstrates, while inyangamugayo and abunzi served as lay judges in ostensibly customary-style courts, they cannot be understood as just elders gathered informally under a tree. Their oath of office explicitly linked their authority and loyalty to the nation-state. The oath stated:

> I solemnly swear to the Nation that I shall: 1, diligently fulfill the responsibilities entrusted to me; 2, remain loyal to the Republic of Rwanda; 3, observe the Constitution and the other laws; 4, work for the consolidation of national unity; 5, conscientiously fulfill my duties of representing the Rwandan people without any discrimination whatsoever; 6, never use the powers conferred on me for personal ends; 7, promote respect for the freedoms and fundamental

rights of the human being and safeguard the interests of the Rwandan people. Should I fail to honour this oath, may I face the rigours of the law. So help me God. (Organic Law N.16/2004, Article 9; Organic Law N.31/2006, Article 7)

Inyangamugayo and abunzi wore sashes that represented their official role when they presided over court sessions. In a context with few other technologies—no dedicated courtroom or dais, rarely even a microphone, no black robes, minimal differentiation among people's clothes—the sash stood out as a significant social marker. It resembled the Rwandan flag, composed of three parallel bands of blue, green, and yellow, with a single yellow sun. The front was marked with INYANGAMUGAYO or UMWUNZI, and the back with INKIKO GACACA (gacaca courts) or COMITE Y'ABUNZI. The presence of the sashes, properly worn, signaled and enacted the start of the trial sessions, and their removal marked closure. By taking the oath and donning the sash, inyangamugayo and abunzi stepped into a specific state-backed role with duties and obligations, including to preside over sessions, investigate, sift through contested facts, decide on the truth or falsity of the charges, determine guilt or innocence, issue judgments, and allocate punishments.

Governing Through Community: Intermediaries Situated in Local Networks

An example from a gacaca session in Ndora reveals the ways lay judges were at the heart of the government-through-community approach—specifically, it illustrates how they were deeply situated within the "communities" the decentralized courts were intended to help rebuild, and thus how they were intermediaries who blurred the boundary between state and community. The presiding judge whom I call Laurence was a returnee who arrived in Ndora a few months after the genocide, as I indicated earlier. Two of the other four judges on the panel, Faustin and Vincent, were born in Ndora and survived the genocide there. The first defendant, a man named Nshimye, was accused of planning genocide, being in a group of killers, and being at a roadblock. Nshimye accepted some of the charges and refuted others. During testimony, Faustin asked Nshimye to provide

Figure 10. Inyangamugayo recessing after a session, 2007 (photo by author).

more information about the planning of the genocide, saying that he frequently saw Nshimye in the company of a notorious genocide leader. Later
Faustin refuted a witness's testimony that Nshimye had participated in a
certain person's death by noting that he saw Nshimye at the time, and that
he was not involved.

Vincent too questioned Nshimye's version of events several times and
pushed Nshimye to accept responsibility for certain charges. After one victim insisted that Nshimye must have information about her brother's
death, Vincent admonished her to stop asking, noting that several people
had just said Nshimye was not responsible. Vincent later corroborated
Faustin's support of the defendant, noting that he and Faustin were trying
to escape together and Nshimye directed them to a place where they could
avoid being caught. In the closing moments of Nshimye's trial, the female
victim whom Vincent admonished spoke up to criticize Vincent for appear-
ing biased in favor of Nshimye. Laurence, the presiding judge, responded
by reminding everyone that the inyangamugayo should not take sides but

Figure 11. Inyangamugayo awaiting start of hearing category 3 property cases (photo by author).

just testify as to what they saw or heard. Vincent countered that if anyone thought he was partial, he would step aside. He put his head in his hands for several minutes and rubbed his eyes, seeming chastised.

In the late afternoon, Laurence summoned a defendant called Paul, whose charges included preparing genocide and joining groups of killers. This time, when Laurence called for witnesses and victims to come forward, Faustin stood up from behind the judges' table, removed his sash, and joined the others who had gathered to provide testimony. When Paul testified, he refuted allegations that he had participated in attacks against Faustin, saying that in fact he had tried to help him. When it was Faustin's turn, he took a few steps forward to stand before the panel of judges. He described how one day during the genocide, Paul came for him with a group of killers. Paul brought Faustin out from his hiding place in a latrine and asked for his identity card. Because the identity card ink was smeared and therefore difficult to read, Paul took Faustin to the commune office. On the way, Paul stopped several people from attacking Faustin preemptively, then while Paul was distracted when talking to a superior, four men seized Faustin. The men tried to kill him, but Faustin escaped. After he finished testifying, Faustin immediately walked back around the wooden table and picked up his sash. He carefully placed it across his chest and took his seat, where he remained for the rest of the afternoon's testimony.[9]

As this example of Faustin and Vincent illustrates, those who wore the sash, representing state power, were people with their own knowledge of the political violence and social dynamics. Lay judges were part of the social fabric being rebuilt. Their knowledge came from their own experience as well as from their outside investigations, which were permitted by their inquisitorial role. They came into case sessions with prior information about general context, or even about a precise crime or disputed point.

In some situations, lay judges carried information into cases that was directly related to particular participants. In cases before comite y'abunzi, the abunzi often knew the particular plot of land in question and had their own independent memories of the land's ownership and provenance, or knew the individuals involved in the dispute. In the Ndora gacaca example, Vincent and Faustin evaluated testimony based on their own memories of the defendant and the events in the charges. Faustin presided over several cases where defendants confessed to involvement in attacks on him.[10] Other judges used knowledge they had gained through conversations and experiences since the genocide. For example, an inyangamugayo named Immaculée, who lost her brother and father in the genocide, described realizing during the course of one trial that the defendant owned land on which she helped exhume a mass grave:

> We asked him to give us the details of what happened at that pit hole, and information on the people who were killed there. He kept denying personal responsibility, and responding that we were asking

the wrong person. He said that besides, there were some pit holes that had been dug to dump in Hutu, so why was he even on trial.[11] When he said all this, what came to my mind immediately were the images of the bodies we exhumed in 1995. Some still had bits of their clothes on. There were even a boy and a girl who had been tied up together and dumped in the pit hole, and their bodies were still tied together when we exhumed them. Straight away, I imagined that it was the defendant who had tied up this boy and girl.[12]

Though no forensic evidence was presented in this defendant's trial, Immaculée's vivid memories of decomposing bodies from a decade earlier influenced her perspective that the defendant was deliberately obscuring the truth, in the absence of a plausible explanation on his part. As this quote shows, testimony provided during any given session was layered onto related information acquired over years. Trials were just one step in a much broader, locally embedded process. In this case, Immaculée found the session so emotionally upsetting that she left the trial early and did not participate in deliberations—reflecting a careful choice to step aside, for someone who otherwise always arrived early and was the last to leave after deliberations.

Much of the lay judges' locally rooted knowledge was more general than Faustin's or Immaculée's, based on living in the area over time. Inyangamugayo and abunzi all had basic familiarity with Rwanda, their own cell and sector, and the dynamics of life there. They knew common family practices, such as whom and when people married, where they lived, and who looked after children when parents died. They knew the general practices and variations in rituals surrounding events like births and deaths. They knew the local landscape and setting of the area under their jurisdiction, including general distances between places, how long it took to walk certain routes, how views could be obscured in the rain, how sound carried between certain hillsides, or what you could see from a given yard.

Lay judges used this general locally rooted information to identify the key issues at stake, and to assess evidence. For example, to analyze quickly flowing testimony during family land disputes, abunzi drew on their insider knowledge of common practices of land use, partitioning, and inheritance, as well as norms of family relationships, and familiarity with the local population dynamics over decades of recurring violence. They used this information to assess, for example, if an adoption that had not been registered was formal or informal, or if failure to formally partition and bequeath land decades earlier was deliberate or inadvertent. They used general fluency that came from living in the area to assess the evidence people provided—such as proof that an adoption had been formal because, despite a lack of official paperwork, the uncle helped find his nephew a wife (a task reserved for a father figure), and the nephew would swear on his uncle's name (in lieu of his father's name). Often when abunzi or inyangamugayo were describing the details of cases and their judgments to other local authorities, they had to provide lengthy explanations on these details of local practices in order to clarify the details, underscoring the local position of the abunzi or inyangamugayo and the outsider status of the others.

Lay judges often conducted explicit investigations outside trials to learn more about specific details of cases, consistent with the requirements of their inquisitorial role. In Ndora, for example, the presiding judge, Laurence, indicated: "When I have someone's trial scheduled, I talk to people who confessed and were released, then I talk to the survivors asking them about the person in question's conduct during the genocide. Sometimes we even share drinks if necessary. I get down to earth and talk to the layman, for example ask him what he thinks about a given accused person. So I always have information about the accused before the trial."[13]

In land disputes, which made up the vast majority of the cases before comite y'abunzi, the abunzi routinely went to the plot in question to better understand, for example, its size, location, what was on it, or where the demarcations were. Often they sought out elders, who could tell stories about who had lived on the land, when and with whom, and how land had been transferred, officially or unofficially, including before independence and the decades of ensuing political violence. Lay judges also gained information from outside sessions simply by being a part of everyday life. As one inyangamugayo noted, with two small children she did not have the time to conduct focused investigations, but nonetheless "I hear stray information when out and about."[14] Inyangamugayo and abunzi often spoke with people outside trials to ask them to have the courage to testify, or to explain the legal justification for particular decisions to help people come to terms with judgments they did not like.

Inyangamugayo and abunzi did not try to overcome this preexisting knowledge of people, places, and events as a liability but rather used it as an asset in how they evaluated and analyzed evidence presented during trials. That is, without professional attorneys trained to identify material facts or hire expert witnesses, lay judges used their deep contextual knowledge to evaluate testimony and resolve contested factual issues. Generally, they knew (or believed they knew) the context well enough to assess what testimony was plausible and which witnesses were reliable. Many told me they felt that their knowing the context helped them to tell whether someone was being consistent with his or her testimony over time, or with commonly accepted details. They felt they were able to identify false allegations if people suddenly changed their story, for example, while those who had said the same thing for more than a decade, corroborated by others similarly consistent, were likely to be speaking the truth. Inyangamugayo and abunzi all noted that they would never make a judgment based on only one or two witnesses, but sought corroboration to resolve contradictions, both between people and with the same individual, over time. Many judges became adept at identifying patterns and inconsistencies within or across complex testimony, even without sophisticated databases for tracking information. Yet, they felt they could determine the plausibility of testimony because they knew culture, context, and lifestyle well enough to understand what was reasonable. For example, they knew what times of day people were likely to take their cows to graze, and therefore if an assertion of having taken cows to graze was a legitimate alibi. Or they could assess the likelihood of particular crops being ready for harvest at specific times, which related to likely yields of a field that had been looted, and therefore how much someone should repay. Finally, they felt they could assess bias and motivations by learning about social relationships, and what kinds of preexisting enmities or relationships there might be. Lay judges saw their task as embedded in ongoing processes of truth seeking that lasted over years, bigger than any one case session or trial.

What I have sought to demonstrate here is how deeply lay judges' positionality within localized social and knowledge networks influenced their work, and how this intermediary positioning blurred the boundary between state and nonstate, and served to extend the state deeply into people's everyday lives. This is consistent with the previous hundred years, according to historian David Newbury, who illustrated that by the late nineteenth century, the central court's influence penetrated directly to the lowest levels of society (D. Newbury 2009:235). The performative action of Faustin removing and redonning his sash made visible the shifts, sometimes subtle, sometimes explicit, between official and unofficial, state and nonstate, legal and nonlegal, that were at the heart of lay judges' role, and that were crucial to understanding the way lay judges enacted the mediation approach. Seeing these uses of the sash as awkward glitches that resulted from using unprofessional judges dismisses as "noise" practices that were in fact crucial to how state power was exercised and experienced in Rwanda. Through these actions, lay judges showed that the state was not distant but embodied and enacted by neighbors, and consequently, community was not apolitical but instead deeply enmeshed with the exercise of state power.

Legal Aid Clinic Staff as Intermediaries

Thus far I have focused predominantly on abunzi and inyangamugayo, in order to emphasize the natural similarities between how their roles were conceptualized within institutions with similar forms. Legal aid clinic staff members, by contrast, were quite different in their structural position—specifically, they were less clearly insiders, and they were not official representatives of the state. I argue that we can nonetheless see them as intermediaries between people and the state, intermediaries whose exercise of state power was distinct from that of the state's professional representatives.

Most rural Rwandans saw inyangamugayo and abunzi as proximate to them in terms of educational status, economic status, and lifestyle, which was in stark contrast with other representatives of the state in Rwanda who were not so intimately connected to people and knowledge in their jurisdiction. This distinction was particularly clear in rural areas but also manifested itself in towns and cities. Most rural Rwandans perceived the national government to be distant from them, and they felt regional and local authorities were only marginally closer. Professional judges and local administrative authorities—such as mayors, gacaca coordinators, executive secretaries at the cell or sector level, or civil affairs administrators—were predominantly university-educated urban residents. They served in short-term appointments throughout the country, and therefore most maintained their personal connections in Kigali or otherwise outside the cell in which they worked, and most hoped to move into more prestigious positions in more central (that is, urban) locations. They spoke a differently accented Kinyarwanda and typically left the area on weekends, all markers of their outside status. They were not farmers themselves and had rarely grown up

in the immediate area. Many were repatriés who had been raised and educated outside Rwanda, returning after the RPF gained power. Most were
only superficially familiar with the mundane concerns of daily life in rural
Rwanda, such as crop schedules or norms of boundary disputes.

Legal aid clinic staff members were somewhere in between. The law
students and permanent staff members were virtually all outsiders to
Butare, and most were a part of Rwanda's emerging or existing elite (given
both that those who attended the National University of Rwanda tended to
have strong political and economic connections already, and that those who
graduated from the university further increased their symbolic and economic capital). On the other hand, they were less tightly linked to the
regime than the state's official representatives. They were not elected
authorities, nor did they have an official state role, even though people
perceived them as proximate to state power. They often knew people
involved in the disputes they addressed.

Legal aid clinic staff members and students also shared an unprofes-
sional/lay status with abunzi and inyangamugayo, insofar as they were students who had some training in law but were new to their role. There were
idiosyncrasies in how they conducted their work, as they learned by doing.
They too were trained explicitly in the mediation approach. Their work
also was unpaid and was scheduled in among other responsibilities. Ultimately, I suggest it is productive to consider legal aid clinic staff members
as intermediaries who, though they were less consistently situated within
local social and knowledge networks than inyangamugayo and abunzi, were
nonetheless dual and ambiguous representatives of both state and community, and that this was crucial to how they conducted their work.

Operationalizing Mediation and Improvising Authority

I turn now to exploring in more detail how lay judges exercised state power
through advocating harmony in harmony legal models, and how they did
so explicitly from their position as intermediaries within local social and
knowledge networks. That is, I focus now on the mediation role of inyangamugayo and abunzi, and the ways they took seriously, and put into practice,
the mediation principles of compromise and unity. I refer to the way these
lay judges and mediators exercised power as improvisational not to underscore an illogical or haphazard use of authority but to demonstrate how

Figure 12. Legal aid clinic staff members with clients, 2008 (photo by author).

they operationalized mediation principles in different and often creative ways, and how this had the effect of increasing the variation in how state power was exercised and experienced.

Laurence, the presiding judge in Ndora, was likely to take a consensus-based, participatory approach. While presiding, he alternated between directing the questioning and yielding the floor to other judges. He had an even-tempered rapport with witnesses, victims, and defendants. He was willing to correct others' behavior, as the example above showed, but also deliberately solicited feedback from the general assembly to guide the iny-angamugayo's decision making. He had a regular back-and-forth style with participants, asking if everyone agreed with the facts and soliciting advice about what the next step should be to try to get to the bottom of a disputed issue, whether it was about property liability or raising questions as to who made an alarm to summon killers. He tried to help the general assembly members to figure out the logical process for themselves, so it did not all come from the judges. He regularly allowed time for extended interactions between victims and perpetrators in hopes of rebuilding the relationships.

Laurence's insider position shaped how he approached case sessions, and how people responded to him. Laurence often permitted discussions that, though they might seem like unnecessary digressions allowed by an inattentive judge, rather were directly relevant to restoring relationships. In one case in Ndora, for example, he allowed more than an hour of conversation about a bicycle during proceedings against a defendant, Gaspard, accused of locally organizing the genocide as well as committing multiple murders.[15] The bicycle served as a proxy for a discussion of the relationship between the victim and Gaspard. It allowed the victim to reveal that she was upset because Gaspard had mistreated her in the aftermath of the genocide, despite being a friend of her late father. Laurence tried to persuade Gaspard to empathize with the victim's loss without directly addressing liability for the bicycle. He also involved Gaspard's daughter in the discussion, in recognition that the victim and Gaspard were embedded in broader social relationships.

Laurence saw this conversation as one episode in an ongoing process, and he measured incremental progress over time. He knew, for example, that the victim and Gaspard's daughter often sat next to one another during gacaca sessions, suggesting that this relationship between former childhood friends, while uneasy, had not been severed. He used a rhetorical style developed in his role as a pastor, one with which the overwhelmingly Christian participants were familiar and respectful. His good reputation as a pastor buttressed his moral authority to counsel people and make social or moral demands of them, even among those not in his immediate congregation.

Further, Laurence's efforts to rebuild social bonds extended beyond case sessions into ordinary life. For example, in cases where a defendant was released on time served, based on a confession, Laurence typically approached the victims after the trial. He explained:

> I tell them I am sorry. I acknowledge that so many people died and I understand their agony. But I try to explain that since they can't bring back their lost relatives, it is no use having perpetrators who have confessed and shown remorse spend their whole lives in prison. Otherwise, the perpetrator's child would always be mad that

he is in prison because of you, and that creates a vicious cycle. I help them follow up with the only thing they can get back, which is the property. About 80 percent of the survivors are convinced, and forgive. We advise them to watch the conduct of the reintegrated prisoners, to converse with them to find out if they still have ideological tendencies. See if he will help, for example, by sending his child to fetch water when you are sick. Some survivors come to us and tell us that a given person who was reintegrated has really changed.[16]

The presiding judge in Nyanza, Elaste, was more likely to dominate the trial proceedings in his court. Elaste had a commanding presence, prone to giving stern lectures to participants and the general assembly, and wielding authority to confiscate ringing cell phones or detain people for false testimony. Some whispered to me that he was authoritarian. Elaste presided in every session I attended in Nyanza, and he was typically the only judge on the panel to question participants. He often used the fact that witnesses were not allowed to hear one another's testimony to his advantage in evaluating testimony. He would alter what one had said and ask another to corroborate or refute it, in hopes of trapping someone in a lie. He was inclined to give speeches consistent with the mediation principles, combining pleas for reconciliation with threats of sanction. For example, this is a typical example of how he spoke with the participants:

You'll never be peaceful if you carry someone's blood on your hands. It even hinders your daily actions, if you are hiding something, because it makes you afraid. To be at peace, you must come forward and confess your crimes. Only then, when you are brave enough to tell of your crimes, will you get some relief. You will no longer be suspicious and fearful of people finding out. If you confess, it also helps the relatives of the victims. People are traumatized, and need to know about how their loved ones died. The goal of gacaca is to resolve these conflicts here. We need the truth in order to build unity and reconciliation. We are building a better, more peaceful Rwanda.[17]

When there were direct conflicts between participants, or when they became upset, Elaste tended to speak sternly to them, reminding them of their duties, of the goals of the process. He was more likely to lecture than to simply give them time to talk to one another.

By contrast, the presiding judge in Butare had a cerebral, academic style. He questioned people on nuanced points of their arguments. For example, he availed himself of reports written by scholars and human rights researchers about the genocide. During a months-long set of complex cases against dozens of defendants accused of participating in genocide at the hospital in Butare,[18] he regularly thumbed through a copy of a noted book by the NGO African Rights, which included detailed narratives about the dynamics of genocide across Rwanda, including several pages centered on events in the hospital in Butare (African Rights 1995:984–989). That book was based on interviews conducted in the immediate aftermath of the genocide—the kind of in-the-moment, recorded witness interviews that the inyangamugayo typically did not have at their disposal.

The abunzi in Ndora said that they operationalized mediation principles through the process itself, as well as their verdicts. The presiding mediator in Ndora described his method, noting: "We get the public itself to convince the parties of the right or wrong thing to do. We do it in the open, so people are convinced it is not a decision taken just by one individual."[19] The abunzi described efforts to find fair solutions that both parties would accept, rather than simply applying the law. For example, in a case where land inheritance was complicated by an informal adoption two generations earlier, they could have simply said that since the adoption had not been formalized, it was not legal and the descendants had no claim to the land. Instead, they sought to learn of the intent of adoption, opting for a more inclusive view of family and shared responsibility. Often they let cases stretch over several weeks, not out of inefficiency, but rather as a deliberate technique to provide time for tempers to settle, and for the disputing parties to change their positions. The abunzi made clear that being rooted in local networks was the basis for their moral authority. As one said, "People have trust in you because they know you, and they know that you actually know their problems."[20]

Even with this shared participatory approach, abunzi varied in their individual styles. The presiding mediator in Ndora, for example, tended to be fairly controlling, imposing his views on the other mediators. Another mediator was typically quiet, interjecting infrequently but with pointed, revealing questions. Yet another was prone to give long monologues to remind participants of customs, practices, norms, or local history. The abunzi in Nyanza tended to be more procedural, focusing heavily on generating a thick paper trail.

Like the lay judges, legal aid clinic staff members tended to position themselves as peers of their clients, as joint problem solvers rather than external decision makers. They sat next to their clients, in chairs at their level, sometimes even seated on the grass. They chatted about clients' families, held their babies on their laps, lent them coins to make photocopies of documents, even as some lectured sternly. Styles of mediation among the legal aid clinic staff members varied as well, as I illustrated in the previous chapter, though variation seemed linked as much to personal style and to the specific dispute as it did to the institutional framing.

Ultimately, as lay judges donned the mantle of state power to facilitate decentralized legal processes, they did so in ways that supported, undermined, and adapted the processes. Lay judges' improvisational exercise of authority was not random, unstructured, or arbitrary but adaptive, evolving, and varied. Because of their unprofessional status—without years of formal legal education or apprentice-based training—and because of the new nature of the legal institutions within which they worked, lay judges learned primarily by doing. This learning while doing was equally true for the legal aid clinic staff and for abunzi and inyangamugayo. Over time, the lay mediators/judges at the center of these harmony models developed their own styles and systems for questioning and analyzing evidence, for deliberating among themselves, and for advocating the mediation approach to participants. These techniques varied between judges, within panels, and between courts, and thus rendered nonmonolithic the exercise of state power.

Professional Judges and State Representatives: Comparative Perspective

Comparison with other judges adjudicating cases about events in Rwanda—specifically ICTR judges in Arusha and professional domestic judges—brings into relief the way lay judges governed through deliberate and unapologetic community embeddedness, and how they were distinct from other professional representatives of the Rwandan state or law.

Faustin and Vincent's personal testimony stands in stark contrast to the conduct of judges at the ICTR in Arusha, who used professional knowledge to evaluate contested facts about events, places, and people about which they did not have personal knowledge. Very few ICTR judges, if any, had been to Rwanda before beginning their work at the tribunal. Consider Judge Robert Fremr, who came to the court in September 2006, after twenty-six years as a judge in the Czech Republic, most recently on the Supreme Court. When he began his work at the tribunal, he had "just rough ideas about the conflict" in Rwanda based on books he read and documentaries he watched in the weeks and months prior to arriving.[21] He proactively continued to read and learn about Rwanda after his arrival, and when we spoke in March 2008, he was scheduled to visit Rwanda on an official site visit the following month for one of the cases he was hearing, at the request of the prosecution and the defense. This visit would be highly controlled to avoid introduction of evidence that was against the tribunal's rules.

Judge Fremr believed his extensive judicial experience and the ICTR procedures made up for his lack of contextual knowledge. In the ICTR's adversarial system, when a particular factual point was in debate—such as whether a witness could have realistically overheard a conversation from where he was standing—judges did not independently assess the accuracy of the witness's comments. Rather, they applied the tenets of international law to make findings of fact on relevant evidence provided in court by attorneys and witnesses from each side. This was consistent with how Western-derived international legal systems valued using objective judges without a stake in the outcome of, or prior knowledge about, cases.

ICTR judges claimed that more important than possessing knowledge of the people or context was having the capacity to be open-minded and analytic in weighing evidence, traits they gained through professional training and judicial experience. Norwegian judge Erik Møse, on the court since its inception and a two-term president of the tribunal, objected strenuously to the idea that as outsiders, ICTR judges were necessarily unable to assess truth. He said:

> It is a challenge to establish the facts, twelve years later, through barriers of language and culture. We are not Rwandan, we do not form a part of Rwandan culture. But I have been in twelve trials over nine years. I am humble in finding out the truth; I do it with great respect. We learn how to ask questions, there is a lot of deliberate repetition, we keep an open mind. We know the kinds of ways people testify now. Maybe Rwandans are better able to determine when people are telling lies. But we are not too bad here.[22]

The elite cadre of international U.N. judges brought different kinds of legal knowledge to their work, and had varying degrees of familiarity with Rwanda and Africa. Overall, judges claimed that the different positions, experiences, and perspectives of judges on each three-judge panel at the ICTR were additive in how they evaluated testimony. At the same time, the judges at the ICTR felt that reshaping relationships could not realistically be part of their task, because they were geographically distant from Rwanda and not part of the society being rebuilt. They noted that the way the ICTR could contribute to reconciliation in Rwanda was more generally through establishing accountability and countering impunity. These comparisons highlight the very different focus of Rwanda's harmony legal models.

By comparison with ICTR judges, professional Rwandan judges in the country's domestic courts used their legal education and specific judicial training, combined with implicit knowledge of people, events, and places in Rwanda, to evaluate contested facts. They spoke Kinyarwanda as well as French or English, and therefore could hear testimony in participants' native languages. They knew the general physical landscape and layout of the country. Yet professional judges were distant from the networks in rural areas of which most inyangamugayo and abunzi were a part. Professional judges were Rwandan, but most of their social and knowledge networks were located in the capital, among economic and political elites, and extended outside the country. Most ordinary Rwandans in rural areas saw professional judges as outsiders.

Consider Judge Julien Ndinda, who was a judge on the Superior Court of Nyanza, located a hundred yards from the courtyard where people sat for gacaca sessions for Busasamana sector. In conversations with me, he underscored that he did not see himself as sharing in the same knowledge bases as the people he was judging or their neighbors. Judge Ndinda said that whenever possible, he preferred to go onsite to hold trials in the location where events occurred, in front of people who participated or knew about it. He did this for a January 2008 trial against suspects accused of murdering a gacaca judge, holding the trial not in the superior court building in Nyanza but in the local sector where the participants resided. He claimed that this was helpful in assessing truth because while case participants might lie before a judge who they thought did not know something, they would be less likely to lie when the case was tried before their neighbors and peers in the audience. He returned to the trial site to read aloud the judgment in February 2008, which he said was to help ensure transparency and clarity in communication.

Much like the ICTR judges, Rwanda's domestic judges did not see their task as one of rebuilding relationships—that is, they differentiated their approach from the government-through-community self-regulatory governmentality of law-based mediation. They emphasized that their contribution to reconciliation was more broadly by establishing accountability and rule of law through fair judgments. For example, Judge Ndinda emphasized the importance of reading the judgment onsite before the people affected so that they would have full information about it, but he did not talk explicitly about relationships and unity consistent with mediation. Trials in his court focused on evidence related to the truth or falsity of the charges.

On the other hand, government authorities like mayors and national-level gacaca officials clearly saw their task as promoting reconciliation through mediation. Mayors held public "reconciliation meetings" to convince people to resolve property disputes amicably. Staff members of the National Service of Gacaca Jurisdictions, like Albert whose words I described in Chapter 2, visited villages and exhorted people to come together to jointly solve outstanding problems. Yet these authorities, like professional judges, conveyed outsider status that distanced them from the people they sought to help, and their efforts often came across as impositions. People were grateful that national-level authorities could expedite a case or resolve a procedural issue, but they typically found the efforts to rebuild relationships to be pro forma and superficial, more easily ignored than their own engagement with lay judges.

Overall, lay judges' insider status and intermediary position were different from those of other professional representatives of the Rwandan state or international legal institutions. While judges in each court found techniques to assess testimony given their jurisdiction's rules and procedures, only lay judges, consistent with the government-through-community approach, intervened to inculcate active practices of self-management, personal ethics, and collective allegiances among their peers.

Insider Status and Concerns of Bias and Corruption

For lay judges and even legal aid staff to be embedded in local social and knowledge networks, part of the "community" being constituted through top-down forms of governance, invited obvious concerns of bias. People had legitimate concerns about partiality and objectivity among lay judges, as the examples I have illustrated thus far suggest. To evaluate debated facts in courts where they were so personally connected was problematic, because judges could have a stake—emotional or financial—in the outcome of a case. Further, people often feared that without sufficient training and with no lawyers, lay judges might be unable to analyze properly which evidence was relevant. This was particularly true in gacaca with its institutionally engrained view of accusations and culpability. Comite y'abunzi as an institution was not seen as favoring one side, so concerns of bias were less intense, though still ever present.

Much of the existing literature on law in Rwanda emphasizes the corruption, bias, and even illegality of gacaca, and how that undermines the process.[23] Without minimizing the real concerns about corruption, I want to consider these discourses of bias and corruption as a key means through which community and the state were imagined and constituted as fraught and contentious (Gupta 1995; Lazar 2008:82, 90). That is, I leave the task of measuring lay judges' fairness versus corruption to other researchers; rather, here I aim to explore what we can understand about the exercise of state power in the hands of people who were prone to allegations of corruption—lay people who were embedded in local, situated social networks. The deep contextualization of the harmony legal models, and the lay judges at their center, meant no one was objective.

It could be tempting to view the example of Faustin and Vincent as proof that lay judges' insider status was inherently prejudicial and reinforced the institutional bias and victor's justice in the gacaca process, as discussed in Chapter 2. On this particular panel of inyangamugayo, four of the five judges were genocide survivors or repatriés, consistent with what some see as the Tutsi domination of gacaca and of government more broadly, and perhaps enabling Tutsi inyangamugayo to wield power arbitrarily over Hutu defendants and to silence them. Yet, entering into the details suggests that information and relationships judges brought into sessions did not necessarily translate into hardened positions, and inyangamugayo did not always act in parallel with the interest of the institution. It would be obfuscating to dismiss lay judges' insider position as inherently prejudicial. Lay judges acted differently over time and across courts, not always in parallel with the broader leaning of the court. The content of Vincent and Faustin's controversial testimony in Ndora was not simply to implicate the accused. They both provided testimony that corroborated the defendants' claims of innocence of specific charges, as well as testimony that suggested guilt on other charges. Ultimately, Nshimye was sentenced to fifteen years in prison, of which he had already served twelve. Paul was sentenced to twelve years but was released immediately based on time he had already served incarcerated. To reiterate, I offer these details *not* to suggest they serve as proof of absence of corruption, but rather, to ensure the focus on corruption does not obscure variation.

Lay judges could moderate one another's conduct, could change their approach over time, and could testify across ethnic divisions. Laurence showed that inyangamugayo could provide a check on one another's potential for bias by advocating publicly, from his position wearing the sash, for his fellow inyangamugayo to follow the rules of the process. He saw this role as a central part of his job, describing himself as neutral because he was a returnee and not directly accusing anyone. Vincent appeared shamed by Laurence's comments. Laurence's critique likely convinced Faustin to explicitly remove his sash to testify in Paul's trial (rather than just speaking from behind the bench as he had in Nshimye's trial). This is particularly noteworthy because it suggests that Laurence could influence Faustin's behavior, even though Faustin might otherwise be seen as above reproach, since he was a genocide survivor, and, having recently served eight years in the army, was tightly linked to the RPF (even as Faustin's presence on the court was a key example of government surveillance and involvement).

In addition, there was variance in inyangamugayo's and abunzi's behavior over time—that is, this example does not reflect how Vincent and Faustin acted in every trial. Lay judges often policed themselves about whether or not to recuse themselves, and their decisions about how and when to testify could be related to procedural and contextual factors. On days when there were enough inyangamugayo alternates available to reach a quorum, Faustin and Vincent were more likely to recuse themselves, testifying against a defendant as an ordinary participant, or sitting in the general assembly when a relative testified as a victim.[24]

It would be a mistake, then, it seems, to see criticisms of lay judges' bias as reflecting only their inexperience or their insider knowledge. Even the so-called objective international judges at the ICTR, as well as the highly trained domestic judges in Rwanda's Superior Court, faced accusations and concerns about being biased, whether as too sympathetic to the accused or to the victims. Each judge to whom I spoke brought up, unprompted, how he or she faced allegations of bias. The fact that lay judges were a lightning rod for constant accusations of bias tells us not only about the fallibility of the judges but, perhaps more centrally, about the dynamics of the sociopolitical context in which people were complaining.

Lay judges' "partiality" bore the brunt of the criticism when people were dissatisfied with the process or outcome of a trial. In gacaca, families of defendants blamed judges for their long prison sentence, or victims blamed judges for releasing someone who had admitted to killing their loved ones. People complained (either formally or in public gossip) that certain inyangamugayo either had participated in genocide and therefore were likely to exonerate their friends, or that they were survivors and therefore likely to impose collective guilt based on emotion. Disputing parties in comite y'abunzi could rarely agree on three abunzi to hear the case (Organic Law N.31/2006, Article 18), and case proceedings were filled with participants' objections that the umwunzi selected by the other side was negatively predisposed toward them, or that an umwunzi they did not trust was participating too assertively. People whispered allegations that abunzi or inyangamugayo were being bribed, or that they must have been biased due to friendship. Some people suggested that young women were elected only because they were easily influenced (even controlled) by their husbands or fathers, consistent with normative assumptions associated with age and gender, as I have discussed throughout the preceding chapters.

Concerns about bias extended into everyday life, given that abunzi and inyangamugayo lived alongside the participants and moved easily between their official duties and ordinary life. For example, even if an umwunzi regularly socialized with a defendant before the defendant came to trial, she might be viewed suspiciously if she did so in the weeks surrounding the case—perhaps suspected of trying to influence testimony, asking for a bribe, or revealing secrets about the deliberations.

Critiques of bias could escalate to the level of threats against lay judges, particularly inyangamugayo. Although relatively rare, incidents where threats escalated to violence kept fear of retaliation at the forefront in even the most relaxed judge's mind. For example, in October 2007, less than fifty kilometers from Nyanza and Ndora, the president of a gacaca appeals court was killed while walking home from a local bar one night. Nine people were arrested and tried (before Judge Ndinda, mentioned earlier), accused of murdering the victim because he had ruled against them in gacaca cases. Five perpetrators were convicted and sentenced to life in prison in February 2008, and four were exonerated (Prosecution vs. Nyirakiromba et al. 2008). These examples were not frequent, but they are nonetheless powerful for the intensity of emotion they reflected, and the emotions they in turn provoked.

Overall, at the heart of the law-based mediation approach in Rwanda's harmony models was the idea that all Rwandans did, and should, have a stake in the outcome of cases. The government-through-community approach was predicated on the idea that everyone had personal experiences to draw on that would shape how they thought about the trials—that is, it would have been against the intent of the legal model to find judges who were disconnected from local social and knowledge networks. Yet, the networks in which inyangamugayo, abunzi, and even legal aid clinic staff were embedded did not create a coherent, cohesive community of which they were uncontested representatives. Critiques about bias revealed deeper divisions, tension, and distrust, and pointed to the politicization of social dynamics in Rwanda and the high stakes associated with legal processes.

Conclusion

At the gacaca meeting with which I began this chapter, one inyangamugayo in particular, whom I call Cyprian, voiced most clearly the tensions of lay judges' positionality, and brought into relief the fact that lay judges are not best seen as a seamless proxy for regime power. Cyprian served as an example of the way judges across all three meetings expressed frustration and anger with the national office's public performance of oversight, and the ways inyangamugayo stood their ground between both the population's complaints and the national office's regulation. In the Butare meeting, as Patrick prepared to turn the floor over to the inyangamugayo to respond to the particular case concerns he had raised, Cyprian stood up from among the other inynamugayo gathered in the stadium stands to object to the meeting's procedure. Beginning politely but growing increasingly animated and angry, he suggested Patrick should have informed the inyangamugayo of the dossiers in advance in order to better enable the inyangamugayo to respond to specific complaints. The inyangamugayo seated around me began to mutter in frustration, agreeing with Cyprian, as Patrick responded that the inyangamugayo should do their best to respond. The continuing dissatisfaction voiced by the inyangamugayo prompted the other national gacaca representative, who had thus far been seated silently in the front, to rise and admonish the inyangamugayo that it did not make sense to call off the meeting just because people did not like the procedure. As a few inyangamugayo flipped through their notes and began to approach Patrick's table to speak, Cyprian spoke up again, this time from the microphone. He spoke angrily, saying that this meeting was just challenging their judgment and setting them up to rehear trials, rather than helping them resolve the questions they in fact had about the process. He then sat down, folded his arms, and did not speak for the remainder of the meeting, as other inyangamugayo began to address the cases.

My goal in this chapter has been to supplement contemporary understandings of state power in Rwanda by drawing attention to lay judges and mediators as people who implemented one dimension of state power, and who therefore brought state power into being—but, crucially, not simply in a way identical to the formal regime.[25] Attention to the lay judges across three forums shows another dimension of how state power was imagined and exercised by people who embodied state power in improvisational—sometimes ambiguous, sometimes arbitrary, sometimes fair, sometimes corrupt—ways.

I further showed here how lay judges' local positioning was integral to the government-through-community approach. It allowed lay judges to engage in ongoing efforts over time, from a structural position shared with other participants. This is consistent with other periods in Rwanda, when, for example, local authorities such as lineage heads had more moral authority and social influence to resolve disputes than outside chiefs (C. Newbury 1978). At the same time, the lay judges' insider status, which did not correspond with the level of social, political, or economic capital necessary to have influence at the national level, limited their ability to impact the root structural causes of past and present conflicts.

Scholars of Rwanda have emphasized that state power has always been strong, from the highly centralized precolonial kingdom, throughout the colonial period, during the First and Second Republics, even during the genocide, and in the postgenocide period.[26] Work on law in contemporary Rwanda tends to emphasize how legal forums, particularly gacaca, serve as sites of "lawfare, the effort to conquer and control . . . by the coercive use of legal means" (Comaroff 2001:2). I concur with critical scholarship that sees postgenocide Rwanda's legal forums as sites for consolidating and further strengthening centralized government power and extending the reach of the authoritarian, dictatorial regime (see Chapter 2), consistent with dominant characterizations of power and politics in Africa as characterized by excess and consumption aimed to sate its own needs (Bayart 1993 [1989]; Mbembe 2001). Current critiques of Kagame's RPF resonate with Achille Mbembe's claim that "struggles for physical survival and the reproduction of life itself are now the principal stakes in the exercise of power and in the imaginaries of war and democracy in Africa" (Mbembe 2006:312) and with the Comaroffs' assertion that the fetishization of law is a displacement of politics, such that the law has become the medium through which politics are played out (Comaroff and Comaroff 2006:22).

I contend that lay judges are provocative sites in which to explore the exercise of power in Rwanda, given their deliberate (idealized) placement as dual representatives of community and state. This positionality allows us to trace how power moved beyond realms perhaps more traditionally associated with the state through being embodied in individuals who were deeply contextualized in local social and knowledge networks, and therefore how while there was no place "beyond the state" (Jones 2008) in rural Rwanda, the state was varied in how it was expressed. Inyangamugayo and abunzi did not see themselves simply as proxies for the state. Lay judges often chafed against the intervention and oversight of state representatives from the capital, arguing that they knew the local conditions better than the national government delegates did. Gacaca and comite y'abunzi sessions occurring in sites far from Kigali diverged from the central goals of the institution and showed both the strengths and limits of state power. I thus concur with Susan Thomson's argument in the conclusion of her groundbreaking book, *Whispering Truth to Power*, detailing the ways the state penetrates rural life in postgenocide Rwanda that, "rather than taking 'the state' as a point of departure, a focus on the effects of state power on the everyday lives of rural people points to a recognition of multiple actors, agencies, organizations and levels that defies straightforward analysis. For example, research into the practices of local officials is necessary, as it is through these individuals that the majority of rural poor come into contact with 'the state' and where their images of the state are forged" (Thomson 2013:195). Lay judges' improvisational authority shows that through the government-through-community approach, the state extended its power while also ceding its uniformity. Decentralization in Rwanda put the exercise of state power into the hands of people who were minimally trained and inconsistently inculcated in the regime ideology. This meant that state power was improvised and not monolithic.

Legal Architectures of Social Repair

This book refers to three strands of remediation that capture multiple dimensions of how law was invoked as a tool of reconciliation in postgenocide Rwanda. The first strand is the correction of a defect, a reversal or cure of a harmful effect. Specifically, I have attended to how the creation of grassroots legal forums was intended to serve as a remedy for the devastation of the genocide, and to help undo a past history of destructive violence. I have shown how gacaca courts, comite y'abunzi, and the legal aid clinic were all purportedly designed to promote nonviolent dispute resolution at local levels to provide a strong foundation on which the new Rwanda would be built. By emphasizing "mediation," the second strand to which I have drawn attention is how these grassroots legal forums were specifically built on having third-party actors—lay judges or mediators—attempt to broker compromises based on unity between disputants across a wide range of disputes. I have explored how this emphasis on harmony was a form of government through community. The final strand that the title emphasizes is "re" in the sense of "again," to remind us that the harmony-based practices we see in grassroots legal forums were a reinvocation of an earlier supposedly traditional or cultural practice. I have shown how this cultural justification was central to the call for a specific kind of unity that defined the terms of naturalized Rwandan-ness.

I have situated the book squarely within the broad literature that analyzes and critiques the humanitarianism, peace-building, and transitional justice industries by laying bare the assumptions under which they operate and the ways these institutions and interventions often paradoxically and perversely reinforce the conditions they intend to repair.[1] In doing so, I take seriously the laudable goals of the policy interventions put in place.

I have shown how within these forums people debated the micropolitics of reconciliation, contesting meanings of family, community, gender, exchange, guilt and innocence, and ultimately citizenship, as related to the genocide. Decentralized legal forums' public, contextualized, ongoing processes enabled interactions that were one part of restoring social connections, alongside divisions and scars. They provided dynamic processes for negotiating bonds in a context of social fragility. They were a powerful, albeit ambivalent, tool for addressing micro-level, situated tensions, which is necessary, though not sufficient, for ending collective violence on the ground and ensuring stability of regional, national, and transnational settlements.[2]

And yet, I have shown the dangers of depoliticization produced by framing law-based reconciliation in terms of interpersonal relationships, especially by an authoritarian state. That is, "love is not enough" to cement a departure from violence (Nader 2003). Focusing law on relationships tends to ignore the political-economic forces, including deep power imbalances, that drove and continue to drive conflict. The emphasis on relationships within grassroots law had parallels in NGO mental health interventions in postwar Liberia, where trauma interventions were similarly aimed to manage, not to cure, and to promote pro-social forms of sociality (Abramowitz 2014:6–7). Merry has shown in other contexts how mediators often invoke moral and therapeutic discourses, even while being deeply embedded in the trappings of the legal, which serves to perpetuate subtle cultural domination (1990:132–133). Indeed, the fact that law is used as much to avert change and maintain status quo configurations of power as it is to produce transformation is one of the "irreconcilable challenges" (Leebaw 2008) of transitional justice. The grassroots legal forums in Rwanda did not address national-level issues which drove the genocide, and which continued to be a problem, such as tight control of political power and economic resources in the hands of few and economic marginalization of large portions of the population.

Further, state-backed involvement in these legal forums was not benign. Harmony had a dark side, and mediation in grassroots legal forums was deeply authoritarian and violent in some of its manifestations. The grassroots legal forums even served as a form of lawfare, exacerbating the pervasive ongoing forms of physical, symbolic, or structural violence, for example, through institutional biases that dominated Hutu men, or through threats or actual violence against survivors who testified before gacaca. They certainly did not stop the Rwandan regime from continuing to export its war to the DRC or to engage in violence against its citizens within national borders; deeply troubling developments in these respects continued even as I was writing this Conclusion in early 2015. Grassroots mediation-based legal forums did not inoculate against all future problems and threats of rupture. They surely could have been designed to better do so, particularly by allowing robust conversations without risk of criminalization for alternate political views.

Yet, beyond pointing out these strengths and weaknesses, many interlocutors have asked me for more specificity in proffering conclusions, particularly those from academic disciplines that are less tolerant of the critical deconstruction at the heart of mainstream contemporary cultural anthropology, those who work daily as peace practitioners in conflict and postconflict zones without the luxury of endless complexifying, as well as the Rwandans living through the morass of the genocide's aftermath. I find it difficult to provide normative solutions; living in Rwanda and conducting ethnographic research there, engaging with and reflecting on Rwanda from the outside for more than a decade, requires (and begets) humility and nuance in learning from people living with the legacy of unthinkable violence, alongside conviction to speak against that violence and its transmutation in the present. Perhaps what the grassroots legal forums examined here and the stories I have told about people within them can best lay bare is conundrums of legalized reconciliation, and how they push us to rethink certain dimensions of law and reconciliation. I close by offering not solutions but suggestions and cautions.

My first suggestive caution is to move beyond the often simplified valorization of "culture" in law given the fluidity of cultural practice and the ways that culture is politicized, and to consider the value of contextualization. What I am reiterating here is that, contrary to the Rwandan government's official discourse, the power of these legal forums did not derive from their being inherently "cultural, Rwandan" institutions, based in customary law and therefore better in an African context. Rather, it lay primarily in their being socially embedded and contexualized. My argument here is consistent with Rosalind Shaw and Lars Waldorf's call for "reframing 'the local'" away from a specific place or culture to instead a "place-based" standpoint that takes into account the perspectives and experiences of people the forums intend to benefit (Shaw and Waldorf 2010a:6, 25). Their being contextualized meant the forums were a relevant—even if hated—part of people's lives. As I showed across the chapters, participation in legal forums was a part of daily practice, intertwined with friends, family, and neighbors, and embedded in the physical landscape. The decentralized legal forums placed individuals and their stories at the center. Wide rules of evidence allowed for broad conversations, in lieu of proceedings narrowly restricted by concerns of relevance to specific points of law or distracted by objections and complex rules of procedure. Case sessions were part of longer-term, deeply situated social processes and interactions, including more multidimensional and iterative reconstruction efforts occurring across a variety of institutional mechanisms. Finding ways to contextualize and embed legal processes—ideally in culturally informed ways—could perhaps serve as a useful point of departure for creating spaces in which people can negotiate productive social transformations.

My second caution is not to allow the emphasis on the very real problems of state intervention in grassroots legal forums to blind us to other sources of division and inequality. Asserting that the state is primarily to blame for the negative effects of legalized reconciliation efforts suggests the corollary, that grassroots, bottom-up processes are the only repository of real social transformation. Valorizing grassroots processes ignores how even the most locally rooted civil society movements are typically interconnected with national and transnational discourses and institutions that cannot be considered free from state intervention, and are suffused with power dynamics, hierarchies, and forms of violence. Even in precolonial and colonial Rwanda, for example, a drumming practice called *ngoma* that was used to address threats to social reproduction by invoking the spirits of the dead was tightly under the king's control (Janzen and Janzen 2000; Janzen 1992).

Centering critiques on "the state" for generating divisive and unequal dimensions of grassroots legal forums echoes the postgenocide government's master narrative in blaming the West for introducing division to Rwanda. Of course, I believe fundamentally in the importance of critiquing and deconstructing both domestic and international interventions, in order to lay bare how power operates through institutions. But, without absolving the Rwandan state, we must recognize how placing primary blame on state interventions for fomenting or exacerbating divisions risks paralleling the government's master narrative in holding dear the core of a romanticized notion that there is a space outside the state (or, prior to Western intervention) where a kinder, gentler reconciliation can occur, absent power relations of class or gender or age, or other forms of silencing. While state-backed legal forums increase coercion and structural violence in efforts to promote unity and provide perverse incentives for instrumentality, they do not create them ex nihilo—akin to the effects of global processes in Rwanda's social history, which promoted conditions to exacerbate ethnic divisions, for example, but did not create them out of nothing.

I suggest that one underexplored dimension in the relationship between state power and existing divisions and inequalities is how the waiting itself in and around the edges of these legal forums produced forms of sociality. The sociality of waiting, I suggest, was a doing of something, an active, performative, communicative practice amid the transitional uncertainties of postgenocide Rwanda. That is, Rwanda's legal processes produced unexpected practices of waiting in which social work happened, similar to how scholars have analyzed how waiting in postwar Bosnia (Hromadžić 2014) or in India (Jeffrey 2010) is a work of forming social solidarity and a means of navigating an ambiguous present.

My third caution grows out of the second: we should consider broadening our notion of reconciliation, including relinquishing the idea that there is a benign reconciliation practice out there, if only we can design the right process to facilitate it. It is an anthropological truism that all forms of community involve power relations, hierarchy, and exclusions. Our ideas of power-free cultural practices in the past or the present are more fiction than empirical fact. There are surely examples of acts of generosity, forgiveness, and redemption between former enemies, but I am unconvinced that they are the norm rather than the exception, or that they can be institutionalized and rendered mandatory. Nonstate, localized processes of social reconstruction can be deeply aggressive and silencing (Das 2007; Theidon 2006). For example, Christy Schuetze has illustrated how spirit possession in Mozambique can redress acts of political violence between neighbors, but in ways in which "the rage and vengeance of the victims of violence—of those who were offended in the deepest possible way—gains expression and the ugliness and violence of war can resurface in people's lives" (Schuetze 2013). Sharika Thiranagama has argued in relation to Sri Lanka that "the constant remaking of life . . . is as much a sign of violence as it is an act of 'healing'" (Thiranagama 2011:104). In the face of such compelling empirical evidence, might we need to acknowledge that reconciliation, like social healing, at its core involves the more unsavory sides of human sociality?

Specifically, I suggest grassroots legal forums had the potential to serve as what Steven Feierman has called institutions of social healing, prevalent in Africa, which address a variety of threats to social reproduction, including poverty, hunger, disease, or violence and are fundamentally about rebuilding networks of relationships between people, creating alliances of mutual support and moral community (Feierman 1995; Feierman and Janzen 1992; Janzen 2010). These ideas are at the heart of the government-through-community approach and the emphasis on harmony in Rwanda's contextualized legal forums. Further, social healing involves ambivalent power, to injure as well as to restore, and is intimately tied up with danger and violence (Ashforth 2000; Schoenbrun 2010). That is, it can escalate tensions even as it resolves others, as we saw in grassroots legal forums. Finally, social healing rituals, movements, or discourses often operate as a kind of public sphere in which public opinion is shaped and ultimately feeds back to influence the state, though the forms of communicative practice may not mirror the rational Enlightenment debate that Habermas imagined.[3] Social healers have historically worked against forms of established political order and authority, and healing movements provided contexts in which people criticized and evaluated their leaders and the sociopolitical context (Feierman 1995). This is akin to how I have traced throughout the book how Rwandans used these legal forums to contest authority and legitimacy of power at multiple levels of scale, and to improvise how authority is exercised.

Overall, considering grassroots legal forums in relation to institutions of social healing historicizes and contextualizes efforts at social repair while also underscoring that "cultural" forms of social rebuilding are always already political, and social repair is inherently tied up with violence and social critique. There is a deep history of contextualized institutions and metaphors of healing in Rwanda, including Nyabingi mediumship, ngoma drumming, and populist religious movements called *Kubordwa*.[4] Yet they were surprisingly absent in the postgenocide period.[5] At the same time, Christopher Taylor (1992) has deftly shown how Rwandan cultural logics of healing have historically blurred the boundaries between physical and social realms, and have changed in relation to political-economic transformations, leading us to ask how social healing might manifest in the present, in relation to contemporary political-economic transformations.

What, then, are we to make of reconciliation in postgenocide Rwanda? Two conclusions about reconciliation seem to emerge from the research: the national policy on unity and reconciliation does not represent the views of ordinary Rwandans in a one-to-one way, and Rwandans themselves hold a wide range of views on reconciliation, with variance of opinion on whether it involves punishment and what its relationship is to revenge;

whether it requires forgiveness; whether *kubana*, living together, sometimes glossed as coexistence, is the only realistic option as distinct from *kwiyunga*, the stronger form of reconciliation; and whether it is forward looking or backward looking.[6] Ultimately, whether "reconciliation" is understood as the sharing of individual narratives of suffering (Burnet 2012) or as "repeated social activity and coexistence but not necessarily about ideas shared and meanings fixed" (Finnstrom 2010:136), the Rwanda example shows that these processes are neither gentle nor teleological. The work of building and rebuilding social networks among "intimate enemies" (Theidon 2012)—including, I would add, within families coping with the hardship and insecurities of violence—in the aftermath of war and amid ongoing political repression was contentious, suffused with hostility and instrumentality. It was not linear. It could come in some areas and not others, emerging in fits and starts. It was patchwork, piecemeal, staggered, with setbacks.

I close with words spoken to me by a Rwandan friend and colleague in July 2008, which capture the complexity of hope, fear of repetition, and the elusiveness of reconciliation. He said,

> Rwanda is facing the same problems as before, it is looking like it did in 1985 and 1986. This is how the struggle started last time. Maybe this is why I survived, so I could bear witness to how it is being recreated in the same way. When you drive around Kigali, you see things that are very troubling. For example, there are lots of very nice cars in Kigali, very nice cars. But who owns all of them? Who is driving them? There are still very few people getting rich. Rwanda is diverse, but the power structure is not. They are starting to open up education, but there are still few job opportunities. That is a problem. If war breaks out again, this time I will get out.

As Agathe had reflected a few months earlier, "We wonder how this will work out."

Notes

Introduction

1. For more on rebuilding postgenocide Rwanda, see Burnet 2012; Clark 2010; Straus and Waldorf 2011; Thomson 2013.

2. For details on the genocide, see for example Des Forges 1999; Fujii 2009; C. Newbury 1995; D. Newbury 1998; Straus 2006; Taylor 1999; Umutesi 2004.

3. Law N.39 of 12/03/99 On the Establishment of the National Unity and Reconciliation Commission. Rwandan Constitution, Article 178.

4. For critiques of the policy of national unity and reconciliation, see especially Lemarchand 2009; Meierhenrich 2008; Thomson 2013.

5. National Service of Gacaca Jurisdictions. http://www.inkiko-gacaca.gov.rw/En/EnObjectives.htm. Accessed February 1, 2011.

6. Interview, Alphonse. June 4, 2008. Ndora.

7. National Service of Gacaca Jurisdictions, http://www.inkiko-gacaca.gov.rw. Accessed February 2, 2011. See online archive: http://web.archive.org/web/20110927164427/http://www.inkiko-gacaca.gov.rw/En/EnObjectives.htm.

8. Interview, legal aid clinic director. June 3, 2008. Ndora.

9. Interview, Ndora resident. February 22, 2008. Ndora.

10. See, e.g., Clark 2010; Cruvellier 2010; Eltringham 2010; Ingelaere 2009; Palmer 2015; Peskin 2008; Thomson and Nagy 2011; Waldorf 2006; Wilson 2011.

11. Interview, mayor. August 2007. South Province. ("Comite y'abunzi n'a rien à voir avec gacaca.")

12. Interview, Ndayisaba. January 25, 2007. Ndora.

13. Government of Rwanda, http://www.gov.rw. Accessed February 2, 2011. See online archive: http://web.archive.org/web/20110421133434/http://www.gov.rw/page.php?id_article =19.

14. National Service of Gacaca Jurisdictions, http://www.inkiko-gacaca.gov.rw. Accessed February 2, 2011. See online archive: http://web.archive.org/web/20110927164212/http://www.inkiko-gacaca.gov.rw/En/Generaties.htm

15. Burnet 2012:196; C. Newbury 1978:20; Reyntjens 1985:150–152; Reyntjens 1990; Rose 1996:6–7.

16. See, e.g., Bohannan 1957; Colson 1953, 1974; Evans-Pritchard 1940; Gibbs 1967; Gluckman 1955; Rose 1999; Schapera 1955.

17. Chanock 1985; Colson 1974; Comaroff and Roberts 1981; Mann and Roberts 1991; Moore 1986; Obarrio 2014; Reyntjens 1990.

234 Notes to Pages 14–44

18. Abel 1982a:270; Abel 1982b:6; Auerbach 1983:15; Merry 1993:56; Merry and Milner 1993:5.

19. Burnet 2010; Ingelaere 2009; Thomson 2011a.

20. See also Nader 2002b:44; Nader and Grande 2002.

21. Mattei and Nader 2008:18, 78; Merry 1993:39; Nader 1999a, 2002a:54, 2002b:44; Nader and Grande 2002.

22. See also Abel 1982:7; Merry 1990:179; Nader 1988:269, 276.

23. Mattei and Nader 2008:77–78; Nader 2002:54; Nader and Grande 2002:591.

24. Abel 1982a; Mattei and Nader 2008:18; Nader 1988:275, 1993:440, 2002:48–49.

25. Buckley-Zistel 2006a, 2006b; Burnet 2009; Lemarchand 2009:99–108; C. Newbury and D. Newbury 1999; Thomson 2011a:374–377. See also Hintjens 2008 and McLean Hilker 2012 for how ethnicity is reinforced.

26. See also Greenhouse et al. 1994:130, 141; Lazarus-Black 2007:139–157; Merry 1990:177–180; Wilson 2003:189.

27. Burnet 2010; Ingelaere 2009; Thomson and Nagy 2011; Waldorf 2010.

28. Research has shown this same effect in psychosocial interventions to address trauma (Abramowitz 2014; Locke 2012), as I discuss in more detail in the Conclusion.

29. See also Bolten 2012a; Englund 2002; Finnstrom 2008; Kelly 2008; Lubkemann 2008; Moran 2006; Neofotistos 2012; Theidon 2012

30. See, e.g., Derrida 2001; Minow 1998.

31. See, for example, Buckley-Zistel and Zolkos 2011; Burnet 2012; Helms 2013; Irvine and Hays-Mitchell 2012; Moran 2010.

32. All other provinces had between 274 (North) and 1,981 (East). National Service of Gacaca Jurisdictions, July 2008, author's files.

33. Interview, Chargé d'État Civil. July 7, 2008. Ndora.

34. GEOHIVE/National Institute of Statistics. http://www.geohive.com/cntry/rwanda .aspx. Accessed January 31, 2011.

35. Interview, Chargé d'État Civil. July 7, 2008. Ndora.

36. Geohive/National Institute of Statistics in Rwanda. http://www.geohive.com/cntry/ rwanda.aspx. Accessed January 31, 2011.

37. Interview, Gacaca coordinator for Nyanza District. January 30, 2008. Nyanza.

38. Burnet 2012; Finnstrom 2010; Greenhouse et al. 2002; Theidon 2012; Thiranagama 2011.

Chapter 1. Silencing the Past

1. The other sites were Gisozi, Bisesero, Nyarabuye, Nyamata, Rebero, Ntarama. ("Memorandum sur les sites mémoriaux du génocide." Musée National du Rwanda. December 2003. In author's possession.)

2. The elderly man's image is featured on the cover of Totten and Ubalbo's *We Cannot Forget: Interviews with Survivors of the 1994 Genocide in Rwanda* (2011, Rutgers University Press).

3. See, e.g., Buckley-Zistal 2006b, Burnet 2012, Thomson 2013, Zorbas 2009.

4. For Rwandan precolonial history, see Jan Vansina and David Newbury. For colonial history, see Catharine Newbury, René Lemarchand, and Filip Reyntjens.

5. See, e.g., Burnet 2012; Eltringham 2004; Ingelaere 2010:53; Lemarchand 2009:99–108; Meierhenrich 2008; Newbury 2009:19; Pottier 2002; Reyntjens and Vandeginste 2005; Straus and Waldorf 2011:11–12; Thomson 2013; Vidal 2001; Zorbas 2004, 2009.

6. To justify the Rwandan kingdom as a basis for unified national identity, the postgenocide government used a version of history that was consolidated and gained legitimacy in the
writings of Abbé Alexis Kagame, a Catholic priest and court intellectual in the 1940s. Scholars
and politicians have drawn on Abbé Kagame's historical works as received truth, and even
ten years after the genocide his legacy was "still rooted in the general historical consciousness
of Rwandans and it still dominate[d] the perception of Rwanda's history" (Vansina 2004:4).
Yet, beginning in the 1960s, several scholars persuasively demonstrated how this official version of court history could not be uncritically accepted as objective historical truth, because
it derived from a "single reservoir of traditions," though masking itself through tautological
corroboration with other sources (Newbury 2009:19; Vansina 2004:4–12). They showed how
Abbé Kagame's history was developed in dialogue with the royal court and therefore should
be understood to reflect the views and interpretations of the royal court and its official ideo-
logues, including the Catholic "white fathers" (De Lame 2005; Des Forges 1995:44; Longman
2010a:63; Newbury 2009:19; Newbury and Newbury 2000; Vansina 1985, 2004:4).

7. Scholars have shown that ubuhake, particularly as it existed in the colonial period,
was not representative of all patron-client institutions across time; it changed over the centuries, and clientship took many forms—whether the exchange centered on land or cattle,
whether the contract was between individuals or corporate groups, and what degree of power
differential existed between patron and client—and the degree of reciprocity and benefit in
the clientship relationship varied (Newbury 1988; Vansina 2004). Patrons were not always
omnipotent and unrestrained because in periods and regions when the central government
was still limited, lineage heads were the main political leaders and could limit patrons' power
(Newbury 1988:90). In early clientship and up to the mid-nineteenth century, there were
often strong social relations between patrons and clients, as clients derived significant benefits
from the relationship, patrons made limited demands, and clients' negotiating position was
fairly strong (Newbury 1988:79–82).

8. Vansina argues that in the eighteenth century, the first direct and institutionalized use
of Tutsi versus Hutu came in relation to combatants and noncombatants in armies that were
part of territorial expansion, meaning Tutsi referred to those with power (Vansina 2004:134).

9. Speke described his view in a section headed "Theory of Conquest of Inferior by
Superior Races": "It appears impossible to believe, judging from the physical appearance of
the [Tutsi], that they can be of any other race than the semi-Shem-Hamitic of Ethiopia. The
traditions of the imperial government of Abyssinia go as far back as the scriptural age of King
David. . . . Junior members of the royal family . . . created separate governments, and, for
reasons which cannot be traced, changed their names. . . . [They] cross[ed] the Nile close to
its source . . . where they lost their religion, forgot their language, extracted their lower
incisors like the natives, changed their national name. . . . We are thus left only the one very
distinguishing mark, the physical appearance of this remarkable race . . . as a *certain* clue to
their Shem-Hamitic origin" (Speke 1863:246–250). Speke's hypothesis was consistent with
prevailing Western understandings of human variation at the time as determined by race,
according to which each race had distinct physical, behavioral, and psychological characteristics, and races were hierarchically organized, reflecting different stages of human evolution.
Speke's analysis had neither empirical evidence nor explanation for how and why these supposed transformations and loss of identity occurred, yet it served as a "convenient paradigm
for others uncritically to follow" (Newbury and Newbury 2000:852) and informed more than
a century of scholarship on, and administrative rule in, Rwanda and Africa more broadly.

10. In a typical example, Westermann wrote in 1934: "The significance of the Hamites in the composition of the African population consists in the fact that as nomads and conquering warriors they have . . . pushed their way into the countries of the Negroes. Owing to their racial superiority they gained leading positions and became the founders of many of the larger states in Africa" (Westermann 1949 [1934]:13–14).

11. Maquet's work—which was widely disseminated to other scholars of Africa, particularly in the works of Lucy Mair (1962; 1974; 1977)—marked a shift from earlier scholarship in that Maquet did not argue that the differences were genetic but instead stressed that Rwandans *believed* these perceptions, which correlated with physical stereotypes, about themselves and others. He reaffirmed that Tutsi were outsiders who "came into Rwanda as conquerors," and who asserted superiority over Hutu (Maquet 1961:10–12, 170; Maquet 1970:106), but rather than try to justify how this rightfully predisposed Tutsi to rule, he aimed to explain the existing deep social inequalities in Rwanda. He called the ethnic stratification a caste system, underscoring how people experienced ethnic group membership as permanent and closed, and linked to power or domination. This perspective thus contributed to emphasizing the rigid and static nature of interethnic relations in Rwanda (Codere 1962).

12. By the 1950s and 1960s, scholars no longer defended views of Tutsi as a biologically superior race, but, with the notable exception of d'Hertefelt (1971), they nonetheless maintained the view that the two groups were physically distinct with separate origins, arguing now that these differences could be attributed to environmental and sociopolitical factors (Hiernaux 1963; Hiernaux 1975 [1974]; Rodney 1972:137–141).

13. See, e.g., African Rights 1995; Des Forges 1999; Fujii 2009; Hatzfeld 2005; Janzen and Janzen 2000; Prunier 1995; Straus 2006; Taylor 1999, 2002.

14. See, e.g., Gourevitch 1998; Lemarchand 2009:49–68; Mamdani 2001; Prunier 1995; Semujanga 2003; Twagilimana 2003.

15. See, e.g., Codere 1962, 1973; Hiernaux 1963, 1975 [1974]; Mair 1962; Maquet 1961, 1970; Seligman 1930; Speke 1863; Westermann 1949 [1934].

16. Debates continue over the precise dates of Rwabugiri's reign (e.g., Vansina 2004:209–211).

17. Uburetwa was the only traditional obligation that remained legal under colonialism. Unlike other taxes and prestations that were monetized by 1934, colonial leaders felt that uburetwa was so central to the sociopolitical order that to replace it "would undermine the chief's authority over the population," and they did not fully convert it to cash payment until 1949 (Newbury 1980a:112, 141; Reyntjens 1985:133–142).

18. Brauman et al. 2000:148; Davenport and Stam 2009; Des Forges 1999; Lemarchand 2009:89–91; Nduwayo 2002:11–16; Prunier 2009:12–24; Ruzibiza 2005:334–336; Straus and Waldorf 2011; Thomson 2013.

19. See Lemarchand 2009:64–65; Newbury 1997:53; Reyntjens 2009; Vansina 2004:52–53. Geographical areas were incorporated into the kingdom at different periods over time, typically by force, and therefore the degree of royal court penetration and resulting sociopolitical impacts varied dramatically by region and period (Newbury 1988:8; Vansina 2004). Conquered peoples were not always easily enfolded, meaning there was variance in who was considered "Rwandan," and how "Rwandan" they were (Newbury 2009:204–228; Vansina 2004:156). These variations were particularly pronounced in the north and northwest, which were incorporated late, and where differences remained relevant in later political developments (De Lame 2005:45; Lemarchand 1970).

20. Even as early as the seventeenth century, class differences were emerging, and some institutional forms were introduced that came to play a role in social stratification later on, such as ubuhake and corvée (forced) labor (Vansina 2004:20, 32–33). During the eighteenth century, the kingdom expanded and centralized, which resulted in the consolidation of an elite class and increasingly rigid, hierarchical social stratification by the end of the century (Newbury 2009:204–228, 319; Vansina 2004:88, 123, 136). Patron-client relations changed, as ubuhake contracts, which were a tool of state expansion, extended deeper into society, adopted first among the king and his allies, then between herders of unequal power (Vansina 2004:48). Further, during this period, corvée labor practices increased, typically falling on the socially weakest people (Vansina 2004:97). The elite versus ordinary person divide and the civil war at the end of the eighteenth century (1796–1801) both belied claims of unity in this period.

21. Particularly in the north and northwest (incorporated late into the kingdom), lineage-based organization related to land ownership remained more vigorous than in other areas of the country (De Lame 2005:45; Reyntjens 1987:93). Family belonging changed with the economic and political changes, particularly with monetization, commodification of labor, and mobility (Jefremovas 2002:85–93). Patronage and client ties—in the form of personal connections more so than formalized contracts—continued to play a role in access to resources, particularly land, political and economic power, and security after independence (Jefremovas 2002; Pottier 2006).

22. North and south were in ongoing opposition beginning with the revolution, where northern Hutu advocated a more conservative agenda than southern; the same division was behind the 1973 coup when northern Hutu took over from southern; and this division fueled competition between regionally based political parties after multipartyism was legalized in the 1990s, which increased political tension in the lead-up to 1994 (Lemarchand 1970; Reyntjens 1985; Twagilimana 2003).

Chapter 2. Escaping Dichotomies

1. See Mary Moran with respect to postwar Liberia, how transformations in gender ideology "must be seen as grounded in *both* pre-war social institutions and forms of authority as well as in the new opportunity structures characterizing both the wartime and post-war contexts" (2012:52, see also 2006).

2. See Ministry of Local Government 2008b:4; Constitution of the Republic of Rwanda 2003, Article 167.

3. Interview, Chargé d'État Civil. July 7, 2008. Ndora.

4. National Service of Gacaca Jurisdictions promotional print materials. Received July 2007. Author's personal files.

5. For analyses of African law under colonial rule, see Chanock 1985; Mann and Roberts 1991; Moore 1986; Nader 2002. For information on Rwandan law under colonial rule, see Reyntjens 1985.

6. See, e.g., Amnesty International 2002:20–21; Clark 2010:52, Gasibirege 2002; Jones 2010:56, Reyntjens and Vandeginste 2005:118.

7. Most authors writing about precolonial gacaca do not cite primary sources or historical material, so it is difficult to locate the historical roots of precolonial gacaca versus the ideas that circulate about it. As several Rwandan studies show, by the late 1990s and early 2000s, most Rwandans believed that gacaca was part of the Rwandan precolonial heritage, that in its

original precolonial form it contributed to rebuilding communities, and even helped eliminate hereditary hatreds (Gasibirege 2002; Runyange 2003).

8. The information I provide throughout this chapter about law under colonial rule, unless otherwise noted, comes from Filip Reyntjens's *Pouvoir et Droit au Rwanda* (1985).

9. It is less clear precisely how the customary courts related to informal gacaca processes in the precolonial period. Were conciliation tribunals an attempt to formalize ad hoc gacaca proceedings, or did the systems continue to exist in parallel? Overall, the colonial period did not erase gacaca but weakened it, primarily by greatly reducing the authority of lineage heads, who were the key leaders of gacaca (Runyange 2003:54). Conventional wisdom suggests that gacaca continued to exist, but in a diluted form that varied by location (Amnesty International 2002; Clark 2010).

10. Ministry of Justice promotional materials. http://www.minijust.gov.rw/spip.php?article23. Accessed December 15, 2010.

11. See Hayner 2011; Hinton 2010; Roht-Arriaza and Mariezcurrena 2006; Shaw et al. 2010; Teitel 2000, 2003.

12. Information on postgenocide domestic legal challenges is compiled from Amnesty International 2002; Prunier 2009; Sibomana 1999; Reyntjens and Vandeginste 2005; Maganarella 2000; Des Forges 1999; Jones 2010.

13. For more detail specifically on legal responses to the genocide—the ICTR and gacaca—see Clark 2010; Jones 2010; Maganarella 2000; Peskin 2008; Wilson 2011.

14. ICTR website, http://www.unictr.org/Cases/StatusofCases/tabid/204/Default.aspx. Accessed December 26, 2010.

15. International Criminal Court website. http://www.icc-cpi.int/en_menus/asp/states%20parties/Pages/the%20states%20parties%20to%20the%20rome%20statute.aspx. Accessed May 20, 2015.

Chapter 3. Gacaca Days and Genocide Citizenship

1. Gacaca session. 2008. Ndora.

2. For an explanation of the creation of gacaca, see Clark 2010.

3. National Service of Gacaca Jurisdictions office. July 2008. Kigali.

4. Information provided by officials at the National Service of Gacaca Jurisdictions office. July 2008. Kigali.

5. Initially there were four categories of crimes but they were streamlined, basically combining Categories Two and Three to make a total of three.

6. Gacaca community meeting. 2008. Ndora.

7. National Service of Gacaca Jurisdictions, http://www.inkiko-gacaca.gov.rw. Accessed February 2, 2011. See online archive: http://web.archive.org/web/20110927164427/http://www.inkiko-gacaca.gov.rw/En/EnObjectives.htm.

8. Gacaca session. 2007. Nyanza.

9. Government of Rwanda. http://www.gov.rw. Accessed February 2, 2011. See online archive: http://web.archive.org/web/20110421133434/http://www.gov.rw/page.php?id_article=19.

10. National Service of Gacaca Jurisdictions, http://www.inkiko-gacaca.gov.rw. Accessed February 2, 2011. See online archive: http://web.archive.org/web/20110927164212/http://www.inkiko-gacaca.gov.rw/En/Generaties.htm.

11. National Service of Gacaca Jurisdictions, http://www.inkiko-gacaca.gov.rw. Accessed February 2, 2011. See online archive: http://web.archive.org/web/20110927164427/http://www.inkiko-gacaca.gov.rw/En/EnObjectives.htm.

12. Gacaca session. 2008. Ndora.

13. Gacaca session. 2007. Ndora.

14. Gacaca session. 2008. Ndora.

15. Gacaca session. 2007. Nyanza.

16. Gacaca session. 2007. Ndora.

17. Gacaca session. 2007. Ndora.

18. Information provided by National Service of *Gacaca* Jurisdictions office, on file with author. July 2008. Kigali. Cases received nationwide between July 15, 2006 and December 31, 2007: 612,151 cases at cell level out of 1,127,706 total.

19. Interview, Ndora resident. May 5, 2008. Ndora.

20. See also Burnet 2012:205; Clark 2010; Ingelaere 2008:51, 55–56; Ingelaere 2009:509, 513; Rettig 2011:195; Thomson 2011:380–381; Waldorf 2006:71.

21. Interview, law student. November 22, 2007. Butare.

22. Interview, Agathe. May 5, 2008. Ndora.

23. Gacaca session. 2007. Ndora.

24. For reification of identity in the master narrative, see Buckley-Zistel 2006a, 2006b; Burnet 2009; Thomson 2011a:374–377.

25. See also Nguyen (2010) for therapeutic citizenship in relation to HIV/AIDS in West Africa, and James (2010) for traumatic citizenship in Haiti, though she steps back from designating it as citizenship, arguing the categorization is produced in relation to more fluid constellations and processes.

26. See, e.g., Bolten 2012 on Sierra Leone; Lubkemann 2008 on Mozambique; Taussig 2003 on Colombia; Theidon 2012 on Peru; Thiranagama 2011 on Sri Lanka.

27. See the Introduction for a discussion of Alphonse's trial.

28. Gacaca session. 2008. Ndora.

29. Gacaca charge sheet, obtained from inyangamugayo in Ndora, and through the Ministry of Justice, author's files.

30. Interview, genocide survivor. June 9, 2008. Kigali.

31. Gacaca sessions. 2007. Butare.

32. Gacaca session. 2007. Kigali.

33. See also Chakravarty 2014 for a similar argument on the existence of a moderate, middle ground among ordinary rural Hutu.

34. For victimhood as politicized in Haiti, see James 2010. For more on the moral purity of the category of victim in Bosnia-Herzevovinia, see Helms 2013.

35. Interview, Nyanza resident. December 28, 2007. Nyanza.

36. Interview, Nyanza resident. November 27, 2007. Nyanza.

37. Gacaca session. 2007. Nyanza.

38. Interview, Jean. May 20, 2008. Nyanza.

39. Information provided by National Service of *Gacaca* Jurisdictions office, on file with author. July 2008. Kigali.

40. Community meeting. December 6, 2007. Ndora.

41. Gacaca meetings with staff of National Service of Gacaca Jurisdictions. December 2007. Butare, Ndora, Nyanza; interview with inyangamugayo. May 5, 2008. Ndora; interview with gacaca coordinator. May 22, 2008. Butare.

42. Interview, Alphonse. June 4, 2008. Ndora.

43. Interview, Agathe. May 5, 2008. Ndora.

44. See, e.g., Burnet 2010; Chakravarty 20015; Ingelaere 2008, 2009, 2010b; Rettig 2008; Thomson 2010, 2011a; Thomson and Nagy 2011; Waldorf 2006, 2010. For alternative views, see Clark and Kaufman 2009.

45. For a similar view, see Clark 2014.

Chapter 4. Comite y'Abunzi

1. See also Obarrio's recent analysis of custom-based community courts in Mozambique (2014:150–175).

2. Interview, umwunzi. January 25, 2007. Ndora.

3. Sally Engle Merry has described this similar dynamic in the United States (Merry 1990:17).

4. Interview, presiding umwunzi. November 9, 2007. Ndora.

5. Fifty percent of Ndora comite y'abunzi cases I attended were explicitly about land. Of the cases brought to the legal aid clinic that had already been heard by comite y'abunzi (i.e., cases where people were dissatisfied with the result), 70 percent were over land. This suggests that people disproportionately appealed land cases.

6. Interviews, Wildlife Conservation Society staff. July 2005, 2007–2008. Kigali.

7. Interview, Ndora resident. May 2008. Ndora.

8. People who acquired land through custom—meaning it was inherited, acquired from competent authorities, or through "any other means recognized by national custom whether purchase, gift, exchange, and sharing"—had equal rights to those who acquired it through "written law" (Organic Law N.8/2005, Article 7).

9. Comite y'abunzi session. November 30, 2007. Ndora.

10. Case before comite y'abunzi, May 2008. All quotes referring to this case are translated from fieldnotes taken during the case sessions, unless otherwise indicated.

11. Interview, Agathe. May 5, 2008. Ndora.

12. Interview, Chargé d'État Civil. July 7, 2008. Ndora. In addition, the Ministry of Justice estimated that 73 percent of cases were not referred to ordinary courts, based on research conducted in two sectors during a trial phase in 2004/2005. See Ministry of Justice. http://www.minijust.gov.rw. Accessed August 12, 2010.

13. Interview, Agathe. May 2008. Ndora.

14. Ubwoko, or clan, was a shared social identity, but not corporate. Ethnic categories historically crosscut clan status (see Chapter 1).

15. The official Kinyarwanda version uses the term "umuryango," and the official English version uses the term "family."

16. Interview, Kibungo family counselor. October 4, 2007. Kibungo.

17. Comite y'abunzi case. 2007. Ndora.

18. Interview, Aloys. May 28, 2008. Ndora.

19. When I left Ndora in July 2008, Aloys's case had still not been heard, though I did not learn why.

20. For a broader discussion of gender in postconflict societies, see Buckley-Zistal 2011; Burnet 2012; Helms 2013; Ni Aolain 2009, 2012; Moran 2010, 2012.

21. See Moran 2012 for discussion of motherhood as a powerful metaphor in peace building and reconciliation.

22. Interview, Ruhengeri resident. May 5, 2008. Butare.

23. Interview, umwunzi. May 9, 2008. Nyanza.

Chapter 5. The Legal Aid Clinic

1. The smallest administrative unit grouping.

2. For more on gender, marriage, and the impact of normative ideas of womanhood and manhood on Rwandans' lives, see Burnet 2012; De Lame 2005; Jefremovas 1991.

3. All quotes from legal aid clinic director are from an interview with the author, including clinic promotional materials provided to the author, in the author's files. June 3, 2008.

4. Interview, legal aid clinic staff member. June 3, 2008. Butare.

5. Interview, law professor. June 3, 2008. Butare.

6. See discussion of old caseload refugees in Chapter 4.

7. Interview with David. February 21. 2008. Butare.

8. Interview with legal aid clinic staff member. June 2008. Butare.

9. Umunani was a small plot of land customarily provided to sons at marriage or unmarried daughters, enough for a small house, distinct from the rest of the cultivable fields (De Lame 2005:126; Vansina 2004:130).

10. Divorce in Rwanda was regulated by the Civil Code adopted in 1988 (Loi N. 42/1988 du 27/10/1988 portant titre préliminaire et livre premier du Code civil). The 1988 civil code required a minimum six-month period during which spouses were required to attempt reconciliation prior to beginning divorce proceedings (see also Mushimijimana 2015, Ntampaka 1997).

11. See, e.g., Hodgson 2011; Lazarus-Black 2007; Merry and Milner 1993.

12. Discussion with David about Antoinette's case. May 15, 2008. Butare.

13. Discussion with staff at legal aid clinic about Tharcisse's case. February 21, 2008. Butare.

14. See the Introduction for discussion of gender and property ownership. See also Burnet 2012:76; Jefremovas 1991.

15. Africa Justice Foundation website. http://africajusticefoundation.org. Accessed May 2013, in author's possession, archived at http://web.archive.org/web/20130728184846/http://africajusticefoundation.org/our-projects/the-legal-aid-clinic/.

16. Africa Justice Foundation website. http://africajusticefoundation.org/our-blog/news-articles/ajf-delivers-mediation-training-to-providers-of-legal-aid-in-rwanda/ Accessed May 19, 2015.

Chapter 6. Improvising Authority

1. See Ferguson and Gupta 2002; Geertz 2004; Gupta 2012; Hansen and Stepputat 2006; Krohn-Hansen and Nustad 2005; Sharma and Gupta 2006; Trouillot 2001; Trouillot 2003.

2. For more on elections and training of lay judges, see Amnesty International 2002; Clark 2010.

3. Inyangamugayo could make "investigations on testimony" provided in trials (Organic Law N.16/2004, Article 36). Abunzi could hear testimony from "any person who can shed light on the matter" (Organic Law N.31/2006, Article 20).

4. Inyangamugayo cannot have been found to have participated in genocide or to have been sentenced to more than six months in prison (Organic Law N.16/2004, Article 14).

5. Interview, inyangamugayo. February 22, 2008. Ndora.

6. Interview, Elaste. November 20, 2007. Nyanza.

7. Organic Law N.16/2004 of 19.6.2004 was amended on June 27, 2006, March 1, 2007, and June 1, 2008.

8. Interview, umwunzi. February 22, 2008. Ndora.

9. Gacaca session. December 2007. Ndora.

10. Gacaca session. January 10, 2008. Ndora.

11. Comments like this are typically understood as referring to the double-genocide theory, which, in its most divisive interpretation, suggests that the RPF and genocide planners were equally culpable because Hutu also died in attacks.

12. Interview, Immaculée. November 16, 2007. Ndora.

13. Interview, Laurence. December 3, 2007. Ndora.

14. Interview, inyangamugayo. January 22, 2008. Nyanza.

15. Gacaca session. 2007. Ndora.

16. Interview, Laurence. December 3, 2007. Ndora.

17. Gacaca session. 2007. Nyanza.

18. Gacaca sessions. 2007. Butare.

19. Interview, presiding umwunzi. December 14, 2007. Ndora.

20. Interview, umwunzi. February 22, 2008. Ndora.

21. Interview, Judge Fremr. March 13, 2008. Arusha.

22. Interview, Judge Møse. March 13, 2008. Arusha.

23. See discussion in Chapter 3.

24. Gacaca session. 2007. Ndora.

25. I build here on Thomson's distinction between the state and the RPF regime (Thomson 2013:8). For more on state power, see discussion in introduction, and especially Straus and Waldorf 2011; Thomson 2013.

26. See the Introduction and Chapter 1.

Conclusion

1. See, e.g., Abramowitz 2014; Beckett 2013; Bornstein 2012; Fassin 2008; Hromadžić 2015; James 2010; Moran 2010; Mose 2013; Redfield 2013.

2. See Autessere 2010 for analysis with respect to Rwanda's neighbor the Democratic Republic of Congo.

3. Comaroff and Comaroff 1993; 1999; Feierman 1995:77; Habermas 1974; 1984.

4. Feierman 1995, 1999; Janzen and Janzen 2000; Janzen 1992; Taylor 1992; 1999.

5. Janzen 2010; Janzen and Janzen 2000; Taylor 1992; 2002.

6. See Buckley-Zistel 2006; Burnet 2010; Chakravarty 2014; Clark and Kaufman 2009; Longman 2010b; Thomson 2013; Zorbas 2009.

Bibliography

Abel, Richard

1982a The Contradictions of Informal Justice. *In* The Politics of Informal Justice (Volume 1). R. Abel, ed. Pp. 267–320. New York: Academic Press.

1982b Introduction. *In* The Politics of Informal Justice (Volume 2). R. Abel, ed. Pp. 1–16. New York: Academic Press.

Abramowitz, Sharon

2014 Searching for Normal in the Wake of the Liberian War. Philadelphia: University of Pennsylvania Press.

Abrams, Philip

1988 Notes on the Difficulty of Studying the State (1977). Journal of Historical Sociology 1(1):58–89.

African Rights

1995 Death, Despair, and Defiance. London: African Rights.

Agamben, Georgio

2005 State of Exception. Chicago: University of Chicago Press.

Allen, Tim

2008 Ritual (ab)use? Problems with Traditional Justice in Northern Uganda. *In* Courting Conflict? Justice, Peace, and the ICC in Africa. N. Waddell and P. Clark, eds. Pp. 47–54. London: Royal African Society.

Amnesty International

2002 Rwanda: Gacaca: A Question of Justice. London: Amnesty International.

Ansoms, An

2009 Re-Engineering Rural Society: The Visions and Ambitions of the Rwandan Elite. African Affairs 108(431):289–309.

Ansoms, An, and Thea Hilhorst, eds.

2014 Losing Your Land: Dispossession in the Great Lakes. Rochester, NY: James Currey (Boydell and Brewer).

Ansoms, An, and Stefaan Marysse

2005 The Evolution and Characteristics of Poverty and Inequality in Rwanda. *In* The Political Economy of the Great Lakes Region in Africa. S. Marysse and F. Reyntjens, eds. Pp. 71–100. New York: Palgrave Macmillan.

Ashforth, Adam

2000 Madumo: A Man Bewitched. Chicago: University of Chicago Press.

Auerbach, Jerold
1983 Justice Without Law? New York: Oxford University Press.
Autesserre, Severine
2010 The Trouble with the Congo: Local Violence and the Failure of International Peacebuilding. Cambridge: Cambridge University Press.
Babo-Soares, Dionisio
2005 *Nahe Biti:* Grassroots Reconciliation in East Timor. *In* Roads to Reconciliation. E. Skaar, S. Gloppen, and A. Suhrke, eds. Pp. 225–248. New York: Lexington Books.
Bayart, Jean-François
1993 (1989) The State in Africa: The Politics of the Belly. New York: Longman.
Beckett, Greg
2013 The Politics of Emergency. Reviews in Anthropology 42(2):85–101.
Birdsall, Andrea
2007 The International Criminal Tribunal for the Former Yugoslavia: Towards a More Just Order? Peace, Conflict, and Development 8:1–24.
Biruta, Vincent
2006 Rwanda: Genocide Ideology and Strategies for its Eradication. Kigali: Republic of Rwanda, The Senate.
Bizimungu, Pasteur
1999 Report on the Reflection Meetings Held in the Office of the President of the Republic from May 1998 to March 1999.
Blumenson, Eric
2006 The Challenge of a Global Standard of Justice: Peace, Pluralism, and Punishment at the International Criminal Court. Columbia Journal of Transnational Law 44:801–874.
Bohannan, Paul
1957 Justice and Judgment Among the Tiv. London: Oxford University Press.
Bolten, Catherine
2012a I Did It to Save My Life: Love and Survival in Sierra Leone. Berkeley: University of California Press.
2012b "We Have Been Sensitized": Ex-Combatants, Marginalization, and Youth in Postwar Sierra Leone. American Anthropologist 114(3):496–508.
Borneman, John
2002 Reconciliation After Ethnic Cleansing: Listening, Retribution, Affiliation. Public Culture 14(2):281–304.
Bornstein, Erica
2012 Disquieting Gifts: Humanitarianism in New Delhi. Stanford: Stanford University Press.
Botte, Roger
1985a Rwanda and Burundi, 1889–1930: Chronology of a Slow Assassination [Part 1]. International Journal of African Historical Studies 18(1):53–91.
1985b Rwanda and Burundi, 1889–1930: Chronology of a Slow Assassination [Part 2]. International Journal of African Historical Studies 18(2):289–314.
Brauman, Rony, Stephen Smith, and Claudine Vidal
2000 Politique de terreur et privilège d'impunité au Rwanda. Esprit 585:147–161.
Briggs, Morgan
2013 Rebalancing Culture and Power Beyond Globalized Liberalism: The Case of Alternative Dispute Resolution. *In* Centaur Conference. McGill University, Montreal.

Buckley-Zistel, Susanne
2006a Dividing and Uniting: The Use of Citizenship Discourses in Conflict and Reconciliation in Rwanda. Global Society 20(1):101–113.
2006b Remembering to Forget: Chosen Amnesia as a Strategy for Local Coexistence in Post-Genocide Rwanda. Africa: The Journal of the International African Institute 76(2):131–150.
2009 We Are Pretending Peace: Local Memory and the Absence of Social Transformation and Reconciliation in Rwanda. In After Genocide: Transitional Justice, Post-Conflict Reconstruction and Reconciliation in Rwanda and Beyond. P. Clark and Z. D. Kaufman, eds. Pp. 125–144. New York: Columbia University Press.
Buckley-Zistel, Susanne, and Magdalena Zolkos
2011 Introduction: Gender in Transitional Justice. In Gender in Transitional Justice. S. Buckley-Zistel and R. Stanley, eds. Pp. 1–33. New York: Palgrave Macmillan.
Burgess, Patrick
2006 A New Approach to Restorative Justice: East Timor's Community Reconciliation Processes. In Transitional Justice in the Twenty-First Century. N. Roht-Arriaza and J. Mariezcurrena, eds. Pp. 176–205. Cambridge: Cambridge University Press.
Burke-White, William W.
2005 Complementarity in Practice: The International Criminal Court as Part of a System of Multi-Level Global Governance in the Democratic Republic of Congo. Leiden Journal of International Law 18:557–590.
Burnet, Jennie
2005 Genocide Lives in Us: Amplified Silence and the Politics of Memory in Rwanda. Dissertation, University of North Carolina at Chapel Hill.
2009 Whose Genocide? Whose Truth? Representations of Victim and Perpetrator in Rwanda. In Genocide: Truth, Memory, and Representation. A. Hinton and K. L. O'Neill, eds. Pp. 80–110. Durham: Duke University Press.
2010 (In)Justice: Truth, Reconciliation, and Revenge in Rwanda's Gacaca. In Transitional Justice: Global Mechanisms and Local Realities After Genocide and Mass Violence. A. Hinton, ed. Pp. 95–118. New Brunswick, NJ: Rutgers University Press.
2012 Genocide Lives in Us: Women, Memory, and Silence in Rwanda. Madison: University of Wisconsin Press.
Butamire, Pan
2010 Rwanda Still Unfolding. The New Times. December 31. P. 1. Kigali.
Cavalli-Sforza, Luigi Luca, Paolo Menozzi, and Alberto Piazza
1994 The History and Geography of Human Genes. Princeton: Princeton University Press.
Chakravarty, Anuradha
2012 Partially Trusting Field Relationships: Opportunities and Constraints of Fieldwork in Rwanda's Postconflict Setting. Field Methods 24 (3):251–271.
2014 Navigating the Middle Ground: The Political Values of Ordinary Hutu in Post-Genocide Rwanda. African Affairs 113(451):232–253.
2015 Investing in Authoritarian Rule: Punishment and Patronage in Rwanda's Gacaca Courts for Genocide Crimes. Cambridge: Cambridge University Press.
Chanock, Martin
1985 Law, Custom, and Social Order: The Colonial Experience in Malawi and Zambia. Cambridge: Cambridge University Press.

Chrétien, Jean-Pierre
1995 Rwanda: Les médias du génocide. Paris: Karthala.
Clark, Phil
2010 The Gacaca Courts, Post-Genocide Justice and Reconciliation in Rwanda: Justice Without Lawyers. Cambridge: Cambridge University Press.
2014 Bringing the Peasants Back In, Again: State Power and Local Agency in Rwanda's Gacaca Courts. Journal of Eastern African Studies 8(2):192–213.
Clark, Phil, and Zachary D. Kaufman, eds.
2009 After Genocide: Transitional Justice, Post-Conflict Reconstruction, and Reconciliation in Rwanda and Beyond. New York: Columbia University Press.
Clarke, Kamari
2009 Fictions of Justice: The International Criminal Court and the Challenge of Legal Pluralism in Sub-Saharan Africa. Cambridge: Cambridge University Press.
Codere, Helen
1962 Power in Ruanda. Anthropologica 4(1):45–85.
1973 Biography of an African Society: Rwanda, 1900–1960. Tervuren: Royal Museum for Central Africa.
Colson, Elizabeth
1953 Social Control and Vengeance in Plateau Tonga Society. Africa: The Journal of the International African Institute 23(3):199–212.
1974 Tradition and Contract: The Problem of Order. Chicago: Aldine.
Comaroff, Jean, and John Comaroff, eds.
1993 Modernity and Its Malcontents: Ritual and Power in Postcolonial Africa. Chicago: University of Chicago Press.
2003 Reflections on Liberalism, Policulturalism, and ID-ology: Citizenship and Difference in South Africa. Social Identities 9(4):445–473.
2006 Law and Disorder in the Postcolony. Chicago: University of Chicago Press.
Comaroff, John
2001 Colonialism, Culture, and the Law: A Foreword. Law and Social Inquiry 26:305–314.
Comaroff, John L., and Jean Comaroff, eds.
1999 Civil Society and the Political Imagination in Africa: Critical Perspectives. Chicago: University of Chicago Press.
Comaroff, John, and Simon Roberts
1981 Rules and Processes: The Cultural Logic of Dispute in an African Context. Chicago: University of Chicago Press.
Connerton, Paul
1989 How Societies Remember. Cambridge: Cambridge University Press.
Constitution of the Republic of Rwanda
2003 Adopted by Rwandan Citizens in the Referendum of 26 May 2003 as confirmed by the Supreme Court in its ruling N.772/14.06/2003 of 02/06/2003.
Cruvellier, Thierry
2010 Courts of Remorse: Inside the International Criminal Tribunal for Rwanda. Madison: University of Wisconsin Press.
Dallaire, Romeo
2003 Shake Hands with the Devil: The Failure of Humanity in Rwanda. Toronto: Random House Canada.

Das, Veena

2007 Life and Words: Violence and the Descent into the Ordinary. Berkeley: University of California Press.

Davenport, Christian, and Allan C. Stam

2009 What Really Happened in Rwanda? Pacific Standard. October 6.

De Lame, Danielle

2005 A Hill Among a Thousand: Transformations and Ruptures in Rural Rwanda. H. Arnold, trans. Madison: University of Wisconsin Press.

Derrida, Jacques

2001 On Cosmopolitanism and Forgiveness. M. Dooley and M. Hughes, trans. New York: Routledge.

Des Forges, Allison

1995 The Ideology of Genocide. Issue: A Journal of Opinion 23(2):44–47.

1999 Leave None to Tell the Story: Genocide in Rwanda. New York: Human Rights Watch.

d'Hertefelt, Marcel

1971 Les clans du Rwanda ancien: Eléments d'ethnosociologie et d'ethnohistoire. Tervuren: Royal Museum for Central Africa.

Dickinson, Laura

2003 The Promise of Hybrid Courts. The American Journal of International Law 97(2):295–310.

Doughty, Kristin C.

2008 Commemoration and Narratives of Community Healing: Ten Years After the Rwandan Genocide. In Health Knowledge and Belief Systems in Africa. T. Falola and M. M. Heaton, eds. Durham, NC: Carolina Academic Press.

2014 'Our Goal Is Not to Punish but to Reconcile:' Mediation in Postgenocide Rwanda. American Anthropologist 116 (4):780–794.

2015 Law and the Architecture of Social Repair: Gacaca Days in Postgenocide Rwanda. Journal of the Royal Anthropological Institute 21(2): 419–437.

Economist

2010. In the Dock but for What? The Economist. November 25.

Eller, Jack David

1999 From Culture to Ethnicity to Conflict: An Anthropological Perspective on International Ethnic Conflict. Ann Arbor: University of Michigan Press.

Eltringham, Nigel

2004 Accounting for Horror: Post-Genocide Debates in Rwanda. London: Pluto Press.

2010 Judging the "Crime of Crimes": Continuity and Improvisation at the International Criminal Tribunal for Rwanda. In Transitional Justice: Global Mechanisms and Local Realities After Genocide and Mass Violence. A. Hinton, ed. Pp. 206–226. New Brunswick: Rutgers University Press.

2011 The Past Is Elsewhere: The Paradoxes of Proscribing Ethnicity in Post-Genocide Rwanda. In Remaking Rwanda. S. Straus and L. Waldorf, eds. Pp. 269–282. Madison: University of Wisconsin Press.

Englund, Harri

2002 From War to Peace on the Mozambique-Malawi Borderland. London: Edinburgh University Press for the International Africa Institute.

2006 Prisoners of Freedom: Human Rights and the African Poor. Berkeley: University of California Press.

Eramian, Laura

2014a Ethnicity Without labels? Ambiguity and excess in "Postethnic" Rwanda. Focaal: Journal of Global and Historical Anthropology 70:96–109.

2014b Personhood, Violence, and the Moral Work of Memory in Contemporary Rwanda. International Journal of Conflict and Violence8(1):2014.

Evans-Pritchard, E. E.

1940 The Nuer: A Description of the Modes of Livelihood and Political Institutions of a Nilotic People. Oxford: Clarendon Press.

Excoffier, Laurent, et al.

1987 Genetics and History of Sub-Saharan Africa. Yearbook of Physical Anthropology 30:151–194.

Fassin, Didier

2008 The Humanitarian Politics of Testimony: Subjectification Through Trauma in the Israeli-Palestinian Conflict. Cultural Anthropology 23(3):531–558.

Feierman, Steven

1995 Healing as Social Criticism in the Time of Colonial Conquest. African Studies 54:73–88.

1999 Colonizers, Scholars, and the Creation of Invisible Histories. In Beyond the Cultural Turn: New Directions in the Study of Society and Culture. L. Hunt, ed. Pp. 182–216. Berkeley: University of California Press.

Feierman, Steven, and John M. Janzen, eds.

1992 The Social Basis of Health and Healing in Africa. Berkeley: University of California Press.

Ferguson, James, and Akhil Gupta

2002 Spatializing States: Toward an Ethnography of Neoliberal Governmentality. American Ethnologist 29(4):981–1002.

Finnstrom, Sverker

2008 Living with Bad Surroundings: War, History, and Everyday Moments in Northern Uganda. Durham: Duke University Press.

2010 Reconciliation Grown Bitter? War, Retribution, and Ritual Action in Northern Uganda. In Localizing Transitional Justice. R. Shaw, L. Waldorf, and P. Hazan, eds. Pp. 135–156. Stanford: Stanford University Press.

Fletcher, Laurel, and Harvey Weinstein

2002 Violence and Social Repair: Rethinking the Contribution of Justice to Reconciliation. Human Rights Quarterly 24:573–639.

Foucault, Michel

1978 The History of Sexuality, Volume 1: An Introduction. New York: Random House.

1982 The Subject and Power. Critical Inquiry 8(4):775–795.

1991 Governmentality. In The Foucault Effect: Studies in Governmentality. G. Furchell, C. Gordon, and P. Miller, eds. Pp. 87–104. Chicago: University of Chicago Press.

Fujii, Lee Ann

2009 Killing Neighbors: Webs of Violence in Rwanda. Ithaca: Cornell University Press.

Gahamanyi, Bibiane Mbaye

2003 Rwanda: Building Constitutional Order in the Aftermath of Genocide. In Human Rights Under African Constitutions: Realizing the Promise for Ourselves. A. A. An-Na'im, ed. Pp. 251–294. Philadelphia: University of Pennsylvania Press.

Gasarasi, Charles, and Herman Musahara
2004 The Land Question in Kibungo Province. Cahiers de Centre de Gestion des Conflits 12.
Gasibirege, Simon
2002 Résultats definitifs de l'enquête quantitative sur les attitudes des Rwandais vis-à-vis des juridictions gacaca. Cahiers de Centre de Gestion des Conflits 6:38–92.
Geertz, Clifford
1973 The Interpretation of Cultures. New York: Basic Books.
2004 What Is a State if It Is Not a Sovereign? Current Anthropology 45(5):577–593.
Gettleman, Jeffrey, and Marlise Simons
2010 International Court Seeks Indictments in Kenya Vote Violence. New York Times. September 4.
Gibbs, James
1967 The Kpelle Moot. In Law and Warfare: Studies in the Anthropology of Conflict. P. Bohannan, ed. Pp. 277–290. Garden City, NY: Natural History Press.
Gluckman, Max
1955 The Judicial Process Among the Barotse of Northern Rhodesia. Manchester: Manchester University Press.
Gourevitch, Philip
1998 We Wish to Inform You That Tomorrow We Will Be Killed with Our Families: Stories from Rwanda. New York: Farrar, Straus and Giroux.
Greenhouse, Carol J., Elizabeth Mertz, and Kay B. Warren
2002 Ethnography in Unstable Places: Everyday Lives in Contexts of Dramatic Political Change. Durham: Duke University Press.
Greenhouse, Carol J., Barbara Yngvesson, and David M. Engel
1994 Law and Community in Three American Towns. Ithaca: Cornell University Press.
Gupta, Akhil
1995 Blurred Boundaries: The Discourse of Corruption, the Culture of Politics, and the Imagined State. American Ethnologist 22(2):375–402.
2012 Red Tape: Bureaucracy, Structural Violence, and Poverty in India. Durham: Duke University Press.
Habermas, Jürgen
1974 The Public Sphere: An Encyclopedia Article (1964). New German Critique 1(3):49–55.
1979 (1976) Legitimation Problems in the Modern State. In Communication and the Evolution of Society. J. Habermas, ed. Pp. 179–205. Boston: Beacon Press.
1984 The Theory of Communicative Action, Volume 1. T. McCarthy, trans. Boston: Beacon Press.
Halbwachs, Maurice
1980 The Collective Memory. F. J. Ditter Jr. and V. Y. Ditter, trans. New York: Harper and Row.
Hansen, Thomas Blom, and Finn Stepputat
2006 Sovereignty Revisited. Annual Review of Anthropology 35:1–21.
Hatzfeld, Jean
2005 Machete Season: The Killers in Rwanda Speak. New York: Farrar, Straus and Giroux.
Hayner, Priscilla
1995 Fifteen Truth Commissions: 1974–1994: A Comparative Study. In Transitional Justice. Kritz, N. ed. Pp. 225–261. Washington, DC: USIP Press.

2011 Unspeakable Truths: Transitional Justice and the Challenge of Truth Commissions. New York: Routledge.

Helms, Elissa

2013 Innocence and Victimhood: Gender, Nation, and Women's Activism in Postwar Bosnia-Herzegovina. Madison: University of Wisconsin Press.

Heyman, Josiah, and Alan Smart

1999 States and Illegal Practices: An Overview. *In* States and Illegal Practices. J. Heyman, ed. Pp. 1–24. New York: Berg.

Hiernaux, Jean

1963 Heredity and Environment: Their Influence on Human Morphology. A Comparison of Two Independent Lines of Study. American Journal of Physical Anthropology 21:575–589.

1975 (1974) The People of Africa. New York: Charles Scribner's Sons.

Hintjens, Helen

2008 Post-Genocide Identity Politics in Rwanda. Ethnicities 8(1):5–41.

Hinton, Alexander Laban, ed.

2010 Transitional Justice: Glocal Mechanisms and Local Realities After Genocide and Mass Violence. New Brunswick, NJ: Rutgers University Press.

Hobsbawm, Eric, and Terence Ranger, eds.

1983 The Invention of Tradition. Cambridge: Cambridge University Press.

Hodgson, Dorothy L., ed.

2011 Gender and Culture at the Limit of Rights. Philadelphia: University of Pennsylvania Press.

Honwana, Alcinda

2005 Healing and Social Reintegration in Mozambique and Angola. *In* Roads to Reconciliation. E. Skaar, S. Gloppen, and A. Suhrke, eds. Pp. 83–100. New York: Lexington Books.

Hromadžić, Azra

2014 "Only When the Spider Web Becomes Too Heavy": Youth, Unemployment, and the Social Life of Waiting in Postwar and Postsocialist Bosnia-Herzogovina. Journal of Social Policy 11 (Special Issue Youth Unemployment: Policies, Measures, and Challenges).

2015 Citizens of an Empty Nation: Youth and State-Making in Postwar Bosnia and Herzegovina. Philadelphia: University of Pennsylvania Press.

Hull, Matthew S.

2012 Government of Paper: The Materiality of Bureaucracy in Urban Pakistan. Berkeley: University of California Press.

Ingelaere, Bert

2008 The *Gacaca* Courts in Rwanda. *In* Traditional Justice and Reconciliation After Violent Conflict: Learning from African Experiences. L. Huyse and M. Salter, eds. Pp. 25–59. Stockholm: International IDEA.

2009 "Does the Truth Pass Across the Fire Without Burning?" Locating the Short Circuit in Rwanda's *Gacaca* Courts. Journal of Modern African Studies 47(4):507–528.

2010a Do We Understand Life After Genocide? Center and Periphery in the Construction of Knowledge in Postgenocide Rwanda. African Studies Review 53(1):41–59.

2010b Peasants, Power and Ethnicity: A Bottom-Up Perspective on Rwanda's Political Transition. African Affairs 109(435):273–292.

Irega, Victor, and Beatrice Dias-Lambranca
2008 Restorative Justice and the Role of Magamba Spirits in Post–Civil War Gorongosa, Central Mozambique. *In* Traditional Justice and Reconciliation After Violent Conflict: Lessons from African Experiences. L. Huyse and M. Salter, eds. Stockholm: International IDEA.

Irvine, Jill, and Maureen Hays-Mitchell
2012 Gender and Political Transformation in Societies at War. Journal of International Women's Studies 13(4):1–9.

James, Erica
2010 Democratic Insecurities: Violence, Trauma, and Intervention in Haiti. Berkeley: University of California Press.

Janzen, John M.
1992 Ngoma: Discourses of Healing in Central and Southern Africa. Berkeley: University of California Press.
2000 Historical Consciousness and a "Prise de Conscience" in Genocidal Rwanda. Journal of African Cultural Studies 13(1):153–168.
2010 The Social Reproduction of Health: Local and Global Idioms in Central African Communal Politics. Social Health in the New Millennium conference, Philadelphia, March 2010.

Janzen, John M., and Reinhild Kauenhoven Janzen
2000 Do I Still Have a Life? Voices from the Aftermath of War in Rwanda and Burundi. Lawrence: University of Kansas Press.

Jeffrey, Craig
2010 Timepass: Youth, Class, and Time Among Unemployed Young Men in India. American Ethnologist 37(3):465–481.

Jefremovas, Villia
1991 Loose Women, Virtuous Wives, and Timid Virgins: Gender and the Control of Resources in Rwanda. Canadian Journal of African Studies 25(3):378–395.
1995 Acts of Human Kindness: Tutsi, Hutu, and the Genocide. Issue: A Journal of Opinion 23(2):28–31.
2002 Brickyards to Graveyards: From Production to Genocide in Rwanda. Albany: State University of New York Press.

Johnson, Marcus
2009 RFP No. 696-RW-09–010-USAID/Rwanda "MCC Threshold Program—Strengthening Civic Participation in Rwanda." Kigali: U.S. Agency for International Development.

Joireman, Sandra
2001 Inherited Legal Systems and Effective Rule of Law: Africa and the Colonial Legacy. Journal of Modern African Studies 39(4):571–596.

Jones, Ben
2008 Beyond the State in Rural Uganda. Edinburgh: Edinburgh University Press.

Jones, Nicholas
2010 The Courts of Genocide: Politics and the Rule of Law in Rwanda and Arusha. New York: Routledge.

Kagame, Paul
2014 Speech at the Africa Innovation Summit: Leading Innovation. Cape Verde.

Kagire, Edmund
2009 World Figures to Light Candles During 15th Genocide Commemoration. New Times. April 7. P. 1. Kigali.

Karemera, Emmy
2004 Kagame Inaugurates *Gacaca* Genocide Trials. New Times. June 25–27. P. 1. Kigali.

Kazoora, Moses
2004 937,000 Genocide Victims Identified. New Times. April 2–4. P. 1. Kigali.

Kelly, Tobias
2008 The Attractions of Accountancy: Living an Ordinary Life During the Second Palestinian Intifada. Ethnography 9(3):351–376.
2011 This Side of Silence: Human Rights, Torture, and the Recognition of Cruelty. Philadelphia: University of Pennsylvania Press.

Kelsall, Tim
2005 Truth, Lies, Ritual: Preliminary Reflections on the Truth and Reconciliation Commission in Sierra Leone. Human Rights Quarterly 27(2):361–391.
2013 Culture Under Cross-Examination: International Justice and the Special Court for Sierra Leone. Cambridge: Cambridge University Press.

Kimenyi, Felly
2007 Forty Lawyers Pledge Loyalty. New Times. November 25. P. 3. Kigali.

Kimenyi, Felly, and Godfrey Ntagungira
2008 Use Land Properly—Kagame: As Land Re-Distribution Kicks Off in Eastern Province. New Times. January 23. Pp. 1–2. Kigali.

King, Elisabeth
2009 From Data Problems to Data Points: Challenges and Opportunities of Research in Post-genocide Rwanda. African Studies Review 52(3):127–148.
2014 From Classrooms to Conflict in Rwanda. New York: Cambridge University Press.

Krohn-Hansen, Christian, and Knut G. Nustad, eds.
2005 State Formation: Anthropological Perspectives. Ann Arbor: Pluto Press.

Kroslak, Daniela
2007 The Role of France in the Rwandan Genocide. London: Hurst.

Latigo, James Ojera
2008 Northern Uganda: Tradition-Based Practices in the Acholi Region. *In* Traditional Justice and Reconciliation After Violent Conflict: Learning from African Experiences. L. Huyse and M. Salter, eds. Stockholm: International IDEA.

Law N.18/2008 of 23/07/2008
Relating to the Punishment of the Crime of Genocide Ideology. Official Gazette of the Republic of Rwanda N.20.

Lazar, Sian
2008 El Alto, Rebel City: Self and Citizenship in Andean Bolivia. Durham: Duke University Press.

Lazarus-Black, Mindie
2007 Everyday Harm: Domestic Violence, Court Rites, and Cultures of Reconciliation. Chicago: University of Illinois Press.

Leebaw, Bronwyn Anne
2008 The Irreconcilable Goals of Transitional Justice. Human Rights Quarterly 30:95–118.

Lemarchand, René
1970 Rwanda and Burundi. New York: Praeger.
1995 Rwanda: The Rationality of Genocide. Issue: A Journal of Opinion 23(2):8–11.
2009 The Dynamics of Violence in Central Africa. Philadelphia: University of Pennsylvania Press.

Levi, Primo
1988 The Drowned and the Saved. New York: Summit Books.

Li, Tanya Murray
2014 Lands End: Capitalist Relations on an Indigenous Frontier. Durham: Duke University Press.

Livingston, Julie
2012 Improvising Medicine: An African Oncology Ward in an Emerging Cancer Epidemic. Durham: Duke University Press.

Locke, Peter.
2012 Appropriating Trauma: Legacies of Humanitarian Psychiatry in Postwar Bosnia-Herzegovina. Intergraph: Journal of Dialogic Anthropology 3(2).

Longman, Timothy
1995 Genocide and Socio-Political Change: Massacres in Two Rwandan Villages. Issue: A Journal of Opinion 23(2):18–21.
2000 State, Civil Society, and Genocide in Rwanda. In State, Conflict, and Democracy in Africa. R. Joseph, ed. Pp. 339–358. Boulder: Lynne Rienner.
2006 Justice at the Grassroots? Gacaca Trials in Rwanda. In Transitional Justice in the Twenty-First Century. N. Roht-Arriaza and J. Mariezcurrena, eds. Pp. 206–228. Cambridge: Cambridge University Press.
2010a Christianity and Genocide in Rwanda. Cambridge: Cambridge University Press.
2010b Trying Times for Rwanda: Reevaluating Gacaca Courts in Post-Genocide Rwanda. Harvard International Law Review 32(2):48–52.

Lubkemann, Stephen
2008 Culture in Chaos: An Anthropology of the Social Condition in War. Chicago: Chicago University Press.

Maganarella, Paul
2000 Justice in Africa: Rwanda's Genocide, Its Courts, and the UN Criminal Tribunal. Brookfield: Ashgate.

Mair, Lucy
1962 Primitive Government. Baltimore: Penguin Books.
1974 African Societies. Cambridge: Cambridge University Press.
1977 African Kingdoms. Oxford: Clarendon Press.

Malkki, Liisa H.
1995 Purity and Exile: Violence, Memory, and National Cosmology Among Hutu Refugees in Tanzania. Chicago: University of Chicago Press.

Mamdani, Mahmood
2001 When Victims Become Killers: Colonialism, Nativism, and the Genocide in Rwanda. Princeton: Princeton University Press.

Mann, Kristin, and Richard Roberts, eds.
1991 Law in Colonial Africa. Portsmouth, NH: Heinemann.

Maquet, Jacques

1961 The Premise of Inequality in Ruanda. London: Oxford University Press.

1970 Rwanda Castes. *In* Social Stratification in Africa. A. Tuden and L. Plotnicov, eds. Pp. 93–124. New York: Free Press.

Mattei, Ugo, and Laura Nader

2008 Plunder: When the Rule of Law Is Illegal. Malden, MA: Blackwell.

Mbembe, Achille

2001 On the Postcolony. Berkeley: University of California Press.

2006 On Politics as a Form of Expenditure. *In* Law and Disorder in the Postcolony. J. Comaroff and J. Comaroff, eds. Pp. 299–336. Chicago: University of Chicago Press.

McCourt, Kerstin

2009 Judicial Defenders: Their Role in Postgenocide Justice and Sustained Legal Development. The International Journal of Transitional Justice 3:272–283.

McLean Hilker, Lyndsay

2009 Everyday Ethnicities: Identity and Reconciliation Among Rwandan Youth. Journal of Genocide Research 11(1):81–100.

2011 The Role of Education in Driving Conflict and Building Peace: The Case of Rwanda. Prospects 41(2).

2012 Rwanda's "Hutsi": Intersections of Ethnicity and Violence in the Lives of Youth of "Mixed" Heritage. Identities: Global Studies in Culture and Power 19(2):229–247.

McMahon, Patrice, and David Forsythe

2008 The ICTY's Impact on Serbia: Judicial Romanticism Meets Network Policies. Human Rights Quarterly 30:412–435.

Meierhenrich, Jens

2008 The Transformation of *lieux de mémoire:* The Nyabarongo River in Rwanda, 1992–2009. Anthropology Today 25(5):13–19.

Merry, Sally Engle

1990 Getting Justice and Getting Even: Legal Consciousness Among Working-Class Americans. Chicago: University of Chicago Press.

1993 Sorting Out Popular Justice. *In* The Possibility of Popular Justice. S. E. Merry and N. Milner, eds. Pp. 31–66. Ann Arbor: University of Michigan Press.

2006a Human Rights and Gender Violence: Translating International Law into Local Justice. Chicago: University of Chicago Press.

2006b Transnational Human Rights and Local Activism: Mapping the Middle. American Anthropologist 108(1):38–51.

Merry, Sally Engle, and Neal Milner, eds.

1993 The Possibility of Popular Justice: A Case Study of Community Mediation in the United States. Ann Arbor: University of Michigan Press.

Ministry of Finance and Economic Planning

2000 Rwanda Vision 2020. Kigali: Government of Rwanda.

Ministry of Local Government, Good Governance, Community Development, and Social Affairs

2008a Community Development Policy. Kigali: Government of Rwanda.

2008b Rwanda Decentralization Implementation Program 2008–2012. Kigali: Government of Rwanda.

Minow, Martha

1998 Between Vengeance and Forgiveness: Facing History After Genocide and Mass Violence. Boston: Beacon Press.

Moore, Sally Falk

1986 Social Facts and Fabrications: "Customary" Law on Kilimanjaro 1880–1980. Cambridge: Cambridge University Press.

1992 Treating Law as Knowledge: Telling Colonial Officers What to Say to Africans About Running "Their Own" Native Courts. Law and Society Review 26(1):11–46.

2001 Certainties Undone: Fifty Turbulent Years of Legal Anthropology, 1949–1999. Journal of the Royal Anthropological Institute 7(1):95–116.

2005 Law and Anthropology: A Reader. Malden, MA: Blackwell.

Moran, Mary

2006 Liberia: The Violence of Democracy. Philadelphia: University of Pennsylvania Press.

2010 Gender, Militarism, and Peace-Building: Projects of the Postconflict Moment. Annual Review of Anthropology 39:261–274.

2012 Our Mothers Have Spoken: Synthesizing Old and New Forms of Women's Political Authority in Liberia. Journal of International Women's Studies 13(4):51–66.

Morgan, Timothy

2005 Purpose Driven in Rwanda. Christianity Today. September 23.

Morrill, Constance

2006 Show Business and "Lawfare" in Rwanda: Twelve Years After the Genocide. Dissent 53(3):14–20.

Mose, David

2013 Anthropology of International Development. Annual Review of Anthropology 42:227–246.

Møse, Erik

2005 Main Achievements of the ICTR. Journal of International Criminal Justice 3:920–943.

Munyaneza, James

2004 Mediators to accelerate justice—Premier. New Times. Pp. 1, 2. July 14–15. Kigali.

Mushimijimana, Diane

2015 Is Divorce Accepted in Rwandan Society? Rwanda Focus. February 20. Kigali.

Musoni, Edwin

2008a 54,000 hectares of land to be re-distributed in Eastern Province. New Times. January 23. P. 3. Kigali.

2008b Rwanda, a Country with a Purpose—Kagame. New Times. March 31. Pp. 1,3. Kigali.

Nader, Laura

1988 The ADR Explosion—The Implications of Rhetoric in Legal Reform. Windsor Yearbook of Access to Justice 8:269–291.

1990 Harmony Ideology: Justice and Control in a Zapotec Mountain Village. Stanford: Stanford University Press.

1999a The Globalization of Law: ADR as "Soft" Technology. American Society of International Law Proceedings 93:304–311.

1999b Pushing the Limits: Eclecticism on Purpose. Political and Legal Anthropology Review 22(1):106–109.

2002a The Life of the Law: Anthropological Projects. Berkeley: University of California Press.

2002b A Wide-Angle on Dispute Management. Willamette Journal of International Law and Dispute Resolution 10(37):37–46.

2003 Departure from Violence: Love Is Not Enough. Public Culture 15(1):195–197.

2005 Coercive Harmony: The Political Economy of Legal Models. Kroeber Anthropological Society 92–93:7–22.

Nader, Laura, and Elisabetta Grande

2002 Current Illusions and Delusions About Conflict Management—In Africa and Elsewhere. Law and Social Inquiry 27:573–594.

Nagy, Rosemary

2008 Transitional Justice as Global Project: Critical Reflections. Third World Quarterly 29(2):275–289.

Ndangiza, Fatuma

2007 Social Cohesion in Rwanda: An Opinion Survey. Kigali: National Unity and Reconciliation Commission.

Nduwayo, Leonard

2002 Giti et le génocide Rwandais. Paris: L'Harmattan.

Nee, Ann, and Peter Uvin

2010 Silence and Dialogue: Burundians' Alternatives to Transitional Justice. In Localizing Transitional Justice. R. Shaw, L. Waldorf, and P. Hazan, eds. Pp. 157–182. Stanford: Stanford University Press.

Neofotistos, Vasiliki

2012 The Risk of War: Everyday Sociality in the Republic of Macedonia. Philadelphia: University of Pennsylvania Press.

Newbury, Catharine

1978 Ethnicity in Rwanda: The Case of Kinyaga. Africa 48(1):17–29.

1980a Ubureetwa and Thangata: Catalysts to Peasant Political Consciousness in Rwanda and Malawi. Canadian Journal of African Studies 14(1):97–111.

1988 The Cohesion of Oppression: Clientship and Ethnicity in Rwanda: 1860–1960. New York: Columbia University Press.

1995a Background to Genocide: Rwanda. Issue: A Journal of Opinion 23(2):12–17.

1998a Ethnicity and the Politics of History in Rwanda. Africa Today 45(1):7–24.

Newbury, Catharine, and David Newbury

1999 A Catholic Mass in Kigali: Contested Views of the Genocide and Ethnicity in Rwanda. Canadian Journal of African Studies 33(2–3):292–328. (Special Issue: French-Speaking Central Africa.)

Newbury, David

1980b The Clans of Rwanda: An Historical Hypothesis. Africa 50(4):389–403.

1995b Guest Editor's Introduction, Rwanda: Genocide and After. Issue: A Journal of Opinion 23(2):4–7.

1997 Irredentist Rwanda: Ethnic and Territorial Frontiers in Central Africa. Africa Today 44(2):211–221.

1998b Understanding Genocide. African Studies Review 41(1):73–97.

2001 Precolonial Burundi and Rwanda: Local Loyalties, Regional Royalties. International Journal of African Historical Studies 34(2):255–314.

2009 The Land Beyond the Mists. Athens: Ohio University Press.

Newbury, David, and Catharine Newbury

2000 Bringing the Peasants Back In: Agrarian Themes in the Construction and Corrosion of Statist Historiography in Rwanda. American Historical Review 105(3):832–877.

Nguyen, Vinh-Kim

2010 The Republic of Therapy: Triage and Sovereignty in West Africa's Time of AIDS. Durham: Duke University Press.

Ni Aolain, Fionnuala

2009 Women, Security, and the Patriarchy of Internationalized Transitional Justice. Human Rights Quarterly 31:1055–1085.

2012 Advancing Feminist Positioning in the Field of Transitional Justice. International Journal of Transitional Justice 6:205.

Niezen, Ronald

2010 Public Justice and the Anthropology of Law. Cambridge: Cambridge University Press.

Nora, Pierre

1989 Between Memory and History: Les Lieux de Mémoire. Representations 26:7–24.

Nordstrom, Carolyn

2007 Global Outlaws: Crime, Money, and Power in the Contemporary World. Berkeley: University of California Press.

Nsanzuwera, François-Xavier

2005 The ICTR Contributions to National Reconciliation. Journal of International Criminal Justice 3(944–949).

Ntampaka, Charles

1997 Rwanda: Family Law in Rwanda. *In* The International Survey of Family Law 1995. Bainham, A., ed. Pp. 415–533.

Obarrio, Juan

2014 The Spirit of the Laws in Mozambique. Chicago: University of Chicago Press.

Organic Law N.08/96 of 30/08/1996

On the Organisation of Prosecution for Offences Constituting the Crime of Genocide or Crimes Against Humanity Committed Since 1 October 1990. Official Gazette of the Republic of Rwanda.

Organic Law N.22/99 of 12/11/1999

Completing the First Civil Code Book and Instituting the Fifth Section Relating to Marriage, Patrimony, and Succession. Official Gazette of the Republic of Rwanda.

Organic Law N.33/2001 of 22/06/2001

Modifying and Completing Organic Law N.40/2000 of 26/01/2001 on the Creation of *Gacaca Jurisdictions* and the Prosecution of Genocide Crimes or Crimes Against Humanity Committed Between October 1, 1990 and December 31, 1994. Official Gazette of the Republic of Rwanda.

Organic Law N.16/2004 of 19/6/2004

Establishing the Organization, Competence, and Functioning of Gacaca Courts Charged with Prosecuting and Trying the Perpetrators of the Crime of Genocide and Other Crimes Against Humanity, Committed Between October 1, 1990 and December 31, 1994. Official Gazette of the Republic of Rwanda.

Organic Law N.08/2005 of 14/07/2005

Determining the Use and Management of Land in Rwanda. Official Gazette of the Republic of Rwanda. Official Gazette of the Republic of Rwanda.

Organic Law N.31/2006 of 14/08/2006
On Organisation, Jurisdiction, Competence and Functioning of the Mediation Committee. Official Gazette of the Republic of Rwanda.
Organic Law N.13/2008 of 19/05/2008
Modifying and Complementing Organic Law N.16/2004 of 19/06/2004 Establishing the Organisation, Competence and Functioning of *Gacaca* Courts Charged with Prosecuting and Trying the Perpetrators of the Crime of Genocide and Other Crimes Against Humanity, Committed Between October 1, 1990 and December 31, 1994, as Modified and Complemented to Date. Official Gazette of the Republic of Rwanda.
Palmer, Nicola
2015 Courts in Conflict: Interpreting the Layers of Justice in Post-Genocide Rwanda. Oxford: Oxford University Press.
Penal Reform
2004 Research Report on the Gacaca: Report VI, From Camp to Hill, the Reintegration of Released Prisoners. Kigali: Penal Reform International.
Peskin, Victor
2008 International Justice in Rwanda and the Balkans: Virtual Trials and the Struggle for State Cooperation. Cambridge: Cambridge University Press.
Petryna, Adriana
2002 Life Exposed: Biological Citizens After Chernobyl. Princeton: Princeton University Press.
Phelps, Teresa Goodwin
2004 Shattered Voices: Language, Violence, and the Work of Truth Commissions. Philadelphia: University of Pennsylvania Press.
Pillay, Navnethem
2010 Report of the Mapping Exercise documenting the most serious violations of human rights and international humanitarian law committed within the territory of the Democratic Republic of the Congo between March 1993 and June 2003. New York: United Nations Human Rights Office of the High Commissioner.
Pottier, Johan
2002 Re-Imagining Rwanda: Conflict, Survival, and Disinformation in the Late Twentieth Century. Cambridge: Cambridge University Press.
2005 Escape from Genocide: The Politics of Identity in Rwanda's Massacres. *In* Violence and Belonging: The Quest for Identity in Post-Colonial Africa. V. Broch-Due, ed. Pp. 195–213. New York: Routledge.
2006 Land Reform for Peace? Rwanda's 2005 Land Law in Context. Journal of Agrarian Change 6(47):509–537.
Power, Samantha
2002 "A Problem from Hell": America and the Age of Genocide. New York: Basic Books.
Prosecution vs. Nyirakiromba et al.
2008 Judgment. High Court of Nyanza.
Prunier, Gerard
1995 The Rwanda Crisis: History of a Genocide. New York: Columbia University Press.
2009 Africa's World War. Oxford: Oxford University Press.
Redfield, Peter
2013 Life in Crisis: The Ethical Journey of Doctors Without Borders. Berkeley: University of California Press.

Renteln, Alison Dundes
2005 The Cultural Defense. Oxford University Press: Oxford.

Rettig, Max
2011 The Sovu Trials: The Impact of Genocide Justice on One Community. *In* Remaking Rwanda. S. Straus and L. Waldorf, eds. Pp. 194–209. Madison: University of Wisconsin Press.

Reyntjens, Filip
1985 Pouvoir et droit au Rwanda: Droit publique et évolution politique, 1916–1973. Tervuren: Royal Museum for Central Africa.

1987 Chiefs and Burgomasters in Rwanda: The Unfinished Quest for a Bureaucracy. Journal of Legal Pluralism and Unofficial Law 25–26:71–97.

1990 Le gacaca ou la justice du gazon au Rwanda. Politique Africaine 31:31–41.

1995 Subjects of Concern: Rwanda, October 1994. Issue: A Journal of Opinion 23(2):39–43.

2005 Rwanda, Ten Years On: From Genocide to Dictatorship. *In* The Political Economy of the Great Lakes Region in Africa. S. Marysse and F. Reyntjens, eds. Pp. 15–47. New York: Palgrave Macmillan.

2009 The Great African War: Congo and Regional Geopolitics, 1996–2006. Cambridge: Cambridge University Press.

Reyntjens, Filip, and Stef Vandeginste
2005 Rwanda: An Atypical Transition. *In* Roads to Reconciliation. E. Skaar, S. Gloppen, and A. Suhrke, eds. Pp. 101–127. New York: Lexington Books.

Richters, Annemiek
2010 Suffering and Healing in the Aftermath of War and Genocide in Rwanda: Mediations Through Community-Based Sociotherapy. *In* Mediations of Violence in Africa: Fashioning New Futures from Contested Pasts. A. Richters and L. Kapeitjns, eds. Pp. 173–210. Leiden: Brill.

Ring, Laura A.
2006 Zenana: Everyday Peace in a Karachi Apartment Building. Bloomington: Indiana University Press.

Rodman, Kenneth
2008 Darfur and the Limits of Legal Deterrence. Human Rights Quarterly 30:529–560.

Rodney, Walter
1972 How Europe Underdeveloped Africa. London: Bogle-L'Ouverture Publications.

Roht-Arriaza, Naomi, and Javier Mariezcurrena, eds.
2006 Transitional Justice in the Twenty-First Century: Beyond Truth Versus Justice. Cambridge: Cambridge University Press.

Rose, Laurel
1992 The Politics of Harmony: Land Dispute Strategies in Swaziland. Cambridge: Cambridge University Press.

1996 Are Alternative Dispute Resolution (ADR) Programs Suitable for Africa? Africa Notes (September):3–7.

2004 Women's Land Access in Post-Conflict Rwanda: Bridging the Gap Between Customary Land Law and Pending Land Legislation. Texas Journal of Women and the Law 13:197–250.

Rose, Nikolas
1999 Powers of Freedom: Reframing Political Thought. Cambridge: Cambridge University Press.

Rosen, Lawrence
2006 Law as Culture: An Invitation. Princeton: Princeton University Press.
Ross, Fiona C.
2003 Bearing Witness: Women and the Truth and Reconciliation Commission in South Africa. Sterling, VA: Pluto Press.
Runyange, Medard
2003 Defis de la justice communautaire comme instrument de résolution des donflits: Cas de acaca traditionnel au Rwanda. Cahiers de Centre de Gestion des Conflits 8:48–74.
Rutayisira, Jean
2004 A Guide to Civic Education: Life Skills for Rwandan Primary Schools. Kigali, Rwanda: National Curriculum Development Center, Ministry of Education, Science, Technology and Scientific Research.
Rutembesa, Faustin
2002 Le discours sur le peuplement comme instrument de manipulation identaire. *In* Peuplement du Rwanda: Enjeux et perspectives. Cahiers du Centre de Gestion de Conflicts No. 5, ed. Pp. 73–102. Butare: National University of Rwanda.
Ruzibiza, Abdul Joshua
2005 Rwanda: L'histoire secrète. Paris: Éditions du Panama.
Schapera, Isaac
1955 A Handbook of Tswana Custom and Law. Oxford: Oxford University Press.
Scheper-Hughes, Nancy, and Philippe Bourgois, eds.
2004 Violence in War and Peace: An Anthology. Malden, MA: Blackwell.
Schoenbrun, David
2010 Healing + Violence = Sovereignty: Historical Contingencies of a Hard Equation. Social Health in the New Millennium conference, Philadelphia, March 2010.
Schuetze, Christy K.
2010 The World is Upside Down: Women's Participation in Religious Movements in Mozambique. Dissertation awarded by University of Pennsylvania Department of Anthropology.
2013 "Reconciliation? A Case Study of Violence, Memory, and the Work of Spirit Mediums in Addressing Intra-Community Violence in Central Mozambique." Violence, Memory, and Social Recovery symposium. University of Rochester.
Scott, James C.
1985 Weapons of the Weak: Everyday Forms of Peasant Resistance. New Haven: Yale University Press.
1990 Domination and the Arts of Resistance: Hidden Transcripts. New Haven: Yale University Press.
1998 Seeing Like a State: How Certain Schemes to Improve the Human Condition have Failed. New Haven: Yale University Press.
Seligman, Charles Gabriel
1930 Races of Africa. London: Oxford University Press.
Semujanga, Josias
2003 Formes et usages des préjugés dans le discours social du Rwanda. *In* Rwanda: Identité et citoyenneté. F. Rutembesa, J. Semuganga, and A. Shyaka, eds. Pp. 13–32. Butare: National University of Rwanda.
Sharma, Aradhana, and Akhil Gupta, eds.
2006 The Anthropology of the State: A Reader. Malden, MA: Blackwell.

Shaw, Rosalind

2005 Rethinking Truth and Reconciliation Commissions: Lessons from Sierra Leone. USIP Special Report (130):1–12.

2007 Memory Frictions: Localizing the Truth and Reconciliation Commission in Sierra Leone. International Journal of Transitional Justice 1:183–207.

Shaw, Rosalind, and Lars Waldorf

2010a Introduction: Localizing Transitional Justice. In Localizing Transitional Justice. R. Shaw, L. Waldorf, and P. Hazan, eds. Pp. 3–26. Stanford: Stanford University Press.

2010b Localizing Transitional Justice: Interventions and Priorities After Mass Violence. Stanford: Stanford University Press.

Shaw, Rosalind, Lars Waldorf, and Pierre Hazan, eds.

2010. Localizing Transitional Justice. Stanford: Stanford University Press.

Shraga, Daphna

2005 The Second Generation UN-Based Tribunals: A Diversity of Mixed Jurisdictions. In Roads to Reconciliation. E. Skaar, S. Gloppen, and A. Suhrke, eds. Pp. 55–82. New York: Lexington Books.

Sibomana, André

1999 Hope for Rwanda. Sterling, VA: Pluto Press.

Sikkink, Kathryn, and Carrie Booth Walling

2006 Argentina's Contribution to Global Trends in Transitional Justice. In Transitional Justice in the Twenty-First Century: Beyond Truth Versus Justice. N. Roht-Arriaza and J. Mariezcurrena, eds. Pp. 301–324. Cambridge: Cambridge University Press.

Smith, James M., and Stephen Smith

2004 Jenocide. Brochure for the Kigali Memorial Centre. Produced in Partnership with Aegis Trust.

Speed, Sharon

2008 Rights in Rebellion: Indigenous Struggle and Human Rights in Chiapas. Stanford: Stanford University Press.

Speke, John Hanning

1863 Journal of the Discovery of the Source of the Nile. London: William Blackwood and Sons.

Starr, June, and Barbara Yngvesson

1975 Scarcity and Disputing: Zero-ing in on Compromise Decisions. American Ethnologist 2:553–566.

Straus, Scott

2006 The Order of Genocide: Race, Power, and War in Rwanda. Ithaca: Cornell University Press.

Straus, Scott, and Lars Waldorf, eds.

2011 Remaking Rwanda: State Building and Human Rights After Mass Violence. Madison: University of Wisconsin Press.

Tambiah, Stanley

1989 Ethnic Conflict in the World Today. American Ethnologist 16(2):335–349.

Taussig, Michael

2003 Law in a Lawless Land. Chicago: University of Chicago Press.

Taylor, Christopher C.

1992 Milk, Honey, and Money: Changing Concepts in Rwandan Healing. Washington, DC: Smithsonian Institutional Press.

1999 Sacrifice as Terror: The Rwandan Genocide of 1994. New York: Berg.

2002 The Cultural Face of Terror in the Rwandan Genocide of 1994. *In* Annihilating Difference: The Anthropology of Genocide. A. L. Hinton, ed. Pp. 137–178. Berkeley: University of California Press.

Teitel, Ruti

2000 Transitional Justice. Oxford: Oxford University Press.

2003 Transitional Justice Genealogy. Harvard Human Rights Journal 16:69–94.

2008 Editorial Note—Transitional Justice Globalized. International Journal of Transitional Justice 2:1–4.

Terrio, Susan J.

2009 Judging Mohammed: Juvenile Delinquency, Immigration, and Exclusion at the Paris Palais de Justice. Stanford: Stanford University Press.

Theidon, Kimberly

2006 Justice in Transition: The Micropolitics of Reconciliation in Postwar Peru. Journal of Conflict Resolution 50(3):433–457.

2009 Editorial Note. International Journal of Transitional Justice 3:295–300.

2010 Histories of Innocence: Postwar Stories in Peru. *In* Localizing Transitional Justice. R. Shaw, L. Waldorf, and P. Hazan, eds. Pp. 92–110. Stanford: Stanford University Press.

2012 Intimate Enemies: Violence and Reconciliation in Peru. Philadelphia: University of Pennsylvania Press.

Thiranagama, Sharika

2011 In My Mother's House. Philadelphia: University of Pennsylvania Press.

Thomas, Kedron, and Rebecca Galemba

2013 Illegal Anthropology: An Introduction. Political and Legal Anthropology Review 36(2):211–214.

Thomson, Susan

2010 Getting Close to Rwandans Since the Genocide: Studying Everyday Life in Highly Politicized Research Settings. African Studies Review 53(3):19–34.

2011a The Darker Side of Transitional Justice: The Power Dynamics Behind Rwanda's Gacaca Courts. Africa 81(3):373–390.

2011b Reeducation for Reconciliation: Participant Observations on *Ingando*. *In* Remaking Rwanda. S. Straus and L. Waldorf, eds. Pp. 331–342. Madison: University of Wisconsin Press.

2011c Whispering Truth to Power: The Everyday Resistance of Rwandan Peasants to Post-Genocide Reconciliation. African Affairs 110(440):439–456.

2013 Whispering Truth to Power: Everyday Resistance to Reconciliation in Postgenocide Rwanda. Madison: University of Wisconsin Press.

Thomson, Susan M., and Rosemary Nagy

2011 Law, Power and Justice: What Legalism Fails to Address in the Functioning of Rwanda's *Gacaca* Courts. International Journal of Transitional Justice 5:11–30.

Trouillot, Michel-Rolph

1995 Silencing the Past: Power and the Production of History. Boston: Beacon Press.

2001 The Anthropology of the State in the Age of Globalization: Close Encounters of the Deceptive Kind. Current Anthropology 42(1):125–138.

2003 Global Transformations: Anthropology and the Modern World. New York: Palgrave Macmillan.

Tunks, Michael A.
2002 Diplomats or Defendants? Defining the Future of Head-of-State Immmunity. Duke Law Journal 52(651):651–682.
Turshen, Meredith, Sheila Meintjes, and Anu Pillay, eds.
2002 The Aftermath: Women in Post-Conflict Transformation. London: Zed Books.
Twagilimana, Aimable
2003 The Debris of Ham: Ethnicity, Regionalism, and the 1994 Rwandan Genocide. Lanham: University Press of America.
Umutesi, Marie Beatrice
2004 Surviving the Slaughter: The Ordeal of a Rwandan Refugee in Zaire. J. Emerson, trans. Madison: University of Wisconsin Press.
United Nations Security Council
1994 Resolution 955 (1994) on establishment of an International Tribunal for Rwanda and adoption of the Statute of the Tribunal, Volume 955: Official Documents System of the United Nations (S/RES/955(1994)).
Uvin, Peter
1998 Aiding Violence: The Development Enterprise in Rwanda. West Hartford, CT: Kumarian Press.
Valji, Nahla
2007 Gender Justice and Reconciliation. Dialogue on Globalization: Occasional Paper 35. Friedrich-Ebert-Stiftung: Berlin.
Van Biema, David
2005 Warren of Rwanda. In Time. August 15.
van Leeuwen, Mathijs
2001 Rwanda's Imidugudu Programme and Earlier Experiences with Villagisation and Resettlement in East Africa. Journal of Modern African Studies 39(4):623–644.
Vansina, Jan
1985 Oral Tradition as History. Madison: University of Wisconsin Press.
2004 Antecedents to Modern Rwanda: The Nyiginya Kingdom. Madison: University of Wisconsin Press.
Venter, Christine
2006 Eliminating Fear Through Recreating Community in Rwanda: The Role of the Gacaca Courts. Texas Wesleyan Law Review 13:577–598.
Vidal, Claudine
1998 Questions sur le rôle des paysans durant le génocide des Rwandais Tutsi. Cahiers d'Études Africaines 38(2–4):331–345.
2001 Les commemorations du génocide au Rwanda. Les temps modernes 613:1–46.
Wagner, Sarah
2008 To Know Where He Lies: DNA Technology and the Search for Srebrenica's Missing. Berkeley: University of California Press.
Waldorf, Lars
2006 Mass Justice for Mass Atrocity: Rethinking Local Justice as Transitional Justice. Temple Law Review 79(1):1–87.
2010 "Like Jews Waiting for Jesus": Posthumous Justice in Post-Genocide Rwanda. In Localizing Transitional Justice: Interventions and Priorities After Mass Violence. R. Shaw, L. Waldorf, and P. Hazan, eds. Pp. 183–202. Stanford: Stanford University Press.

2011 Instrumentalizing Genocide: The RPF's Campaign Against "Genocide Ideology." *In* Remaking Genocide. S. Straus and L. Waldorf, eds. Pp. 48–66. Madison: University of Wisconsin Press.

Warren, Rick
2002 The Purpose-Driven Life: What on Earth Am I Here For? Grand Rapids, MI: Zondervan.

Weber, Max
1968 Economy and Society, Volume 1. G. Roth and C. Wittich, eds. Berkeley: University of California Press.

Weeks, Sindiso Mnisi
2011 Securing Women's Property Inheritance in the Context of Plurality: Negotiations of Law and Authority in Mbuzini Customary Courts and Beyond. Acta JuridicaPp.140–173.
2013 Women's Eviction in Msinga: The Uncertainties of Seeking Justice. Acta Juridica Pp. 118–142.

Westermann, Diedrich
1949 (1934) The African To-Day and To-Morrow. New York: International African Institute.

Wilson, Richard A.
2001 The Politics of Truth and Reconciliation in South Africa: Legitimizing the Post-Apartheid State. Cambridge: Cambridge University Press.
2003 Justice and Retribution in Postconflict Settings. Public Culture 15(1):187–190.
2011 Writing History in International Criminal Trials. Cambridge: Cambridge University Press.

Worden, Scott
2008 The Justice Dilemma in Uganda. United States Institute of Peace Report. Pp. 1–15. Washington, DC: United States Institute of Peace.

Zorbas, Eugenia
2004 Reconciliation in Post-Genocide Rwanda. African Journal of Legal Studies 1(1):29–52.
2009 What Does Reconciliation After Genocide Mean? Public Transcripts and Hidden Transcripts in Post-Genocide Rwanda. Journal of Genocide Research 11(1):127–147.

Index

old-caseload refugee Tutsi/s (repatriés), 156, 158, 174–176. *See also* new-caseload refugee Hutu/s
outsider status, 181–182, 207, 209–210, 216–218. *See also* insider status

pacification, 8, 19, 169, 185
paternity cases, 160–162, 168–172, 178
peace and peace building, 3, 17, 20, 26, 39, 52–53, 55, 64. *See also* mediation principles
penalty reductions/amnesties for perpetrators, 90–91, 101
perpetrators: amnesties/penalty reductions for, 90–91, 101; contestation and, 112; family and, 149–150; gacaca courts and, 31, 112–118, 122–123; government narrative and, 16, 31, 64, 67–68, 70–71; Hutu/s as génocidaires or, 16, 64, 67–68, 70–71; military forces as, 31, 61–62, 72, 242n11; Tutsi/s as, 67–68, 117
Petryna, Adriana, 112
poetics, 128
political elites. *See* elites
political violence: comite y'abunzi and, 127–128, 134, 137, 139, 148, 152; criminal tribunals and, 84, 89; everyday lives and, 11, 21, 38; gacaca courts and, 118; "gray zone" and, 69, 113; Kagame, Paul and, 55, 57, 62, 64; lay judges and, 205, 207; mediation, 11; punishment and, 89; transitional justice after, 89–90; victimhood and, 118. *See also* violence
politics: democratization and, 49, 51–52, 62–63, 237n22; law versus, 33–34, 224, 227; multipartyism and, 51–52, 71, 237n22; politics of memory and, 37–38, 42–44; sociopolitical goals and, 15, 224. *See also* micropolitics of reconciliation; state authority
postgenocide period. *See* government (dominant) narrative; grassroots legal forums (forums); law-based mediation
power. *See* hierarchies of power and inequality; state authority
precolonial period, 45–47, 50, 60–61, 65–66, 76–78, 80–81, 235n6, 236n16, 236n19, 237n20
"pretending peace," 17, 20. *See also* peace and peace building

private versus public spaces, 36, 108, 116–117
production of history, 37–38, 42–44, 56–57, 59–60, 64–66, 68, 70. *See also* government (dominant) narrative; historiography; 1994 genocide; Rwandan Patriotic Army (RPA); Rwandan Patriotic Front (RPF)
professional judges (judges), 18–19, 86, 209–210, 215–218, 220–221. *See also* lay judges
property: comite y'abunzi and, 134–135, 154; communal marriage system and, 184–185; gacaca courts and, 30–32, 75, 100, 105–106, 121, 151, 239n18
protectors/heroes ceremonies, 67–68, *69*
public sphere: legal spaces in, 91, 96–97, 105, 117, 125; private versus, 36, 108, 116–117
punishment: comite y'abunzi and, 1, 6–7, 38, 95, 128–131, 154–157, 162; forums and, 25, 38, 59, 95; gacaca courts and, 1, 5, 89, 93–94, 97–102, 122, 124, 158–159, 162; government through community and, 97; harmony/harmony legal models and, 10–11, 18, 38–39, 76, 95, 97, 128, 131, 154–157, 162, 164–172, 185–186; law-based mediation and, 1, 3, 10, 158; laws and, 1, 10, 93; lay judges and, 200, 202; legal aid clinics and, 1, 7, 39, 95, 162, 164–172, 168, 171, 181, 183, 185–186; state authority and, 10; transitional justice and, 38, 76, 82–84, 86, 89; truth commissions and, 90; truth/truth telling and, 82, 93; unity and, 8, 10, 18, 25

race, 47–48, 52, 59–61, 64–65, 235n9, 236n10, 236n12. *See also* ethnicity; *and specific ethnic groups*
reconciliation (ubwiyunge): overview of, 2–3, 230–232; comite y'abunzi and, 10, 39, 129, 131, 154; contextualization and, 22, 77; divorce and, 178–179, 181–183, 241n10; forgiveness and, 93, 230, 232; gacaca courts and, 10, 91, 125; government narrative and, 3, 43, 70, 185; institutions of social healing and, 3, 9, 30, 74, 130, 230–231, 233n3; judges and, 218; lay judges and, 101, 191, 200–201; legal aid clinics and, 10, 185; resistance and, 21; truth telling and, 74. *See also* conciliation;

13–14, 16, 20; lawfare and, 16, 76, 80, 223–224, 227–228; law versus politics and, 33–34, 224, 227; lay judges and, 195–196, 201–202, 208–209, 219; legal aid clinics and, 7, 11, 166, 168, 174; mediation principles and, 13–14; punishment and, 10; resistance and, 20, 107; tribunals and, 78–79. *See also* government (dominant) narrative; politics

structural violence, 80, 94, 195, 226–227, 229–230

suffering, hierarchy of, 26, 67, 71, 112

Tanzania, 29, 52–53, 55, 64, 85–86, 91, 215

Taylor, Christopher C., 231

ten-year anniversary of 1994 genocide, 38, 40, 43–44, 57–59, *58*, 61–65, 67–68, 70, 116. *See also* 1994 genocide

Theidon, Kimberly, 2, 12, 15, 18, 22–23, 112–113, 232

thick description, 35, 164, 169, 173, 179, 186–187, 190

thinkable versus unthinkable, 38, 44, 71–72

Thiranagama, Sharika, 21, 230

Thomson, Susan, and topics: economics of memory, 111; everyday lives, 21, 27, 224; everyday resistance, 21, 107; government's version of events, 34; mediation and pacification, 185; reconciliation, 3; state authority, 125, 224; Tutsi/s as perptrators, 117; unity versus divisions, 17; withdrawn muteness, 107

TIG (travaux d'intérêt général, or community service), 6, 100–101, 124

top-down policies, 9, 11, 153, 218–219. *See also* bottom-up processes

"total environment" of postgenocide transformation, 3, 43, 70, 185

training, for lay judges, 99, 196, 199–201

transitional justice: overview of, 1–2, 14, 38–39, 81–82; accountability for crimes and, 84–85, 93; coercion and, 18; compromises and, 90–91; contextualization and, 38, 91; criminal tribunals and, 27, 82–89, 92, 93, 215–218, 220–221; customary law and, 38, 76; everyday and genocide-related disputes connection and, 38, 95; harmony/harmony legal models and, 76; healing and, 14–15, 85, 90–91; human rights violations and, 84–89, 91; justice and, 18,

76, 82, 90–91, 93–94; laws and, 14, 87–88; multiple models and, 89, 91–93; national versus international sovereignty and, 81, 88–89, 91–92; punishment and, 38, 76, 82–84, 86, 89; silences/silencing and, 18, 91; truth commissions and, 14–15, 18, 85, 89–91; universal legal-based norms and, 38, 87–89; victim narratives and, 14, 18, 90–91

Trouillot, Michel-Rolph, 43–44, 56–57

truth and reconciliation commissions, 14–15, 18, 85, 89–91

Truth and Reconciliation Commission (TRC), 15, 18, 90

truth/truth telling: comite y'abunzi and, 128, 136, 138, 141, 175, 193; documentation and, 175; forums and, 23, 74, 91, 93–94; gacaca courts and, 91, 93–94, 106–108, 111–113; judges and, 216–218; punishment and, 82, 93

Tutsi/s: family and, 149; 1994 genocide statistics and, 54; as perpetrators, 67–68, 117, 119, 242n11; as refugees, 50, 55, 156, 158, 169, 174–176; South Province and, 28–29; stereotypes and, 48, 236nn11–12; as victims, 16, 67, 118–120, 124, 149, 242n11. *See also* government (dominant) narrative; historiography

Twa, 46–48, 60

ubuhake (cattle clientship), 46, 48, 66, 235n7, 237n20

uburetwa (mandatory unpaid labor), 60–61, 124, 236n17

ubwiyunge (reconciliation). *See* conciliation; reconciliation (ubwiyunge)

Uganda, 18, 22, 29, 50–51, 55, 81–82, 88–89, 93

umuryango (family). *See* family (umuryango)

umwunzi (mediator). *See* abunzi (mediators)

United Nations, 18, 49, 53–54, 82, 85–89, 92–93, 217

United States, 16, 54, 75, 178

unity (ubumwe): overview of, 2–3, 5, 11–12, 20–21, 25; comite y'abunzi and, 131, 150, 156, 161–162; conversations/discussions and, 21–22; culture/local culture and, 3, 17, 19, 72, 95; family and, 179–180; forums and, 2, 8, 25; gacaca courts and, 5,

Acknowledgments

This book emerges, first and foremost, from time given by people in Rwanda. Out of respect for the privacy of the individuals from Ndora, Nyanza, Butare, Kigali, and elsewhere in Rwanda whose stories fill these pages, I do not name them here, and have given them pseudonyms in the text. It has been my privilege to learn from them, and I am grateful they shared their lives with me. I hope that they recognize their experiences in my retelling and that I accurately captured the complexity of their experiences living simultaneously with loss alongside hope in the possibility of new futures.

Special thanks to David Moussa Ntambara, with whom I first visited Rwanda and jointly conducted research in 2002, and to the Collaborative for Development Action, who sponsored our trip. Moussa's gracious collegiality and friendship exposed me to the beauty and intricacy of his country, and have endured through the years. During my research from 2007 through 2008, I received support from my affiliation with colleagues at the Center for Conflict Management at the National University for Rwanda. Staff members of the university's Legal Aid Clinic and the National Services for Gacaca Jurisdictions provided valuable support and information, as did local authorities in Ndora, Nyanza, Butare, and Kigali. Special mention goes as well to my research assistant, David Karima, who adeptly guided me through the complexities of legal research in Rwanda. Thanks also go to friends who housed, fed, and guided me, and later my husband and children, in Rwanda, most specifically Saidati, Dani, Immaculée, Miriam, Diana, William, Shamsi, Anna, Michel, and Marie-Claire.

Fieldwork for this project in 2007 and 2008 was made possible through support from a Fulbright Foreign Scholarship and the National Science Foundation and the Wenner-Gren Foundation. In addition, it built on summer research grants for work in Rwanda in 2004 and 2005 from the

University of Pennsylvania through the Department of Anthropology, the Browne Center for International Relations, and the Health and Society in Africa programs. My years at Penn were supported financially through the University of Pennsylvania's William Penn Fellowship and two Foreign Language and Area Studies fellowships through the African Studies Center. Subsequent trips have been supported by the University of Rochester. The Humanities Project at the University of Rochester provided support for a symposium focused on themes in the book in 2013 (Violence, Memory, and Social Recovery), and the dean's office provided support for costs associated with publication. Portions of the Introduction have been published in *American Anthropologist*, and portions of Chapter 2 have been published in the *Journal of the Royal Anthropological Association.*

A gracious thank-you to Sandra Barnes, Steve Feierman, and Kathy Hall for their sage advice and guidance throughout the process of fieldwork and writing from which this book emerged. Thanks at Penn extend also to Lee Cassanelli, Paul Kaiser, and Ali Dinar, whose work with the African Studies Center at Penn was deeply meaningful during my time there. Further thanks go to Linda Hill, who provided invaluable insight into how to be a teacher, a writer, and a mentor.

This book has only emerged because of the critiques (both gentle and pointed) and suggestions from so many people, named and not named here. I am humbled to be a part of such a community of scholars, and such meaningful processes of knowledge production. I feel lucky to have worked with editors Peter Agree, Tobias Kelly, and Noreen O'Connor-Abel at University of Pennsylvania Press. They have been patient and unflaggingly supportive of this book. I am indebted to the time, careful consideration, and astute comments provided by the Press's three anonymous referees. I also extend thanks to the many anonymous referees who have commented on my work in recent years in other venues. Thanks also to J. Naomi Linzer Indexing Servies.

Ideas in this book have been shaped by conference panels, discussant comments, and informal conversations with a wide range of colleagues. Any errors that remain are my own. I have benefited from colleagues working on and in Rwanda, whether in hurried conversations or extended exegeses, in Rwanda or in conference rooms, in person or via e-mail, including Jennie Burnet, Phil Clark, John Janzen, Mark Geraghty, Timothy Longman, Susan Thomson, and Lars Waldorf. I have learned from colleagues working on overlapping questions in other regions in Africa, including Crystal

Biruk, Catherine Bolten, Sara Byala, Kamari Clarke, Wendi Haugh, Niklas Hultin, Jennifer Kyker, Benjamin Lawrance, Julie Livingston, Marissa Mika, Mary Moran, Jennifer Riggan, Christy Schuetze, and Catherine van de Ruit. Colleagues studying law, memory, and/or postconflict dynamics outside Africa have enriched my analysis here as well, including John Borneman, Brian Daniels, Josh Dubler, Kerry Dunn, Elizabeth Greenspan, Azra Hromadzic, Rabia Kamal, Naeem Mohaiemen, and Kimberly Theidon.

I am grateful to my colleagues in the Department of Anthropology at the University of Rochester for creating an environment that fosters genuine scholarship: Ayala Emmett, Robert Foster, Tom Gibson, Eleana Kim, John Osburg, Dan Reichman, and Llerena Searle, as well as Ro Ferreri, who makes administrative magic happen so that I can focus on teaching and writing. Further support came from the University of Rochester's Frederick Douglass Institute for African and Africana Studies, which fosters vibrant engagement with Africa. Last, I am grateful to have had the chance to engage with ideas at the core of the book with a wide range of students. Special thanks go to Jonathan Johnson and Brynn Champney for their careful edits of the penultimate manuscript.

I am indebted to my family, who taught me early on that there are many ways to understand the world, that collective belonging is adaptive, that conflict is not inherently dysfunctional, and that disputes can be resolved through a range of mechanisms. My parents, Katherine Conner, Robert Doughty, Cris Doughty, and Marc Ross, all inspired me to question and learn from others.

Final thanks go to my husband and partner in life, Josh Mankoff, whose support of this endeavor deserves its own chapter. I am grateful daily for our shared intellectual and political commitments, his adaptability in supporting a life that spans continents, and his help navigating work-life commitments that, though rarely in balance, are always fulfilling. And last, Natalie and Noah fill my world with love and laughter and with constant challenges to explain why and how the world is as it is, especially when it is not fair. Sharing my world with these three has helped me to become a more focused and perceptive researcher-scholar. I dedicate this book, with great love and appreciation, to them.